MODERN LIBRAR

Seventeenth-Century

FRENCH DRAMA

THE CID by *Corneille*

THE PRECIOUS DAMSELS by *Molière*

TARTUFFE by *Molière*

THE WOULD-BE GENTLEMAN by *Molière*

PHAEDRA by *Racine*

ATHALIAH by *Racine*

Introduction by

JACQUES GUICHARNAUD

YALE UNIVERSITY

THE MODER

Library of Congress Catalog Card Number: 67-17879

THE MODERN LIBRARY

is published by Random House, Inc.

Manufactured in the United States of America

Contents

INTRODUCTION BY *Jacques Guicharnaud* vii

THE CID *by Corneille,*
TRANSLATED BY KENNETH MUIR 1

THE PRECIOUS DAMSELS *by Molière,*
TRANSLATED BY MORRIS BISHOP 63

TARTUFFE *by Molière,*
TRANSLATED BY MORRIS BISHOP 89

THE WOULD-BE GENTLEMAN *by Molière,*
TRANSLATED BY MORRIS BISHOP 153

PHAEDRA *by Racine,*
TRANSLATED BY KENNETH MUIR 225

ATHALIAH *by Racine,*
TRANSLATED BY KENNETH MUIR 283

Introduction BY JACQUES GUICHARNAUD

Classicism is a state of mind which, in France, at first permeated and then dominated all the branches of art during the greater part of the seventeenth century and a portion of the eighteenth, and its influence can still be felt today, even in its supposed enemies. In literature that state of mind found its most complete and exemplary expression in theatre. Even more than works in other genres, a great number of seventeenth-century plays may be said to typify the success of classicism's aspiration: to attain universality and thus to assure its own survival in the sight not only of the learned but of the public in general. Furthermore, historically it was around theatre that the most fruitful (and sometimes the most absurdly pedantic) disputes took place, and around theatre that the main elements of the so-called classical "doctrine" were formulated and developed. The works themselves absorb and obviously transcend the theories and aesthetics of the period, but the works do stem from them, illustrate them, and were very often at the roots of them. A knowledge of the doctrine is therefore essential to bringing out, as a preliminary, certain specific tendencies of the classical spirit.

The French classical theatre of the seventeenth century was the outcome of a happy encounter between a certain number of rules and the taste of a particular period. Taken in themselves, the rules often seem petty, superficial, or pedantic. In France it took lengthy disputes before they were imposed and finally accepted, and some of them, again attacked early in the eighteenth century, were rejected altogether, at least in theory, by the Romantics in the first half of the nineteenth. But from the 1630s to the first third of the eighteenth century, they corresponded for the most part to a living phenomenon: they met the demands of a public that, over long years of aesthetic evolution, had gradually become unified.

These rules are well known. They were clearly formulated by the theorists of the time and by the playwrights themselves in their prefaces, and were picked up by all the critics of French classicism. Apart from certain occasional concessions and exceptions, they define what a play *should* be, by means of principles without which there *can* be no beauty or public success. The most famous rule is that of the three unities—the result of a more or less correct interpretation of Aristotle's *Poetics*. Rather belatedly, in 1674, Boileau stated it very concisely in his *Art poétique* (*Art of Poetry*):

> That unity of action, time, and place
> Keep the stage full, and all our labours grace.
> [TRANS., Sir William Soames, 1683]

Other rules were just as imperative: for example, the distinction of genres, which above all carefully separated comedy from tragedy. In comedy, which is defined more supplely than tragedy, the nonheroic characters (that is, bourgeois and contemporary) generally struggle with their domestic problems or their pursuit of love in such a way as to bring out the ridiculous side of their natures or of contemporary customs; there is no danger of death; and there is always a happy ending. In tragedy, the "higher" genre, the characters are heroic (they belong to the race of princes, great politicians, or war leaders) and are generally borrowed from Greco-Roman antiquity, sometimes from the biblical past, and more rarely from recent but foreign history; they are prompted by "noble" interests, whether political, military, or dynastic, and/or by the passion of love, in adventures that result in catastrophe.

This distinction between the genres led to another rule of

unity—that of tone or style—according to which the language and behavior of tragedy are always kept on a noble level, both through an exclusive choice of objects—sword, dagger, poison; no clubs or handkerchiefs (when Shakespeare became known to the French, he shocked them by, among other things, the use of "lowly" objects in his "tragedies")—and through a rhetoric that was free of familiar vocabulary and constructions. Comedy had, on the contrary, to make use of familiar elements. Further, we discover degrees in the familiar: within the familiar style of a "high comedy" like *Tartuffe,* a dignity of language and gesture is maintained throughout and is far more elevated than the liberties and burlesque of a farce such as *Les Précieuses ridicules* (*The Precious Damsels*).

Still another rule: theatre must be "decorous." The rule varies according to the genre of the play, and is closely linked to that of the unity of tone and style. Its stipulations range from the elimination of obscenity and foul language (some small traces of both were accepted in the little farces) to the elimination of the spectacle of violence, even heroic violence, in tragedy: no duels on stage, not even any bloody deeds. In the name of propriety also, the behavior or decisions of certain heroes of tragedy were to be judged severely. For example, Corneille is blamed by theorists of his time for having imagined that Chimène would accept Rodrigue's presence in her room, that being contrary to the role of a well-born young lady.

Finally, to give only the more striking rules, the crowning principle, which in a way embraces all the others, is that of verisimilitude or probability. Since the concept is not absolutely clear and since interpretations of it vary from period to period, it would be well to go into it in some detail. With the rule of probability we leave the pure realm of form and touch on that of the very spirit of classical theatre. It is certainly the justification for the other rules. Unity of place, for example, is necessary because, for a spectator seated in the same place throughout an entire performance, it is hardly probable that other human beings, whom he sees directly across from him, would be moving from palace to palace or from country to country. Although the example may seem naïve, it shows that one of the underlying principles of playwrights and theorists was to convince the spectator of the reality of the performance, to eliminate any obstacles that might keep him from "participating," as we would put it today. Thus probability is a logic concerning both the action of the play and the spectator's relationship to the play. Such logic is not necessarily that of truth: miraculous or fantastic events are perhaps true historically, but being exceptional, abnormal, or monstrous, they fall outside the realm of probability. If they are performed, they turn the spectator's attention toward the question: How can what is true be contrary to reason?; whereas for the classical mind the function of a work of art was to show the mechanism of what is normal and consistent with the rational structure of the universe. This requirement corresponds to a vision of reality which was interpreted in very different ways by Corneille, Molière, and Racine. It was, above all, the expression of a basic element of the classical spirit. Probable applies to that which does not shock common sense and which the mind immediately recognizes as possible, even while it is moved to laughter or tears, or struck with terror; art is not a free projection of the imagination, but submission to (and the revelation of) what is universal, actively or potentially, in reality—a reality whose structure is consistent with or parallel to that of human reason.

In explaining the formulation of these rules, great emphasis has been put on the role of critics, theorists, the French Academy, etc. And no doubt such influences were of the highest importance. But they would surely have led to the production of pedantic and ossified works had the demands of an alive public not supported them and introduced meaningful nuances. Thus this part of the doctrine is not at all negligible.

First of all, it is clear historically that Corneille, for example, did not change from a free and baroque theatre to a theatre of "regular" form in order to obey a few grammarians. Rather, he grasped the taste of the new spectators and was able to satisfy their demands for rigor and unity. There is no point here in making a sociological study of the theatre public; but it is true that around 1635 the most successful plays, those that had the biggest box-office receipts, were the new so-called "regular" plays—a fashion due no doubt to the novelty of the plays, but also to a new spirit in a public that was weary of violence and disorder, and increasingly taken by a sense of dignity and simple harmony, civility and clarity. These elements were to be lumped together under the category of "taste"—an apparently vague term, but one that points up the true nature of classicism: a synthesis of intellectual exigencies and the intuitive demands of sensibility, an alliance of the mind and the heart. In the 1660s an "irregular" play did not represent the discovery of a new freedom, but was the reminder of a disordered and outmoded art. It was obviously the contrary that occurred around 1830 and again around 1920.

Thus the public and the theorists were in agreement on a certain level. But at the same time the public provided a living influence that checked, distorted, and sometimes opposed pure theory. The disputes concerning Corneille's *Le Cid* and Molière's *L'Ecole des femmes* (*The School for Wives*) are ample proof that *true* classicism cast about and found itself with the help of the theorists, but also in going against them. For the public wanted, above all, to be amused or deeply moved. While extravagance and escapades outside a universe of common sense did not interest them any more, they refused, on the other hand, to sacrifice their pleasure for more formal exigencies. The "rules" were good not in themselves but because they helped satisfy a dual desire: to understand and to be affected. That is why, in the minds of the civilized public, the enlightened critics, and the great playwrights, the notion of what is agreeable took precedence over the rules. To those who, in 1637, attacked *Le Cid* because the play did not blindly conform to the new literary code, the stern essayist Guez de Balzac answered: "Having satisfied a whole kingdom is greater than having written a play according to the rules . . . Knowing the art of pleasing is worth less than knowing how to please without art" (Letter to Monsieur de Scudéry, August 27, 1637). Today we consider Molière's *The School for Wives* (1662) as the first masterpiece of classical high comedy; yet the pedants found it defective in that it showed little respect for the rules drawn from Aristotle. Molière answered that, to begin with, his comedy was not contrary to the rules, but that, most of all, "the great art is to please, and that having pleased those for whom it was written, this comedy is satisfied and . . . needs not be much concerned about the rest" (*Critique de l'Ecole des femmes*, scene VI; 1663). In his *Art of Poetry* of 1674 Boileau proclaimed that "the secret is, first of all, to please and to affect," and he then went on to present the various rules for tragedy as a means by which to discover that secret. There are many examples of this kind, showing that classicism was not merely the subservience to an aesthetics invented by theorists but the use of that aesthetics to create a living art, which corresponded to the contemporary public's appetite for logic, emotion, and entertainment. Of course, the formulation of a new aesthetics and the development of a taste were mutually influential. But while forming their public, the great classical writers knew, above all, how to be in tune with its demands.

We are thus dealing with dramatic production that is both the fruit of aesthetic reflection and the response to a real demand. The major works are neither curiosities nor literary museum pieces (as one might consider the early tragedies of the French Renaissance), nor are they pure examples of short-lived entertainments (like most of the plays on Broadway or the Parisian Boulevard). They have the dignity and the eternal appeal of all great works of art. The tragedies are still very often and very successfully performed in France, not only before educated and experienced audiences but, at the price of some modernization of the staging, before the masses. As for Molière's comedies, they are performed today in almost all the countries in the world. Since such works are alive, they have that characteristic element of life—diversity. While unified by one general spirit, French classical theatre is remarkably individual and varied.

The plays included in this anthology date from 1637, first performance of *Le Cid*, to 1691, first performance of *Athalie* (*Athaliah*). That is to say, they are samples of dramatic production during a particularly fruitful half-century. In his book *La Dramaturgie classique en France*, Jacques Scherer makes a choice and draws up a catalogue of plays that he considers "of a certain historical importance"; between 1637 and 1691 he mentions some 300 of them—an incredible number given that, outside the facilities at Versailles and some temporary or private accommodations, playwrights had available in Paris only two stages from 1634 to 1658, three from 1658 to 1673, two from 1673 to 1680, and one from 1680 on. Since the first half of the eighteenth century it has been traditional to call all the dramatic production "classical"—a term which is justified but which dangerously evokes the naïve image of a harmonious group of wise, interchangeable writers, all assembled around Louis XIV, patron of the arts and letters. Now historically, from 1637 to 1691 a great many things were happening; moreover, the great seventeenth-century writers were very distinct individuals, each with his own temperament and particular genius.

When Corneille first had *Le Cid* performed, Louis XIV was not yet born (he came into the world in 1638). The period was turbulent and individualistic; heroism was then often gratuitous; and resistance to the authority of the great ministers (Richelieu; later, Mazarin) was energetic and chaotic: it blew up into a rebellion which might have turned into a revolution, the Fronde (1648–53), a confused and triangular struggle between the monarchic powers, the nobility defending its privileges, and an *haute bourgeoisie* of magistrates attached to its prerogatives. After the Fronde, the French monarchy continued on its way toward absolutism, centralization, and the establishment of the personal power of young Louis XIV. The outcome of this movement became evident after 1660: the modernization of certain institutions and of the economy was accompanied by a mystique of the personal glory of the monarch, symbolized by a sumptuous court organized around the Sun King and by a stupendous embellishment of the palaces and gardens of Versailles (the work went on from approximately 1664 to 1695). A minority of nobles became the worldly satellites of the King, and from then on, the top of the pyramid was the focal point of all eyes, including those of foreign countries. On the other hand, the bourgeoisie experienced a radical change in structure, not only because of the development of the economy, but through its proximity to the central power because of its accession to high offices. Needless to say, there was no lack of attendant ideological upheavals, characterized by the transition from a quasi-feudal individualism to the search for new wisdom and even a religious consciousness, as has been shown, from very different points of view, by the French critics Paul Bénichou (*Morales du Grand Siècle*) and Lucien Goldmann (*Le Dieu caché*). By the time Versailles was almost completed, the reign of Louis XIV was on the wane: foreign wars, the death of the minister Colbert (1683), religious disputes, the mass exile of the Huguenots following the Revocation of the Edict of Nantes (1684), and many other factors resulted in the impoverishment of the country. The inflexibility and aging of both individuals and institutions created a general atmosphere of gloom. Even Versailles, the symbol of grandeur and wealth, became what Jean Cocteau was to call "an empty shell."

It was normal, then, for dramatic production, from the youth of Corneille to the maturity of Racine, to be diversified and to range from the turbulence of the adventures in *Le Cid*, for example, to the anguished rigor of *Phèdre* (*Phaedra*) and *Athaliah*. But whatever the values of historical explanations, we are struck most of all by the pure and simple fact of the variety in the works themselves.

Le Cid (1637) is an essentially young play. While the Spanish subject matter corresponds to the fashion of the time, it is mostly a pretext for presenting ardent and uncompromising forces, using the exacerbated form of Spanish "honor." Rodrigue and Chimène are emerging from adolescence, and with all the passion of their youth, are at the same time smitten by love and bound by very high moral standards, which reject the compromises offered them by the adult world (the King). They seem—but on the surface only—to be torn between duty and passion; in fact, the two are not contradictory: both are governed by the same impulse of the heart and will. The way they choose to behave is the only possible way if they are to be proud both of themselves and of one another. They are what at the time was called *les généreux*—that is, those who aim at being satisfied with themselves through having reconciled their passion and their will. They belong to a race of truly tragic characters because, although the initial circumstances are independent of them, the catastrophic course they adopt within their situation is the fruit of their own decisions. Their fate, given what they have decided to be in their own eyes and in the eyes of one another, is that they cannot do anything other than what they are doing. They want to do what they are doing, and they can do only what they want.

However—and this is a very Cornelian touch—such heroic and dangerous behavior does not necessarily lead to the characters being crushed: the glorious image they would like to have of themselves may perhaps finally be realized; they have exhaustively shown themselves and others what they really are and what they want to be. Rodrigue has done so much and Chimène has dogged him so relentlessly that they have proved their point. At the end of the play any additional "demonstrative" acts would not make much sense, for the bounds have been reached and both young people are elevated to a higher level at which the bloody incident at the beginning is no longer worth considering. We are thus dealing with an "open" tragedy—or what was then called a tragicomedy.

We are dealing also with a play that seeks to awaken in the spectator not only Aristotelian terror and pity but, above all, admiration—that is, a kind of astonishment at the consequences to which the power of youth may lead. Such elevated demands on oneself and others provoke sympathy; but in the person of the King, we are constantly reminded of the level of pragmatic maturity, with just the touch of a smile. While *Le Cid* is a coherent and admiring portrait of the idealism of youth, a slight but lucid distance adds a dimension to the tableau: a more realistic and wiser power ends by having the last word, which is not without irony.

In Molière's plays—*Les Précieuses ridicules*, 1659; *Tartuffe*, 1669; *Le Bourgeois Gentilhomme* (*The Would-Be Gentleman*), 1670—the question is no longer one of admiration or even of irony but of straight comedy. The protagonists do their best to correspond to a higher image, but they fail. And they fail because they make the mistake of taking the most outward signs for the very essence of the ideal they aspire to. At the same time, they don't effect an alliance between their will and their passion: they take their blind bursts of passion for manifestations of their will. Finally, whereas Corneille's hero succeeds in being satisfied with himself only after superhuman efforts, Molière's characters, who are taken in by appearances, are only too easily satisfied. Three borrowed and pretentious sentences from a valet disguised as a marquis are enough to make the provincials Cathos and Magdelon think they have made Parisian *précieuse* society; a few sighs out of Tartuffe in a church are enough to make Orgon believe he has finally met a real saint; a luxurious dressing-gown is enough to give Monsieur Jourdain the impression of belonging to the nobility. Such mistakes about oneself and about the reality of things, such an obvious want of proportion, are among the basic elements of Molière's comedy and, in fact, of comedy in general.

Molière's heroes create around themselves a universe of fantasy, which is, in truth, devoid of any invention. They impose already existing forms. They think they create and that they create themselves—that is to say, they think they are Cornelian—when actually they are imitating, and imitating badly. And most often they imitate in the worst way possible what is worst in their model—whence the double-edged satire of Molière's comedies: the satire of lunatics who are continually mistaken, and indirectly, a satire of the pretensions of the models they choose. In other words, these lunatics are the extreme—or, as it were, the metaphor—of the human comedy: prisoners of themselves, driven by appetites, by a fundamental desire for domination, and by self-love, they are under the illusion of saving themselves by calling everything that feeds their egotistical self-satisfaction a "value." The two protagonists in *Tartuffe* are particularly characteristic in that respect. One of them, lucid about his motives, hides his coarse appetites behind the mask of a saintly man and then of a patriot, and uses his masks to satisfy his greed: that one is Tartuffe. The other, Orgon, unconsciously sets up as his highest standard certain religious commands which are in fact no more than pretexts for indulging, without remorse, his desire for domination, his tyranny over the family, and his self-satisfaction. Both are comical because of the obvious contradiction between what they seek to imitate or strive to achieve (charity, asceticism, etc.) and their true natures (materialistic, domineering, contemptuous of others, etc.). The same might be said for the Precious Damsels, Mascarille, and Monsieur Jourdain. But one serious question comes to mind: Are not the contradiction and the comic element metaphors for all of man's ambitions? We live in an illusion. We live, of course, with the idea of nature being good, reasonable, and altruistic. But it is merely an idea, which fails in reality, for it never manages to break down the obstinate mechanism of our mask-making self-love.

However, for Molière, the actor-director-playwright, there is a solution—a poetic solution: if life is a true comedy, then one may, with him, joyously rise above it by accepting it in the form of a comedy on stage.

Inspired by Euripides' *Hippolytus*, Racine's *Phaedra*, first performed in 1677, represents a very characteristic shift in emphasis from its Greek source: instead of killing herself in the middle of the tragedy, Phaedra is the center of the play until the very end, and her self-torture somewhat pushes into the background the character of Hippolytus and the goddesses' quarrel which determines his fate. The Racinian heroine thus bears the whole weight of the play, and the subject of the tragedy is the necessary course toward the catastrophe of a sinful love. Phaedra and all the other characters are condemned by an inner fate to doing what they must not or do not want to do. The ancient gods, when they are mentioned, serve only to give the whole an unobtrusive Greek coloring and to express metaphorically the psychological and moral forces that prompt the characters, all of whom succumb to an irremediable and destructive malady, despite the occasional spurts of will and moral conscience that might stop them. Hippolytus, dedicated to virtue and an athletic purity, has become imperceptibly the prey of Aricia's charms; Theseus, a kind of mythological Casanova, is finally a victim of passion—his wrath—because of which he condemns his son to death; and above all, Phaedra, although lucid and wanting to be saved from her sinful love for Hippolytus, is able to do no more than sink deeper and deeper into her passion.

More than the rest of seventeenth-century drama, Racine's stresses the absolute irreversibility that marks each stage of the progression toward catastrophe. Once the infernal machine within Phaedra has started working, every outward circumstance is but an opportunity for the machine to speed up. When, out of passion, Racine's characters have reacted immediately to certain events with words or acts, they become aware of the consequences, but then it is too late. Whatever happens, the situation can only grow worse. Moreover, in *Phaedra* Racine clearly expressed one aspect of his conception of tragedy that was merely hinted at in his earlier plays. Phaedra not only suffers from being aware of her ineluctable fate, but she knows she is guilty. Such passion and its catastrophic outcome is thus somewhat a Christian theme: weighing on Phaedra is a curse for which she is responsible; her blood is tainted by the sin of an entire race, which is also her sin. Certain critics have therefore considered Phaedra's passionate love an expression of the corruption of human nature, resulting from the original sin committed at the beginning of time, and for which man continues to bear the responsibility. The universe of *Phaedra* would thus be a Christian universe devoid of grace.

An anguished play in which everything is sin, *Phaedra* shows us creatures who vainly try to hide the evil: most of the action consists in the characters' hesitancy to speak. For Hippolytus to speak of his love for Aricia, or for Phaedra even to pronounce Hippolytus' name, means betraying a shameful secret, bringing the evil out into the light of day. If they do not speak, they nearly die from it; if they do speak, they commit an irreparable act; if they speak indirectly (in front of Theseus, for example), they necessarily create monstrous misunderstandings. But the tragedy is given its final grandeur by a privileged speech: Phaedra's confession at the end, when she is dying. Thanks to the combination of her suicide and her last words—a clear explanation of what has happened—the black flame that has been devouring her becomes high and bright as it finally consumes its victim.

Athaliah, first performed in 1691, is in a class by itself. Written about a religious subject by order of the King, specifically to be performed by the young ladies of Saint-Cyr, this tragedy is made up of rather uncommon elements: the reintroduction of a chorus, the great spectacle (transformable sets, a mob on stage), and the collective display of weapons in the fifth act. But what strikes us most of all is the tension between the sweet praise addressed to "the lovely law" of God and the frenzied nature of the action, leading to sheer butchery. At first glance the play would seem to be based on a somewhat naïve conflict between the good characters (Joad, Josabeth, Joas) and the wicked (Athaliah, Mathan); but it is a merciless struggle to the death on both sides, during which there are constant reminders of the slaughterers, daggers, and blood of the past, with predictions of bloody combats to come. In fact, *Athaliah* is essentially the presentation of two clans settling their accounts. A counterpart to the tortured passion of Athaliah, who is aware of the catastrophe that hangs over her, is the revengeful passion of Joad. The heads of the two clans are led inevitably to open battle by reason of a vocation or a predestination by which they are wholly governed. Being one of the chosen is as much a fatality as being one of the damned.

Clearly, the universes of these plays are greatly diverse. Yet they have in common several characteristics and a general spirit. To begin with, all sentimentality is excluded. Also, through a more or less rigorous respect for certain rules, they all aim at concentration, at creating a precise focus of interest: in the few privileged hours during which the action unfolds, we witness the climax *par excellence* of a life or an adventure. While it may be exalting, hilarious, or bloody, it always reveals—through the precipitation or final exasperation of the forces in play, which are never obscured by any accidental detail—an essential reality, sought after or hidden. Thus French classical theatre concentrates on the bare and austere presentation of moments of truth. That is to say, things suddenly come to light through the objective and ordered exteriorization of inner realities. The basic instrument of that exteriorization is language: an act or a thought does not exist objectively and intelligibly until it is expressed in a narration or in dialogue. Language is the light that dissipates doubts, organizes reality, and displays it for all to see, including God, in the case of Racine.

The ambition or terror of the characters of classical theatre is to be thus exposed. Actually they represent a complete image of man's condition: their inner mechanism, consisting of will and passion, exists only in relation to the outer world. The glory of Rodrigue and Chimène lies in the perfect combination of their self-satisfaction and the image they present to others; the happiness of Mascarille or Monsieur Jourdain is dependent on the admiration of society; Phaedra's remorse is due to the fact that she both judges herself and is obsessed with how the world of men and gods will judge her. All these plays are an affirmation of that human reality, of that game between will, blind forces, and the objective image. A weapon for clarification, whether creative or deadly, the well-ordered language of the classical writers is the affirmation of man's superiority over his condition—the superiority of intelligence. In one of his *Pensées* Pascal sums up rather well the tragic (and comic) essence of the classical spirit: "If the universe were to crush him, man still would be more noble than that which killed him, because he knows that he dies . . . the universe knows nothing of this"—and doesn't speak of it.

Selected Bibliography

I. *General*

Bénichou, Paul. *Morales du Grand Siècle*. Paris: Gallimard, 1948.

Lancaster, Henry C. *A History of French Dramatic Literature in the Seventeenth Century*, 9 vols. Baltimore: Johns Hopkins, 1952.

Peyre, Henri. *Le Classicisme français*. New York: Editions de la Maison Française, 1942.

Scherer, Jacques. *La Dramaturgie classique en France*. Paris: Nizet, n.d. [1950].

Turnell, Martin. *The Classical Moment: Studies of Corneille, Molière, and Racine*. London: Hamilton, 1947.

II. *On Corneille*

Boorsch, Jean. "Remarques sur la technique dramatique de Corneille," *Studies by the Members of the French Department, Yale University*. London: Oxford University Press, 1941, pp. 101–162.

Doubrovski, Serge. *Corneille ou la dialectique du héros*. Paris: Gallimard, 1964.

Nadal, Octave. *Le Sentiment de l'amour dans l'oeuvre de Pierre Corneille*. Paris: Gallimard, 1948.

Nelson, Robert J. *Corneille, His Heroes and Their Worlds*. Philadelphia: University of Pennsylvania Press, 1963.

III. *On Molière*

Bray, René. *Molière, homme de théâtre*. Paris: Mercure de France, 1954.

Fernandez, Ramon. *Molière, the Man Seen through His Plays*. Wilson Follett, trans. New York: Hill and Wang, 1958.

Gossman, Lionel. *Men and Masks, a Study of Molière*. Baltimore: Johns Hopkins, 1963.

Guicharnaud, Jacques. *Molière, une aventure théâtrale: Tartuffe, Dom Juan, Le Misanthrope*. Paris: Gallimard, 1963.

———, ed. *Molière, a Collection of Critical Essays*. Twentieth Century Views. Englewood Cliffs, N.J.: Prentice-Hall, 1964.

Gutwirth, Marcel. *Molière ou l'invention comique* Paris: Minard, 1966.

Hubert, J. D. *Molière and the Comedy of Intellect*. Berkeley and Los Angeles: University of California Press, 1962.

Moore, W. G. *Molière, a New Criticism*. New York: Doubleday, Anchor Books, 1962.

IV. *On Racine*

Barthes, Roland. *Sur Racine*. Paris: Seuil, 1963.

Goldmann, Lucien. *Le Dieu caché*. Paris: Gallimard, 1956.

Hubert, J. D. *Essai d'exégèse racinienne, les secrets témoins*. Paris: Nizet, 1956.

Maulnier, Thierry. *Lecture de Phèdre*. Paris: Gallimard, 1943.

———. *Racine*. Paris: Gallimard, 1936.

Picard, Raymond. *La Carrière de Jean Racine*. Paris: Gallimard, 1961.

Vinaver, Eugène. *Racine et la poésie tragique*. Paris: Nizet, 1951.

Weinberg, Bernard. *The Art of Jean Racine*. Chicago: University of Chicago Press, 1963.

V. *On Corneille and Racine*

May, Georges. *Tragédie cornélienne, tragédie racinienne*. Urbana: University of Illinois Press, 1948.

Starobinski, Jean. *L'Oeil vivant*. Paris: Gallimard, 1961.

The Cid

by PIERRE CORNEILLE

NEWLY TRANSLATED BY *Kenneth Muir*

Dramatis Personae

DON FERNAND (FERDINAND), *first king of Castille*

THE INFANTA, *his daughter, in love with Rodrigue*

DON DIÈGUE (DIEGO), *Rodrigue's father*

DON GOMÈS (THE COUNT), *Chimène's father*

DON RODRIGUE (RODERIGO) } *in love with Chimène*

DON SANCHE (SANCHO) } *in love with Chimène*

DON ARIAS

DON ALONSE (ALONSO)

CHIMÈNE (CHIMENA)

LÉONOR (LEONORA), *the Infanta's confidante*

ELVIRE (ELVIRA), *Chimène's confidante*

A PAGE

The scene is laid in Seville.

Act I

Scene 1—*Chimène's house.*

(*Enter* CHIMÈNE *and* ELVIRE.)

CHIMÈNE: Elvire, have you given a true account,
Disguising nothing that my father said?
ELVIRE: My senses still are charmed by what they heard,
For he esteems Rodrigue whom you love,
And if I don't misread his very soul,
He will command you to return his love.
CHIMÈNE: Then tell me, I beseech you, once again
What makes you think that he approves my choice.
Tell me afresh how much I ought to hope
From what he said—for such enchanting words
Cannot be heard too often; nor can you promise
Too great a freedom to my hidden love
To come into the light. What did he say
About the approach Don Sanche and Don Rodrigue
Have made through you? Did you not make him see
Too plainly that of these unequal suitors
I favor only one?
ELVIRE: No, for I painted
Your heart as neutral, neither giving joy,
Nor quite destroying hope: not viewing them
With too severe nor yet too kind an eye,
But simply waiting on your father's will
To choose a husband. This delighted him;
His lips and countenance bore witness to it,
And if you make me tell the tale again,
This, then, is what he said of them and you.
"She shows a proper duty; both of them
Are worthy of her; both of noble blood;
Brave, loyal, young; but in their eyes one reads
The shining virtue of their ancestors.
Rodrigue especially in his face displays
The signs of lofty courage; sprung from a house

So rich in warriors that they take their birth
In the midst of laurels—for his father's valor,
Unequaled in his day, was thought a miracle
While his strength lasted; on his brow, the furrows
Are graven by his deeds, and so remind us
What he was once. The son takes after him;
And so my daughter may return his love,
And please me well." Here he cut short his speech
To attend the council, but from those few words
I think he is not equally inclined
To both your lovers. The King is choosing now
A tutor for his son, and there's no doubt
Your father will be chosen for this honor.
His matchless valor and his noble deeds
Make him without a rival in his claim.
And since Rodrigue's father is persuaded
To make the proposal when the council rises
I leave you now to judge if he will seize
The opportunity, and if all your wishes
Will soon be satisfied.

CHIMÈNE: And yet it seems
My troubled soul will not accept this joy,
But feels oppressed. Fate at one moment wears
A double face; and in this happiness
I fear a great misfortune.

ELVIRE: You will see
This fear of yours is happily proved false.

CHIMÈNE: Well, come what may, let us await the outcome.

[*Exeunt.*]

Scene 2—*The Infanta's house.*

(*Enter the* INFANTA, LÉONOR *and* PAGE.)

INFANTA: Go, sirrah, and inform Chimène from me
That she has left it rather late today
For seeing me, and that my love complains

Of her neglect. [*Exit* PAGE.]

LÉONOR: Each day, madame, you're driven
By the same desire, and every day I see you
Inquire about the progress of her love.

INFANTA: Not without reason. I have almost forced her
To accept the arrows which have pierced her heart.
She loves Rodrigue and takes him at my hands,
And Rodrigue conquered his disdain through me;
So as I've forged the chains which bind these lovers
I ought to wish to see their trials end.

LÉONOR: And yet, madame, the more their love has prospered,
You've shown increasing grief. And does this love
Which fills their hearts with joy make your heart sad?
And does the interest which you take in them
Make you unhappy even while they're happy?
But I am indiscreet and go too far.

INFANTA: My sadness doubles, keeping it a secret.
Listen how I have fought, what fierce assaults
Attack my virtue still. Love is a tyrant
Who spares no one. This young knight, this lover
I give to her, I love myself.

LÉONOR: You love him!

INFANTA: Put now your hand upon my heart, and feel
How it is beating at my conqueror's name
The moment it is uttered.

LÉONOR: Pray forgive me
If I presume to blame this love of yours.
What! A great princess so to forget herself
As to admit a simple nobleman
Into her heart! What would your father say?
What would Castille? Do you remember still
Of whom you are the daughter?

INFANTA: I remember
So well that I will shed my blood before
I sink so low as to renounce my rank.
I could reply that in the finest souls
Merit alone should be the cause of love;

And if my passion sought to be excused,
A thousand famous cases could be cited;
But yet I would not blot my reputation
By following such a course: my senses' ambush
Does not abate my courage. I tell myself
That as I am the daughter of a King,
Only a King is worthy of my hand;
And when I saw my heart about to yield
I gave away the thing I dared not take.
I put Chimène in these bonds of love
In place of me; kindled their mutual flame
To put out mine. So do not be surprised
If my tormented soul should eagerly
Await their nuptials: for my repose
(As you will see) depends on it today.
If love lives upon hope, it dies with it.
It is a fire that's quenched by lack of fuel;
Despite the harshness of my wretched lot,
If Chimène should have Rodrigue for husband
My hope would die, my spirit then be cured.
Yet I endure an unbelievable pain.
Rodrigue, until he weds, attracts my love:
And from this comes my secret misery.
I see that love is forcing me to sigh
For one that I disdain; I feel my mind
Is split in two: for if my will is strong,
My heart's ablaze. This wedding's fatal to me—
I dread it, yet I wish for it, not daring
To hope for more than an imperfect joy.
My love and honor draw me different ways,
So that I'll die whether they wed or not.

LÉONOR: After your words, I've nothing more to say
Except to sympathize with your distress.
Till now I blamed you, now I pity you.
But since your virtue combats with the power
Of this sweet ill, repelling its assaults,
It will appease the tempest in your mind.

Then rest your hope in it and on the help
That time will bring; and put your trust in heaven
Which is too righteous to abandon virtue
To endless punishment.

INFANTA: My fondest hope
Is to lose hope.

(*Enter* PAGE.)

PAGE: By your command, Madame,
Chimène comes to see you. [*Exit.*]

INFANTA: Entertain her
In the gallery yonder.

LÉONOR: Do you wish to stay
Day-dreaming here?

INFANTA: No, I only wish,
Despite my grief, to recompose my face
A little more at leisure. I will follow. (*Exit* LÉONOR.)
Just heaven, from which I wait my remedy,
O set at last some limit to the ill
Which now possesses me. Secure my peace
And honor; in another's happiness
I seek my own. This marriage equally
Concerns three people: make it swiftly settled,
Or make my soul more strong. Join these two lovers
In bonds of wedlock: that will break my fetters
And end my torments. But I have delayed
Too long already. I'll go and find Chimène,
For talking with her may assuage my pain. [*Exit.*]

Scene 3—*In front of the Palace.*

(*Enter* DON GOMÈS *and* DON DIÈGUE.)

DON GOMÈS: So you have won: the favor of the King,
In making you the Prince of Castille's tutor,
Promotes you to a place which I alone

Deserved to have.
DON DIÈGUE: This mark of honor, sir,
Bestowed upon my house, displays to all
That he is just, and knows how to reward
Past services.
DON GOMÈS: However great they are,
Kings are like us; and they can make mistakes
Like other men; and this choice serves to prove
To all the court, they know ill how to pay
For present services.
DON DIÈGUE: Let us say no more
About a choice with which you are incensed.
Favor, as well as merit, played a part:
But absolute power demands we should not question
A king's decision. To this honor, then,
That he has done me, add another now.
Join with a sacred knot my house and yours.
You have an only daughter, I one son.
Their marriage now can make us more than friends;
Do me this honor and accept my son
As son-in-law.
DON GOMÈS: This noble son of yours
Should seek a loftier match than you suggest;
And the new brilliance of your dignity
Should swell his heart with further vanity.
Enjoy your honor, and instruct the Prince;
Show him the way to rule a kingdom, sir.
Make all tremble underneath his law,
Filling the good with love, the bad with fear.
Add to these virtues those of a warrior:
Show him how he must learn to suffer hardship,
To be unrivalled in the trade of Mars;
To pass whole days on horseback and whole nights;
To sleep in armor, and to storm the walls,
And owe a victory only to himself.
Instruct him by example; make him perfect,
By showing to his eyes the things you teach.

DON DIÈGUE: Despite of envy, sir, to learn by example
He'll simply read the story of my life;
And there, in a long chain of splendid deeds,
He'll see how to defeat rebellious peoples,
How to attack a place, command an army.
And on great exploits to erect his fame.

DON GOMÈS: Living examples have a greater force.
A prince will learn the lesson of his duty
But feebly from a book. What, after all,
Have all your years achieved?—which cannot equal
A single day of mine. If you were valiant,
I am valiant still: and this right arm
Is of the kingdom now the main support.
Granada and Aragon both tremble
When my sword flashes; and my very name
Serves as a rampart to protect Castille.
For you would soon pass under other laws,
And have your foes for kings, without my aid.
Each day, each instant, to enhance my fame,
Set laurels upon laurels, victory
On victory; the Prince would at my side
Make trial of his courage, underneath
The shelter of my arm; he'd learn to conquer
By watching me, and being what he is,
He'd quickly see . . .

DON DIÈGUE: I know how well you serve the King;
I've seen you fighting under my command.
Now age has frozen all these nerves of mine.
Your matchless valor has filled up my place;
In short, you are today what I was once.
And yet you see in this decision now
A monarch puts some difference between us.

DON GOMÈS: You've gained what I deserved.

DON DIÈGUE: The one who gained it
Deserved it better.

DON GOMÈS: He who best can fill it
Is worthiest for the post.

DON DIÈGUE: To be refused
Is not a good sign.
DON GOMÈS: You obtained the post
By court intrigues.
DON DIÈGUE: The fame of my deeds alone
Solicited for me.
DON GOMÈS: Let us say rather
The King paid honor to your age.
DON DIÈGUE: The King
Measured the honor by my bravery.
DON GOMÈS: If so, the honor should have come to me.
DON DIÈGUE: He who could not obtain did not deserve.
DON GOMÈS: Did not deserve it?
DON DIÈGUE: No.
DON GOMÈS: Such insolence,
You rash old man, will have its just reward.
[*Strikes him.*]
DON DIÈGUE: (*Drawing his sword*) Go on and take my life after such shame;
None of my family has blushed till now.
DON GOMÈS: What would you do, all feeble as you are?
DON DIÈGUE: O God! My strength deserts me in my need.
[DON GOMÈS *disarms him.*]
DON GOMÈS: I have your sword: but you would be too vain
If I should keep it. Farewell. In spite of envy,
Read to the Prince for his instruction now
The story of your life—this punishment
Of insolence will serve as ornament! [*Exit.*]
DON DIÈGUE: Rage and despair! O treachery of age!
Have I then lived so long only to end
In infamy? Have I grown white in war
Only to see my laurels all are withered
In a single day? And did my arm—that arm
All Spain admired, which has so often saved
This empire, propped its throne—betray my cause
And fail me in my need? O cruel remembrance
Of my past glory! Work of many days

Effaced in one! New dignity which proves
Fatal to happiness! A lofty crag
From which my honor falls! Must I behold
The Count thus triumph, and die without revenge
Or live in shame? Count, be the Prince's tutor,
That post will not admit a man dishonored;
Despite the choice of the King, your jealous pride
By this flagrant insult rendered me unworthy.
And you, the glorious instrument of my deeds,
But now the useless ornament of a body
Frozen with age, you sword, which once was feared,
But in this crisis proved a useless show,
Not for defense, go, leave the least of men,
And pass, to avenge me, into better hands.

(*Enter* DON RODRIGUE.)

DON DIÈGUE: Rodrigue, are you brave?
DON RODRIGUE: I soon would prove it
On any man but you.
DON DIÈGUE: Your anger's welcome!
Worthy resentment, sweet for me to see!
In this noble wrath I recognize my blood;
My own youth lives again in this prompt courage.
Come, my son; come, my blood; come to repair
The shame I suffer. Come to avenge me.
DON RODRIGUE: For what?
DON DIÈGUE: A cruel insult, which to both our honors
Carries a mortal blow—a slap on the face.
I would have slain him, but my age betrayed
That brave desire; and so this sword of mine
Which my arm could not keep, I hand to yours
For you to avenge me. Prove your courage now
Against his arrogance. His blood alone
Can wash away this outrage. Die or kill.
Not to deceive you, I must tell you too
That your opponent is a man to fear;
I've seen him, smeared with blood and dust, bring terror

To a whole army; I have seen his valor
Scatter a hundred squadrons—and, one thing more,
This valiant soldier and this famous captain
Is . . .

DON RODRIGUE: For God's sake, tell me.

DON DIÈGUE: The father of Chimène.

DON RODRIGUE: The . . .

DON DIÈGUE: Do not reply; I know too well your love,
But he who lives in infamy is unworthy
To live at all. The dearer the offender
The worse the offense. You know the insult now;
You have the instrument of vengeance there.
I say no more. Avenge me and yourself;
Now show yourself a worthy son of mine.
Crushed with misfortunes, I am going now
To weep for them. Go, fly to avenge us both. [*Exit.*]

DON RODRIGUE:

Pierced to the heart
By such an unforeseen and mortal blow,
To be an avenger is my wretched part,
And yet it is a righteous cause, I know.
I stand here motionless; and in amaze
Yield to the stroke which slays
My love about to have its recompense!
O God, the dreadful pain!
It is my father suffers this offense,
His injurer the father of Chimène.

A war is in my heart:
Against my honor now my love takes part.
I must avenge a father, lose my love.
One fires my courage, one puts out the flame.
The dreadful choice is to betray my love
Or live in shame.
An infinite harm both courses now present.
O God, the dreadful pain!
Must an insult have no punishment?
Must I punish the father of Chimène?

Father, mistress; love, fame;
Noble and hard constraint, sweet tyranny;
My fame will tarnish or my pleasure die.
One brings me misery, the other shame.
Dear, cruel hope of a brave yet loving heart,
  Allotting me my part,
The noble foe of my best happiness,
  Sword which brings my pain,
Are you given me my honor to redress?
Or are you given me to lose Chimène?

Better by far to die,
My mistress should not plead her rights in vain,
By vengeance I will earn her enmity
And I shall earn her scorn should I refrain.
One makes me faithless to my nobler part,
  And one unworthy of her heart.
My ill increases by its remedy
  And all augments my pain:
Come, soul, and since I needs must die,
Let's die without offending my Chimène!

To die unsatisfied!
To seek a death so mortal to my fame!
Let Spain upon my memory put the blame
Of having ill upheld my house's pride!
And if love's path, not honor's, I should choose
  Love also I should lose.
I will not listen to this treacherous thought
  Which but augments my pain,
Come, let me save my honor, as I ought,
Since, after all, I'll have to lose Chimène.

Yes, I have thought amiss—
To him, and not to her, the debt is chief.
Whether I die in combat or of grief
The blood I shed will be as pure as his.
Already I must blame my negligence,—
  I'll run to purge the offense.

Ashamed that I have wavered for so long,
Let me not stay in pain,
Because today my father suffered wrong,
His injurer the father of Chimène.

[Exit.]

Act II

Scene 1—*A room in the Palace.*

(*Enter* DON ARIAS *and* DON GOMÈS.)

DON GOMÈS: I admit between us that my heated blood
Was roused too much by a word, and that I acted
With too much pride; but since the blow was given,
There is no remedy.

DON ARIAS: Let your courage yield
To the King's wishes. He is much concerned;
His wrathful heart with full authority
Will act against you soon. You've no defense
To serve your turn; the rank of the injured man,
The greatness of the injury, demand
Your dutiful submission, and satisfaction
Beyond the common rate.

DON GOMÈS: The King, at his pleasure,
Can of my life dispose.

DON ARIAS: Your fault is followed
By too much anger. But the King still loves you.
Appease his wrath. He has said "This is my will."
Will you disobey?

DON GOMÈS: To preserve my reputation
To disobey is not so great a crime;
And if it were, my present services
Are more than enough to win an amnesty.

DON ARIAS: However illustrious your services,

However they deserve consideration,
A king is never indebted to a subject.
You're much deceived, sir, and you ought to know
A man who serves his king does but his duty.
You will destroy yourself by this illusion.
DON GOMÈS: I will believe you after I have tried.
DON ARIAS: You ought to fear the puissance of a king.
DON GOMÈS: One day does not destroy a man like me.
Let the great King prepare to punish me:
The state itself will perish if I die.
DON ARIAS: How, sir! You fear the sovereign power so little . . . ?
DON GOMÈS: Of a scepter which without me he'd let fall.
The King has too much interest in my life—
My head in falling would bring down his crown.
DON ARIAS: Listen to reason. Make a right decision.
DON GOMÈS: I have decided.
DON ARIAS: What shall I say to him?
I must report to him.
DON GOMÈS: That I will not
Consent to shame.
DON ARIAS: Remember that kings wish
To be absolute.
DON GOMÈS: No, sir, the die is cast.
Let's speak no more of it.
DON ARIAS: I'll say good-bye.
Since I have tried in vain to change your mind,
Despite your laurels, fear the thunderbolt.
DON GOMÈS: I will await it without fear.
DON ARIAS: But not
Without effect.
DON GOMÈS: Then by that we shall see
That Don Diègue will get satisfaction. [*Exit* DON ARIAS.]
The man who fears not death does not fear threats.
My heart can bear the cruellest disgrace.
I can be driven to unhappiness
But not be forced to live without my honor.

(*Enter* DON RODRIGUE.)

DON RODRIGUE: My lord, a word with you.
DON GOMÈS: Speak.
DON RODRIGUE: Tell me this:
Are you acquainted with Don Diègue?
DON GOMÈS: Yes.
DON RODRIGUE: Let us speak quietly. Listen. Do you know
That this old man exemplified the valor
And honor of his time? Do you know this?
DON GOMÈS: Perhaps.
DON RODRIGUE: This flame which flashes from my eyes
Shows that I am his son—do you know this?
DON GOMÈS: How does this concern me?
DON RODRIGUE: Four paces hence
I'll teach you.
DON GOMÈS: Foolish youth!
DON RODRIGUE: Speak calmly, sir.
It's true I'm young, but in the nobly born
Valor waits not for age.
DON GOMÈS: To match yourself
With me? What can have given you this conceit,
Who never fought before?
DON RODRIGUE: Men of my kind
Need no apprenticeship; their trial strokes
Are also master-strokes.
DON GOMÈS: Do you indeed
Know who I am?
DON RODRIGUE: Yes, anyone but me
Would tremble at the mere sound of your name.
The laurel-wreaths with which your head is crowned
Seem to foretell my doom. I'm rash enough
To attack an ever-conquering warrior;
But as I'm brave enough, I'll have the strength.
To one who fights to avenge his father's honor,
Nothing's impossible. You are unconquered,
But not unconquerable.
DON GOMÈS: The lofty courage
Your speech displays I've noticed in your eyes;

And thinking that I saw in you the honor
Of all Castille, my soul has destined you
To wed my daughter. I know your love for her,
And I'm delighted that it yields to duty,
And has not weakened yet your noble ardor;
That your high virtue answers my esteem,
And—wishing a perfect knight for son-in-law—
That I was not mistaken in my choice.
But yet my heart is moved with pity for you:
Your courage I admire; your youth I pity.
Seek not to make a fatal first attempt;
And from an unequal combat free my valor.
This victory would bring me little honor—
To conquer without danger has no glory.
People would always think that you were conquered
Without an effort; and I would only have
The sorrow of your death.

DON RODRIGUE: An unworthy pity
Succeeds your bragging: do you steal my honor,
And fear to take my life?

DON GOMÈS: Go, leave this place.

DON RODRIGUE: Come, no more talk.

DON GOMÈS: Are you so tired of life?

DON RODRIGUE: Are you afraid to die?

DON GOMÈS: Come, you do your duty;
The son degenerates who for one moment
Survives his father's honor. [*Exeunt.*]

Scene 2—*The Infanta's room.*

(*Enter the* INFANTA, CHIMÈNE *and* LÉONOR.)

INFANTA: Chimène, assuage your sorrow. Bear this blow
With constancy. For you will see a calm
Follow this squall. Only a little cloud
Covers your happiness, and you'll lose nothing

By having it deferred.

CHIMÈNE: Worn with despair,
My heart dare hope for nothing. A sudden storm
Troubling a placid sea brings us the threat
Of certain shipwreck; and I do not doubt
That I shall perish within sight of port.
I loved, and I was loved, with the approval
Of both our fathers; and I told you this
At the very moment when their quarrel started;
And when I heard of it my hopes were ruined.
Cursed ambition, the detestable folly
To which the noblest are enslaved! and honor,
Cruel to my dearest hope, what will you cost me
In tears and sighs!

INFANTA: You have no cause for fear,
Because the quarrel flared up in a moment
And will be quenched in another. It has made
Too great a stir not to be settled soon;
The King already wishes for a peace;
I feel for your sorrow, and I will perform
The impossible to stem this quarrel's current.

CHIMÈNE: To reconcile them is impossible:
Such deadly insults cannot be repaired.
Both prudence and compulsion are in vain,
And even if it seemed the ill was cured
It would be but appearance: for the hatred
Hidden within the heart feeds secret fires
Which nonetheless are fierce.

INFANTA: The holy knot
Which joins you with Rodrigue will dissipate
The fathers' hatred, and your stronger love
Will end this discord with a happy marriage.

CHIMÈNE: I long more than I hope, for Don Diègue
Is far too haughty, and I know my father.
I cannot staunch my tears. The past torments me;
I dread the future more.

INFANTA: What do you fear?

An old man's impotence.

CHIMÈNE: Rodrigue has courage.

INFANTA:.He is too young.

CHIMÈNE: But yet the brave are brave
From their first youth.

INFANTA: You should not fear too much.
He is too much in love to do you harm;
And two words from your lips would be enough
To arrest his anger.

CHIMÈNE: If he obeyed me not,
The grief would shatter me; and if he does,
What will be said of him? A noble son
To suffer such an outrage! whether he yields
To the love which binds him to me, or resists,
My mind can only be ashamed for him,
Or torn by his refusal.

INFANTA: Your soul is noble,
And though your heart's involved, you cannot harbor
A thought that's base. But if until the day
When they are reconciled, I make your lover
My prisoner, and so prevent his courage
From doing harm, your loving spirit then
Would suffer no disquiet?

CHIMÈNE: Ah, Madame!
In that case you would set my mind at rest.

(*Enter* PAGE.)

INFANTA: Page, find Don Rodrigue and bring him here.

PAGE: The Count and he . . .

CHIMÈNE: Good God! I tremble.

INFANTA: Speak.

PAGE: Together left the palace.

CHIMÈNE: Alone?

PAGE: Alone.
They seemed to be quarrelling in a low voice.

CHIMÈNE: Doubtless, they're fighting. It is now too late

To intervene. Forgive this haste, Madame.
(*Exeunt* PAGE *and* CHIMÈNE.)

INFANTA: I feel my spirit troubled. I weep for her,
But yet I am enraptured by her lover.
Calmness abandons me—my love revives.
What separates Don Rodrigue and Chimène
Even at the same time makes my hope and pain
To be reborn. Though I regret their severance,
It fills my heart with secret happiness.

LÉONOR: Does that high virtue reigning in your soul
Give way so easily to this base love?

INFANTA: Call it not base, for glorious and triumphant
It legislates for me. Speak well of it,
Since it is precious to me. Although my virtue
Still fights with it, I hope; and ill-defended
Against so mad a hope, my heart flies after
A lover that Chimène has lost.

LÉONOR: And so
You shed your glorious courage, and your reason
Ceases to function.

INFANTA: Reason speaks in vain
When the heart's reached by that enchanting poison!
And when the sick man loves his malady
How hardly will he let himself be cured!

LÉONOR: Your hope seduces you because you find
Your illness sweet; but Rodrigue is unworthy
To be your husband.

INFANTA: I know it but too well;
But if my virtue yields, then learn how far
Love can flatter a heart which it possesses.
If Rodrigue should emerge victorious,
If that great warrior is beaten down
Beneath his valor, I can give him credit
And love him without shame. What won't he do
If he can overcome the Count? I dare
To think that by the least of all his deeds
Whole kingdoms will be brought beneath his laws.

And now already my flattering love persuades me
I see him on the throne of Granada,
The subjugated Moors adoring him,
And trembling as they worship; Aragon
Humbly receiving this new conqueror;
Portugal at his feet; until at last
Bearing his conquering sword across the seas
He sprinkles with the blood of Africans
His destined laurels. All that may be said
Of famous champions, I expect of him
After his victory, and so my love
Will add to my renown.

LÉONOR: But see, Madame,
This fine career that you carve out for him
Comes from a duel which may not take place.

INFANTA: Rodrigue has been insulted; and the Count
Was guilty of an outrage. They have left
The palace together. What would you have more?

LÉONOR: Well, they will fight, if you require it so,
But will your Rodrigue go as far in fact
As in your thoughts?

INFANTA: Yes, you are right.
I'm mad; my mind is wandering: you see
By this what ills my love prepares for me.
Come to my chamber to console my griefs,
And do not leave me now in my distress. [*Exeunt.*]

Scene 3—*The Court.*

(*Enter* DON FERDINAND (*the King*), DON ARIAS *and* DON SANCHE.)

DON FERDINAND: Is the Count then so proud, so blind to reason?
Dares he suppose his crime so pardonable?

DON ARIAS: I have conversed with him for a long time
On your behalf, Sire; I have done my best

And obtained nothing from him.

DON FERDINAND: Righteous Heaven!
Has a rash subject, then, such small respect,
Such little care to please me? He insults
Don Diègue, and scorns his king; lays down the law
In the middle of my Court. However brave,
However great a captain, I know well
How to bring down his pride. For, were he Valor,
Nay, Mars himself, he'll learn the penalty
Of disobeying. Whatever such insolence
Deserved, I wished at first to treat it mildly.
But since my leniency he thus abuses
Go now, and whether he resists or not,
Arrest him.

DON SANCHE: Perhaps he will be less rebellious
After a little while. He was approached
Still heated from his quarrel. A heart so brave
Would find it difficult to yield at first.
He knows that he is wrong, but yet his pride
Prevents him from admitting it.

DON FERDINAND: Be silent,
Don Sanche; be warned now that the man who takes
His part, is guilty too.

DON SANCHE: I will obey,
Sire, and be silent; but yet let me speak
Two words in his defense.

DON FERDINAND: What could you say?

DON SANCHE: I'd say a soul accustomed to great deeds
Cannot abuse itself by such submissions
Involving him (as he believes) in shame.
Therefore the Count resisted. He finds his duty
A trifle harsh, and would obey you, Sire,
If he were not great-hearted. Make his arm,
Strengthened in war, repair this injury
At his sword's point. He'll give satisfaction.
Meanwhile, I'll answer for him.

DON FERDINAND: You forget

The respect you owe to me; but I forgive
Your youthful ardor. Nevertheless, a king
Must prudently consider what is best,
Not waste his subjects' blood. My fatherly care
Protects them, watches over them—the head
Needs members in its service. So your reason
Cannot be mine. You speak as a soldier; I
Should act as a king. Whatever you may say,
Whatever he presumes to think, the Count
Loses no status in obeying me.
Besides, his insult also touches me;
The man I've made the tutor to my son
Has lost his honor. To attack my choice
Is to impugn me, and to undermine
The supreme power. Say no more. Enough of this.
Ten vessels have been sighted, flying the flag
Of our old enemy: they've dared to appear
At the mouth of the river.

DON ARIAS: The Moors have learnt by now
What you are made of; and, so often conquered,
They've lost the heart to pit themselves again
Against so great a victor.

DON FERDINAND: They will never
Behold without some jealousy my scepter
Rule Andalusia in their despite;
And that fair country which they owned so long
Is always looked at with an envious eye.
The only reason why, ten years ago,
I set my throne in Seville, was to be near them,
And so frustrate their warlike undertakings.

DON ARIAS: They've bought the knowledge dearly that your presence
Assures your conquest. You have nought to fear.

DON FERDINAND: And nothing to neglect. Danger is bred
From too much confidence; and you well know
How easily a tide can bring them here.
And yet it would be wrong to cause a panic;

The news is not yet certain. A false alarm
Would in the coming night cause needless fear.
Double the guards at the gates, and on the walls.
For tonight that will be enough.

(*Exit* DON ARIAS. *Enter* DON ALONSO.)

DON ALONSO: Your majesty,
The Count is dead. Don Diègue by his son
Has avenged his insult.
DON FERDINAND: When I was informed
About the insult, I foresaw the vengeance
And tried to prevent it.
DON ALONSO: Chimène brings her grief
To lay it at your feet. She comes in tears
To demand justice of you.
DON FERDINAND: Though my soul
Pities her sorrow, yet the Count deserved
This punishment of rashness. Nonetheless,
However just his fate, I cannot lose
A captain such as him without regret.
After his service rendered to the state,
And since his blood was shed a thousand times
In my defense, however I deplored
His arrogance, his loss will weaken me,
His death afflicts me.

(*Enter* DON DIÈGUE, DON ARIAS *and* CHIMÈNE.)

CHIMÈNE: Justice, Sire, Justice!
DON DIÈGUE: Listen to me, Sire.
CHIMÈNE: I throw myself before you.
DON DIÈGUE: I embrace your knees.
CHIMÈNE: I ask for justice, Sire.
DON DIÈGUE: Hear my defense!
CHIMÈNE: Punish the insolence
Of this audacious man; he has destroyed
The stay of your scepter. He has killed my father.
DON DIÈGUE: He has avenged his father.

CHIMÈNE: A king owes justice
To the blood of his subjects.
DON DIÈGUE: There's no penalty
For righteous vengeance.
DON FERDINAND: Rise up, both of you,
And speak at leisure. Chimène, I sympathize
With your distress and feel my soul is touched
With an equal grief. (*To* DON DIÈGUE) You will speak afterwards,
So do not interrupt her pleadings.
CHIMÈNE: Sire,
My father's dead; my eyes have seen his blood
Gush from his noble side; that very blood
Which often was a safeguard to your walls,
That blood which gained your victories so often,
Now smokes in fury that it should be shed
And not for you; war would not dare to shed it,
But Rodrigue has now within your court
Covered the earth with it. Nerveless and pale
I ran to the spot and found my father lifeless . . .
Forgive my tears, Sire; in this tragic tale
My voice is failing me. My tears and sighs
Will tell the rest more plainly than my words.
DON FERDINAND: Take courage, my child, and know that from today
Your king will act as father in his stead.
CHIMÈNE: My grief is followed, Sire, by too much honor.
I found my father lifeless, as I said;
His side was open, and, to move me more,
His blood inscribed my duty in the dust,
Or (shall I say?) his valor thus reduced
Spoke to me through his wound and urged me on
To seek revenge, and to your righteous ears
My voice speaks through that mouth. Do not allow
Such license, Sire, to reign before your eyes,
And that the bravest, with impunity,
Should be exposed to such a rash attack;

That a presumptuous youth should overcome
A man of such renown, bathe in his blood,
And so affront his memory. When such a warrior
Is snatched away from you, and not avenged,
It will extinguish the desire to serve you.
And so, my father's dead. I ask for vengeance
More for your sake than to relieve my soul.
Yours is the loss when such a great man dies.
Take vengeance, blood for blood; and sacrifice—
No, not to me, but to your crown, your power,
Your person; sacrifice, Sire, to the welfare
Of the whole state, the man that such an outrage
Has filled with pride.

DON FERDINAND: Don Diègue, reply.

DON DIÈGUE: How lucky is the man who ends his life
When he has lost his strength! And how old age
Can bring disaster to an honored man
At the end of his career! I whose long toils
Accumulated glory, I who once
Was followed everywhere by victory,
Now see myself, since I have lived too long,
Receive an insult and remain defeated.
What never battle, siege, nor ambuscade,
Nor Aragon, nor Granada, nor all
Your foes, nor envious rivals could accomplish,
The Count, at court, almost before your eyes,
Has done to me, being jealous of your choice,
And proud of the advantage he possessed
Through age's impotence. And thus the hairs,
Grown white beneath my helmet, and this blood
Poured out so freely in your service, Sire,
This arm, the terror of the enemies' ranks,
Would have descended powerless to the tomb,
Laden with infamy, had I not had
A son who was worthy of me, and of his country,
And worthy of his king. He lent his hand;
He killed the Count. He has restored my honor

And washed away my shame. If to show courage,
If to resent wrongs, if to avenge a blow
Deserves a punishment, on me alone
Should fall the tempest's fury. When the arm
Commits a fault, the head is punished for it.
Whether or not the matter in dispute
Is criminal, Sire, I am the head and he
Is but the arm. And if Chimène complains
That he has killed her father, he did it only
Because I could not do it. Sacrifice
The head, then, that the years will snatch away,
And keep his arm to serve you. Satisfy
Chimène, with blood of mine. I don't resist.
I willingly consent to punishment,
And far from murmuring at a harsh decree,
Dying without dishonor, I shall die
Without regret.

DON FERDINAND: The matter is important,
And, well considered, ought to be debated
In open council. Don Sanche, take Chimène home.
Don Diègue will stay here at my court,
Upon parole. Find his son. I'll do you justice.

CHIMÈNE: It's just, great King, for a murderer to die.

DON FERDINAND: Take some rest, my child, and calm your griefs.

CHIMÈNE: To order rest is to increase my woes. [*Exeunt.*]

Act III

Scene 1—*Chimène's house.*

(*Enter* DON RODRIGUE *and* ELVIRE.)

ELVIRE: Rodrigue, what are you doing? Unhappy man,
Why have you come here?

DON RODRIGUE: I am following
My tragic destiny.
ELVIRE: What possesses you,
To show such pride and rashness as to appear
In the house you've filled with sorrow? Do you come
To confront the phantom of the man you killed?
DON RODRIGUE: His life was my reproach: honor required
That I should slay him.
ELVIRE: But to seek asylum
In the house of death! Has it ever been before
The refuge of the murderer?
DON RODRIGUE: I have come here
Only to surrender to my judge.
Don't look at me with an astonished face!
I seek death after having given it.
My love is judge, my judge is my Chimène.
Since I deserve her hatred, I deserve
To die; and I have come here to receive,
As a sovereign boon, the sentence from her lips,
Quietus at her hands.
ELVIRE: Flee from her sight;
Flee from her violence. Take away your presence
From her first fury. Don't expose yourself
To the first heat of her resentment.
DON RODRIGUE: No,
No, my wronged love cannot have too much anger
For my deserts; and if I can increase it,
I shall die sooner, and by this escape
A hundred deaths that threaten me.
ELVIRE: Chimène
Is at the palace now, prostrate with weeping;
And will return here well accompanied.
Fly, Rodrigue, fly; deliver me
From apprehension. What will not be said,
If you are seen here? Do you wish a slanderer,
To crown her misery, to accuse her now
Of tolerating one who killed her father?

She's coming back—I see her—at least, Rodrigue,
Hide, for her honor's sake.

(DON RODRIGUE *hides; Enter* DON SANCHE *and* CHIMÈNE.)

DON SANCHE: Madame, it's true,
You must have blood for blood; your anger's just,
Your tears are natural; and I will not try
To soften or console you. But if I'm able
To serve you, then employ my sword to punish
The guilty one; employ my love to avenge
This death. My arm will certainly be strong
Under your orders.
CHIMÈNE: Unhappy that I am!
DON SANCHE: Accept my service.
CHIMÈNE: I would offend the King
Who promised me justice.
DON SANCHE: Justice, as you know,
Saunters so slowly that the crime goes free
While the poor plaintiff weeps. Let me avenge you.
That way is surer and more swift to punish.
CHIMÈNE: That's the last remedy; and if it's needed,
And you still pity my misfortunes then,
You will be free to avenge my injury.
DON SANCHE: That's the one happiness to which I aspire,
And as you let me hope, I go contented. [*Exit.*]
CHIMÈNE: At last I'm free to act without restraint
And show you how I suffer; give free passage
To my sad sighs; open my heart to you,
And tell you my distress. My father's dead,
Elvire; and, with the first sword he has wielded,
Rodrigue has cut his thread. Eyes, weep your fill,
And drown yourselves in tears! Half of my life
Has put into the grave the other half,
So that I must avenge, after this deed,
What I have lost on what remains to me.
ELVIRE: Rest, Madame.
CHIMÈNE: Ah! How inopportunely

In this misfortune do you speak of rest!
How will my sorrow ever be appeased
If I cannot hate the cause? What can I hope for,
Except an eternal torment, if I must
Pursue a crime and love the criminal?

ELVIRE: Can you still love the man who slew your father?

CHIMÈNE: It is not love, Elvire; I adore him.
My passion and resentment are at strife.
Within my enemy I find my lover;
Despite my anger, feeling in my heart
Rodrigue is fighting with my father still;
He attacks, he drives him back, and then gives ground;
Defends himself, now strong, now weak, and now
Triumphant; but in this hard fight between
Anger and love, he tears my heart in twain,
But does not alter my determination.
Whatever power my love has over me,
I do not hesitate to follow duty,
But run unwavering where my honor drives me.
Rodrigue is very dear, my love torments me,
My love still takes his side, but all in vain.
I know myself, and that my father's dead.

ELVIRE: Do you mean to pursue him still?

CHIMÈNE: Ah! Cruel thought!
And cruel pursuit which I am forced to make!
For I demand his head and fear to get it:
My death will follow his, and yet I wish
To punish him.

ELVIRE: Give up, Madame, give up
A plan so tragic; do not upon yourself
Impose a law so cruel.

CHIMÈNE: What, Elvire,
My father dead, and almost in my arms,
And I not hear his blood that cries aloud!
My heart, infatuated, think it owes him
No more than useless tears! To suffer passion
To smother honor under cowardly silence!

ELVIRE: Believe me, Madame, you would be excused,
If you were less incensed against a lover
Who is so dear to you. You've done enough.
You've seen the King. Do not press home your plea,
And don't persist in this peculiar humor.
CHIMÈNE: My honor is at stake. I must take vengeance.
However passion may deceive our hearts,
To noble natures all excuse is shameful.
ELVIRE: But you love Rodrigue and cannot hate him.
CHIMÈNE: That I confess.
ELVIRE: What do you mean to do?
CHIMÈNE: To guard my reputation and to end
This torture: to pursue him, to destroy him,
And then die after him.

(*Enter* DON RODRIGUE.)

DON RODRIGUE: I will not give you
The trouble of pursuit. Assure your honor
By slaying me.
CHIMÈNE: What do I see, Elvire?
Rodrigue in my house! Rodrigue in my presence!
DON RODRIGUE: Don't spare my blood, but taste the sweetness now
Of your revenge. I shan't resist.
CHIMÈNE: Alas!
DON RODRIGUE: Hear me, one moment.
CHIMÈNE: Go, and let me die.
DON RODRIGUE: Only four words, and afterwards reply
But with this sword.
CHIMÈNE: Oh! With my father's blood
Still stained!
DON RODRIGUE: Chimène.
CHIMÈNE: Remove that hateful thing
Which blames your crime and blames me that you live.
DON RODRIGUE: Look at it rather to excite your hate,
To increase your wrath and hasten my despatch.
CHIMÈNE: It's colored with my blood.

DON RODRIGUE: Plunge it in mine,
And make it lose the tincture of your own.
CHIMÈNE: How cruel you are, that in one day can kill
Father with sword, and daughter by its sight.
Take it away, I cannot bear to see it.
You'd have me listen, and you make me die.
DON RODRIGUE: I do your will, but do not lose the wish
To finish by your hands my wretched life;
But yet do not expect from my affection
A base repentance of a worthy deed.
The irreparable effect of a quick temper
Disgraced my father, covered me with shame.
You know quite well the effect of such a blow
Upon a man of spirit. I shared the insult
And sought the author of it. So I found him,
Avenged my honor and my father both.
I'd do it again, if I had it to do.
Not that my love did not contend for you
For long, against my father and myself.
Judge of its power: in spite of the offense
I could deliberate if I should take
Vengeance or not. Confronted with the choice
Of hurting you or suffering an insult,
I thought that my arm too had been too prompt;
I accused myself of too much violence;
Your beauty would have doubtless tipped the balance,
If I had not set up against your charms
The knowledge that a man bereft of honor
Would not deserve you; that despite the place
I held within your soul, you loved me noble,
But you would hate me infamous; that to obey
The voice of love would render me unworthy,
Discrediting your choice. I say this still;
And, though with painful sighs, till my last gasp
I would repeat it. I've offended you,
But driven to do it to blot out my shame,
And so deserve you; honor's satisfied,

So is my father, but now I come to you
To offer satisfaction. You see me here
To offer you my blood. I did my duty;
I do it now. I know a slaughtered father
Arms you against my crime. I did not wish
To rob you of your victim. Sacrifice
With courage to the blood that he has spilled,
The one whose honor was in shedding it.

CHIMÈNE: Ah! Rodrigue, it is true, although your foe
I cannot condemn you that you fled from shame.
And in whatever way my griefs burst forth,
I don't accuse you, I lament my woes.
I know what honor, after such an outrage,
Demanded of a noble heart. You've done
Only the duty of a man of worth.
But also, doing it, you've taught me mine.
Your tragic valor by your victory
Instructs me now. It has avenged your father,
Upheld your honor. Now it is my turn
Though it afflicts me, to uphold my honor,
And avenge my father. But alas! my love
Makes me despair: if any other fate
Had snatched my father from me, then my soul,
In the happiness of seeing you, would have found
Its one relief; and when so dear a hand
Had wiped away my tears, I would have felt
A charm against my grief. But I must lose you,
Having lost him. To overcome my love
Is due to honor; and this dreadful duty,
Murderous to me, compels me to take pains
To destroy you. But yet do not expect
From my affection any cowardly feelings
To stay your punishment. Although our love
Pleads in your favor, my nobility
Must answer yours. Since you have shown yourself,
Even in offending me, worthy of me;
I, by your death, must likewise show myself

Worthy of you.

DON RODRIGUE: Defer no longer then
What honor asks of you—it asks my life,
And I resign it to you. Sacrifice it
To this noble aim. The stroke will be sweet to me
Even as the sentence. To await slow justice
After my crime, is to postpone your glory
As well as my punishment. I will die happy
Dying of such a stroke.

CHIMÈNE: Go, I'm your accuser,
And not your executioner. If you
Offer your life to me, is it for me
To take it? I should attack it, but you ought
To defend it; and it's from another man
I must obtain it; I should prosecute you,
Not punish you.

DON RODRIGUE: Although our love pleads for me,
Yet your nobility should answer mine;
And to use other arms to avenge a father,
Chimène, believe me, does not answer it.
My hand alone was able to avenge
The insult to my father; and your hand
Alone should avenge yours.

CHIMÈNE: Oh, cruel! Why
Do you insist on this? You took your vengeance
Unaided, and you wish to give me mine!
I'll follow your example, and I have
Too great a spirit to allow my glory
To be shared with you. My father and my honor
Would not owe anything to the love you bear me,
Nor yet to your despair.

DON RODRIGUE: Harsh point of honor!
Whatever I do, shall I not in the end
Obtain this mercy? In a dead father's name,
Or in our love's name, punish me, for vengeance,
Or else for pity. Your unlucky lover
Will suffer less in dying by your hand

Than living with your hate.
CHIMÈNE: Go, I don't hate you.
DON RODRIGUE: You should do so.
CHIMÈNE: I cannot.
DON RODRIGUE: Do you fear
So little the blame, so little the false rumors?
When it is known your love survives my crime
What will not envy and imposture publish?
Silence them now, and without further talk,
Save your renown by making me to die.
CHIMÈNE: It shines much better if I let you live;
I hope that blackest envy will exhalt
My glory to the skies, and mourn my griefs,
Knowing I persecute the man I love.
Go now, and show no more to my deep sorrow
The man I must destroy, although I love him.
Hide your departure in the shades of night.
If you are seen to leave, you jeopardize
My honor; for the only chance for scandal
Is to discover that I let you stay.
Don't give it cause to speak ill of my virtue.
DON RODRIGUE: Alas!
CHIMÈNE: O let me die!
DON RODRIGUE: What have you decided?
CHIMÈNE: Despite my passion which resists my anger,
I will do all I can to take revenge;
But yet despite the strictness of my duty,
My sole wish is that I accomplish nothing.
DON RODRIGUE: Miracle of love!
CHIMÈNE: O heap of miseries!
DON RODRIGUE: How many woes and tears our fathers cost us!
CHIMÈNE: Who would believe . . .
DON RODRIGUE: Chimène, who would have said . . .
CHIMÈNE: That happiness which seemed within our grasp
Would be destroyed so soon?
DON RODRIGUE: That so near harbor,
A sudden storm would break our hopes in pieces?

CHIMÈNE: Deadly sorrows!
DON RODRIGUE: Vain regrets!
CHIMÈNE: Once more,
Be gone, I will not listen to you more.
DON RODRIGUE: Farewell, I'll drag around my dying life,
Till by your efforts it is taken from me.
CHIMÈNE: If I succeed, I swear I will not breathe
A moment after you. Farewell. Take care
That no one sees you.
DON RODRIGUE: Chimène, whatever evils
The heavens send us . . .
CHIMÈNE: Trouble me no more.
Leave me to sigh. I seek for night and silence
In which to weep. [*Exeunt.*]

Scene 2—A *public square.*

(*Enter* DON DIÈGUE.)

DON DIÈGUE: Our joy is never perfect; happiest things
Are mixed with sadness; and in all events,
Our pure content is sullied with some care.
So is it now. In the midst of happiness
I feel a touch of doubt. I swim in joy
And yet I shake with fear. Though I have seen
My enemy slain who had insulted me,
I cannot see yet the avenger's hand.
I try in vain, all broken as I am,
To seek him through the town. The little vigor
Old age has left me is spent fruitlessly
In searching for this victor. Every hour,
In every place, in this dark night, I think
To embrace him, but embrace a shadow only;
And so my love, thus cheated, forms suspicions
By which my fear redoubles. I can find
No traces of his flight. I fear the friends

And servants of the Count: they terrify me
And overturn my reason. Rodrigue is dead,
Or breathes in prison. Am I still mistaken,
Just Heaven, or do I now behold at last
My only hope? It's he. There is no doubt.
My prayers are answered, all my fear is scattered,
And my distress is ended.

(*Enter* DON RODRIGUE.)

Rodrigue, at last
Heaven lets me see you.

DON RODRIGUE: Alas!

DON DIÈGUE: O! Do not mingle
Sighs with my joy. Let me get back my breath
Before I praise you. My valor has no cause
To disavow you. You have copied it,
And your illustrious courage makes the heroes
Of our great family live again in you.
It is from them you descend; it is from me
You take your birth. Your first fight equals mine;
And animated by a noble spirit,
Your youth, by this great proof, has reached already
The fame I had before. Prop of my age,
Crown of my happiness, touch these white hairs
Which you have honored; come and kiss this cheek
And recognize the place on which was printed
The insult which your courage has effaced.

DON RODRIGUE: Yours is the honor; I could do no less,
Come of your blood, and nourished by your cares.
May my first feat of arms be pleasing to you
To whom I owe my life. But in your pleasure
Do not be jealous if I satisfy
Myself in turn. Let my despair break forth;
It has too long been flattered by your speech.
I don't repent of serving you, but now
Restore the happiness this glorious blow
Has snatched from me. For armed against my love,

I, by this very blow, have lost my soul.
Say no more, for I've lost everything,
And paid you all I owed you.

DON DIÈGUE: Bear more proudly
The fruit of victory: I gave you life,
And you restore me my integrity,
And as my honor is more dear to me
Than life itself, I owe you in return
So much the more. But from a noble heart
Dismiss such weaknesses; we have one honor,
But there are many mistresses. Love
Is but a pleasure, honor is a duty.

DON RODRIGUE: What are you saying?

DON DIÈGUE: What you ought to know.

DON RODRIGUE: My honor now takes vengeance on myself;
And you presume to urge me to the shame
Of faithlessness. But infamy pursues
The warrior without courage equally
With the unfaithful lover. Do not injure
My constancy; let me be noble still,
But do not make me perjured. No, my bonds
Are too strong to be broken in this way;
My word still binds me, though I hope no longer;
And as I cannot leave, or have, Chimène,
The death I seek now is my sweetest pain!

DON DIÈGUE: It is not yet the time to seek for death.
Your prince and country need your sword. The fleet
Which threatened, in the river mouth already,
Thinks to surprise the town and waste the country.
The Moors are upon us; and the tide and night
Will bring them noiselessly unto our walls
Within the hour. The Court is in disorder,
The people fearful. Cries alone are heard,
And only tears are seen. In this disaster,
My good luck had enabled me to find
At home five hundred of my friends, who came,
Knowing my insult, with united zeal

To offer vengeance. Though you have forestalled them,
Their valiant hands will better steep themselves
In blood of Africans. March at their head
Where honor calls you, for this noble band
Desires you as their leader. Go and withstand
The onslaught of our ancient enemies.
There, if you wish to die, you may seek out
A noble death. Seize now the chance that offers;
Make the King owe his safety to your death,
Or rather, come back with victorious laurels.
Don't circumscribe your fame by this revenge
Of a private insult; carry it further now.
By your valor, compel the King to pardon,
Chimène to silence. If you love her still,
Know that the one way to regain her heart
Is to return a conqueror. But time
Is far too precious to be wasted thus
In words, when you should fly. Come, follow me,
Go off to fight,
And show your King the loss that he sustained
By the Count's death, in you he has regained. [*Exeunt.*]

Act IV

Scene 1—*Chimène's house.*

(*Enter* CHIMÈNE *and* ELVIRE.)

CHIMÈNE: Is it not a false report? Are you sure of it?
ELVIRE: You'll hardly credit how all wonder at him
And with a common voice laud to the skies
This hero's glorious deeds. The Moors before him
Exhibited their shame. Swift was their onslaught,
Swifter their flight. After three hours of battle
Our warriors gained a total victory

With two kings prisoner. Their leader's valor
Knew no obstacles.
CHIMÈNE: And Rodrigue's hand
Has wrought these miracles?
ELVIRE: His noble prowess
Obtained these kings as prize. It was his hand
That conquered them and took them prisoner.
CHIMÈNE: Who gave you these extraordinary tidings?
ELVIRE: People who sing his praises, naming him
The object and the author of their joy,
Their guardian angel and their liberator.
CHIMÈNE: With what eyes does the King regard his valor?
ELVIRE: Rodrigue has not yet dared to appear before him;
But Don Diègue has joyfully presented
In the victor's name these captive kings in chains,
And asked permission of this noble prince
That he would deign to see his kingdom's savior.
CHIMÈNE: Is he not wounded?
ELVIRE: I have nothing heard.
But you change color. Recover your spirits now.
CHIMÈNE: Recover also, then, my weakened anger.
Thinking of him, must I forget myself?
He is acclaimed and my heart echoes it.
My duty's powerless, my heart is dumb.
Silence, my love, let anger do its work.
If he has vanquished kings, he killed my father;
And these sad clothes, the emblems of misfortune,
Are the first fruits his bravery produced.
However much they praise his noble courage,
Here every object tells me of his crime.
You, who restore my feelings of revenge,
The veil, crepe, clothes, and the funereal pomp,
Which his first victory prescribed for me,
Uphold my honor now against my passion;
And when my love's too powerful, speak to me
Of my sad duty, fearlessly attack
The victor in his triumph.

ELVIRE: Calm yourself.
Here comes the Infanta.

(*Enter the* INFANTA *and* LÉONOR.)

INFANTA: I have not come here
To offer consolation, but to mingle
My own sighs with your tears.
CHIMÈNE: Rather take part
In the common joy, and taste the happiness
That heaven sends you; no one has the right
To weep, save I alone. The threatened danger
That Don Rodrigue was able to repulse
And the public safety that his arms insured
Allow to me alone the right to weep.
He has saved the city, he has served the King,
And his brave arm is fatal but to me.
INFANTA: My dear Chimène, it's true he has performed
Miraculous deeds.
CHIMÈNE: Already I have heard
This sorry rumor; everywhere they cry
He's a brave warrior, but unlucky lover.
INFANTA: Why should this common talk be vexing to you?
This youthful Mars they praise once pleased you well.
Your soul was his, he lived beneath your laws;
Praising his valor, they applaud your choice.
CHIMÈNE: Everyone can acclaim him with some justice:
For me the praise is but a new ordeal;
My sorrow's sharpened: I see what I lose
When I see how he's valued. Cruel griefs
To a lover's spirit! The more I learn his worth,
And the more my love increases, yet my duty
Is always stronger and, despite my love,
Will prosecute his death.
INFANTA: You were esteemed
For this duty yesterday; the effort you made
Appeared so worthy of a noble heart
That everyone at court admired your courage

And mourned your love. But will you take the advice
Of a true friend?

CHIMÈNE: Not to obey you, Madame,
Would make me criminal.

INFANTA: What was right then
Is so no longer. Rodrigue is now
Our only stay, the people's hope and love,
Castille's protector, the terror of the Moor.
The King himself agrees, and thinks your father
Is born again in him. And if you wish
That I should briefly tell you what I mean,
Seeking his death, you seek the public ruin.
Is it ever permitted, to avenge a father,
To deliver one's country to its enemies' hands?
Is it right to do us harm, that we should suffer
For your father's death, who had no part in it?
That does not mean that you should wed the man
Whom you are forced to accuse. I wish myself
That you would uproot your passion; take away
Your love, but leave to us his life.

CHIMÈNE: Ah, no!
I cannot show such mercy, for the duty
Which spurs me on is limitless. Although
My love pleads for this conqueror; although
People adore him and the King himself
Looks kindly on him; though he is surrounded
By the most valiant warriors, I will go
Under my cypresses to overcome
His laurels.

INFANTA: It is noble when our duty,
To avenge a father, attacks the man one loves.
But it is yet more noble to give up
Personal vengeance to the public interest.
Believe me, it is enough for you to extinguish
Your love for him. He will be sorely punished
If you expel him from your heart for ever.
I hope the country's welfare will impose

This law upon you. And why should you suppose
The King will hear your plea?

CHIMÈNE: He can refuse me,
But I cannot be silent.

INFANTA: Think well, Chimène,
Of what you mean to do. Farewell. I'll leave you
To think of it alone.

CHIMÈNE: My father's dead
And so I have no choice. [*Exeunt.*]

Scene 2—*The King's Palace.*

(*Enter* DON FERDINAND, DON DIÈGUE, DON ARIAS, DON RODRIGUE *and* DON SANCHE.)

DON FERDINAND: Noble inheritor of a famous house
Which always was the glory of Castille
And its defender; sprung from ancestors
Renowned for valor, which your first assay
Has so soon equaled, my strength is too little
To recompense you, and I have less power
Than you have merit. The land you have delivered
From a barbarous foe; my scepter in my hand
By your hands firmly placed; the Moors defeated
Before I had the time to give the order
To drive them back—these are not deeds which give
Your king the means or hope to do you right.
But the two kings, your prisoners, shall serve
As your reward. They've named you in my presence
Their Cid, and since the word means in their tongue
Their lord, I will not envy you the title.
Henceforth you are the Cid. May everyone
Give precedence to this great name; may it
Strike fear into Granada and Toledo
And may it signify to all my subjects
What you are worth to me and what I owe you.

DON RODRIGUE: Sire, spare my shame. You take too much

account
Of my weak service; and you make me blush
Before so great a king, that I so little
Deserve this honor. For I know full well
That to the welfare of your realm I owe
The blood that's in my veins, the air I breathe;
And should I lose them for so fine a cause
I should be doing but a subject's duty.

DON FERDINAND: All those that duty brings into my service
Do not acquit themselves with equal courage;
And if the valor runs not to excess,
It does not have results of such a kind.
Then let us praise you; and recount in full
The story of your victory.

DON RODRIGUE: As you know,
Sire, in that pressing danger, when the town
Was thrown into a panic, a band of friends
Assembled at my father's, and they urged me—
My soul being much disturbed . . . But Sire, forgive
My temerity in daring to employ them
Without authority from you. The danger
Was near at hand; the troops were ready; to show
Myself at Court, I should have risked my head;
And if I had to lose it, it were sweeter
To die in fighting for you.

DON FERDINAND: I excuse
Your haste to avenge your insult; and the state
You have defended speaks in your defense.
Believe me that, from this time forth, Chimène
Will plead in vain; and I will listen to her
Only to comfort her. But pray continue.

DON RODRIGUE: Under me, therefore, did this troop advance
Showing a manly confidence. At first
We were five hundred strong, but we became
Three thousand in arriving at the port,
By a prompt reinforcement. Seeing us march
With such a bearing, even the most fearful

Regained their courage! As soon as they arrived
I hid two thirds of them in the holds of ships
Which we found there; the rest—whose numbers grew
From hour to hour—all burning with impatience,
Lay on the ground around me and kept silence,
Until a good part of the night had passed.
The guard, at my command, all did the same,
And helped my stratagem. I had pretended
This order came from you. Then the faint light
Which falls from the stars revealed to us at last
Thirty ships on the tide. The swelling waters
Brought the Moors to the port. We let them pass.
All appeared quiet to them: no soldiers
There in the port, none on the city walls.
Our utter silence tricked them: they assumed
They had surprised us. Fearlessly they stopped,
They anchored, disembarked and ran at once
Into the hands of those who waited for them.
Then we arose together and at once
Shouted to heaven a thousand deafening cries.
Our men, in our vessels, answered. They appeared
In arms. Then panic seized the Moors; forthwith
They fell into confusion, half-embarked;
And, before fighting, thought that they were lost.
They came to pillage and encountered war.
We pressed them back on water and on land.
Many were slain and streams of blood were flowing
Before they even fought or formed their ranks.
But soon their princes rallied them: their courage
Revived, their fear forgotten; and the shame
Of dying without fighting stayed their panic
And gave them back their courage. So they drew
Their scimitars and bravely faced our men.
Our blood with theirs was mingled horribly;
And earth and river, fleet and port were fields
Of carnage, where Death triumphed. Many actions
And many notable deeds must be unfamed,

Lost in the darkness, in which everyone,
Sole witness of the great blows he had struck,
Could not discern to which side fate inclined.
I went about encouraging our men,
To urge some to advance, to support others,
To draw up new arrivals, rank by rank,
And urging them, in their turn, to advance;
I did not know the outcome of the battle
Until the break of day; but then at last
Light showed us our advantage, as the Moors,
Seeing their losses, suddenly lost courage;
And seeing a reinforcement which arrived
To succor us, the burning lust of conquest
Gave way to fear of death. They gained their ships,
They cut their cables, screaming to the heavens
Their horrid cries. And routed as they were,
And terrified, they did not think at all
Whether their kings were with them. The tide had brought
them,
The ebb now carried them away; meanwhile
Their kings still fought amidst us, and a few
Of their soldiers, wounded, still fought valiantly,
And well they sold their lives. In vain I urged them
To yield to me—for, scimitar in hand,
They would not listen. But, at last, beholding
Their men all lying slain, and hope being lost,
They asked for our captain. So I named myself,
And they surrendered. I despatched them to you,
And so, for lack of foes, the battle ended
Thus, in your service . . .

(*Enter* DON ALONSO.)

DON ALONSO: Sire, Chimène is come
To ask for justice.

DON FERDINAND: What untimely news!
Her duty's too importunate. Go, Rodrigue,
I do not wish her to be forced to see you.

In place of all the thanks that you have earned,
I have to send you off. Before you leave,
Come, let your King embrace you. [*Exit* DON RODRIGUE.]

DON DIÈGUE: Although Chimène
Still seeks his life, she yet would wish to save him.

DON FERDINAND: I'm told she loves him. I will test it now.
Pretend to grieve.

(*Enter* CHIMÈNE *and* ELVIRE.)

Be satisfied, Chimène,
Your hopes are answered; though Rodrigue has conquered
Our foes, yet since then he has died of wounds.
Give thanks to heaven by whom you are avenged.
(*To* DON DIÈGUE) She has turned pale already.

DON DIÈGUE: See, she is fainting.
And wonder, Sire, at the effects of love.
Her grief betrays the secrets of her soul,
So that no longer can we doubt her love.

CHIMÈNE: Rodrigue is dead then?

DON FERDINAND: No, no, he is alive,
And still keeps for you an unaltered love.
Calm this distress which shows your love for him.

CHIMÈNE: But, Sire, one faints from joy as well as grief.
Excess of pleasure takes away one's strength,
And taken by surprise one's senses swoon.

DON FERDINAND: You wish us to believe the impossible?
Chimène, your grief was visible to all.

CHIMÈNE: Add, then, this crowning woe to all the rest,
And say my swoon was the effect of grief.
I have been brought to this by righteous anger.
His death would rob me of the thing I sought.
Were he to die thus for his country's good
My vengeance would be lost, my plans upset.
To die so nobly is a wrong to me.
I ask his death, but not a glorious one,
Not with such glory lifting him so high,
Not on a bed of honor, but on a scaffold,

Die to avenge my father, not for his country,
Die with a tarnished name and blighted memory.
To die for one's country is not a sad fate:
No, it is to immortalize oneself
By a noble death. I therefore like his victory,
And I can do so without crime: it makes
Our country safe and renders me my victim,
But noble now and famous among warriors,
His head is crowned, instead of flowers, with laurels,
And, in a word, a worthy sacrifice
To my father's spirit . . . Alas! to what fond hope
Have I been carried! Rodrigue now has nothing
To fear from me: what could the tears you scorn
Avail against him? All your empire now
Is sanctuary to him; under your power
All is allowed him. He triumphs over me
As over your enemies. In their blood he spilled,
Stifled Justice serves as a new trophy
To the crime of the victor: we augment its pomp,
And scorn of law makes us between two kings
Follow his chariot.

DON FERDINAND: This passion you display
Is much too violent. When one metes out justice
Everything must be weighed. Your father's slain;
He was the aggressor, and equity itself
Commands me to be lenient, and before
You criticize me, look into your heart.
Rodrigue is master of it, and your love
Secretly offers thanks unto your king
Whose favor has preserved your lover for you.

CHIMÈNE: For me! my foe! the object of my wrath!
The author of my woes! My father's killer!
You take so little notice of my suit,
You think to oblige me by not listening to me.
Since to my tears you deny justice, Sire,
Let me appeal to arms—that was the way
By which he outraged me, and so by this

I ought to be avenged. Of all your knights
I ask his head. Yes, let one bring me it
And I will be his prize. Let them fight him, Sire,
And when the combat's over, I will marry
The victor, if Rodrigue should be defeated.
With your authority, let this be proclaimed.

DON FERDINAND: This ancient custom of my realm, designed
To punish unjust killing, makes the state
Lose its best fighters. Often the result
Is to oppress the innocent and uphold
The guilty. I exempt Rodrigue from it.
He is too precious to me, to expose him
To the blows of fickle chance; and whatsoever
He has committed, the Moors in flying from him
Have taken away his crime.

DON DIÈGUE: Will you reverse
For him alone laws which the Court's observed
So many times? What will your people think,
Sire, what will envy say, if he remains
Under your safe protection, making it
A pretext not to appear when men of honor
Would seek a noble death? Such royal favors
Would stain his reputation. Let him taste
Without a blush the fruits of victory.
The Count was insolent—he punished him;
He proved his courage then, and should maintain it.

DON FERDINAND: Then since you wish it, I agree to it.
But for each warrior vanquished, there will be
Hundreds to take his place: the prize Chimène
Has promised to the victor will make foes
Of all my knights. But for Rodrigue alone
To fight with all of them would be unfair.
To enter the lists once will be enough.
Choose whom you wish, Chimène, and choose him well;
After this combat ask me nothing more.

DON DIÈGUE: Sir, do not thus excuse all those who tremble
At Rodrigue's prowess. Leave an open field,

Since there will not be any challengers.
After today, what heart will be so vain
As to encounter him? Who'll risk himself
With such an adversary? Who will be
This valiant—nay, rather, this foolhardy man.
DON SANCHE: Let the field be opened. Here is the challenger!
I'm that foolhardy, nay, that valiant man.
Madame, accord that grace to my keen ardor.
You know your promise.
DON FERDINAND: Chimène, do you remit
Your cause into his hands?
CHIMÈNE: Sire, I have promised.
DON FERDINAND: Be ready tomorrow.
DON DIÈGUE: No, Sire, this delay
Is needless: one is always ready, when
One has the courage.
DON FERDINAND: To come straight from battle
To fight a duel!
DON DIÈGUE: Rodrigue has taken breath
While he recounted it.
DON FERDINAND: At least, I wish
That he, for an hour or two, should take some rest.
But lest this fight should be a precedent,
To show that I permit reluctantly
A bloody proceeding which I never liked,
It will not have the presence of myself
Nor any of my court. (*To* DON ARIAS) You, sir, alone
Shall judge the valor of the combatants.
See that they act as honorable men;
And when the combat's over, bring me the victor.
Whoever he is, his efforts will achieve
The self-same prize. From my hands he'll receive
Chimène, and take her as reward.
CHIMÈNE: What! Sire!
To impose on me so harsh a ruling!
DON FERDINAND: Though
You complain of it, your love—far from approving

Of your complaint—if Rodrigue is victor
Will gratefully accept him. Cease to murmur
Against so mild an order. Whichever wins,
I'll make your husband. [*Exeunt.*]

Act V

Scene 1—*Chimène's house.*

(*Enter* CHIMÈNE *and* DON RODRIGUE.)

CHIMÈNE: Rodrigue! In broad daylight! What is the cause
Of this audacity! Go! You'll stain my honor.
Go, I beseech you.

DON RODRIGUE: As I am going to die,
I come before the fatal stroke to see you
And bid a last farewell. The constant love
Which binds me to your laws dare not accept
My death, until I've paid you homage first.

CHIMÈNE: You're going to die!

DON RODRIGUE: I run to meet the moment
Which will deliver me from your resentment.

CHIMÈNE: You're going to die! Is Don Sanche then so terrible
That he can scare a heart that never quailed?
What weakens you, or what makes him so strong?
Rodrigue goes off to fight and thinks himself
Already dead! The man who did not fear
My father or the Moors, goes now to fight
Don Sanche, and is already in despair!
So, in your need, your courage has abated!

DON RODRIGUE: I run to meet my death, and not to fight;
Since you still seek my death, my faithful love
Well knows how to deprive me of the wish
To defend my life. My courage is the same
As ever; but I have no strength at all

When it would but preserve what does not please you;
Last night already had been fatal to me
If I had fought for my own cause alone;
But since I was defending then my King,
His people and my country, to fight badly
Would have betrayed them. For my noble spirit
Does not so hate my life that it would wish
To leave it by such perfidy. But now
The only interest at stake is mine,
Since you demand my death, I must accept
What you decree. You choose another's hand
For your revenge—I did not deserve to die
By yours—no one shall see me try to parry
His blows. I owe him more respect, who fights
On your behalf; and overjoyed to think
That the blows come from you—since it's your honor
His arms uphold, I will present to him
My naked breast, and worship in his hand
Yours which destroys me.

CHIMÈNE: If the righteous violence
Of a sad duty, which, despite myself, compels me
To prosecute your valor, to your love
Prescribes so stern a law that you are left
Without defense against my champion,
Yet in this blindness do not lose this thought:
Your honor's at the stake as well as life;
And that, however famous while you lived,
When you are dead, they will believe you vanquished.
Your honor is more dear to you than I am,
Since in my father's blood it stained your hands,
And made you then renounce, despite your love,
Your sweetest hope of soon possessing me:
And yet I see you reckon it so little,
That, without fighting, you would wish to lose.
What strange caprice has weakened now your courage?
Why has it gone, or why did you have it once?
What! Are you noble only to injure me?

When you're not hurting me, do you lack courage?
And did you treat my father with such harshness,
So that, when he was conquered, you could suffer
A conqueror? Go, do not wish to die;
Let me still prosecute you, and defend
Your honor, if you have no wish to live.

DON RODRIGUE: After the Count's death, and the Moors' defeat,
Were other actions needed for my fame?
It can disdain the need of self-defense:
It's known my courage dares to undertake
Anything, and that underneath the heavens
Nothing is as dear to me as honor.
No, in this combat, whatever you may think,
Rodrigue can die without a loss of fame.
Without his being accused of lacking courage,
Without being thought defeated, without submitting
To a conqueror. It will be merely said:
"He loved Chimène: he did not wish to live,
And still deserve her hatred; he has yielded
Himself to the harsh fate that forced his mistress
To seek his death. She wished to have his head,
And if he had refused to give it her
His noble heart would think it was a crime.
To avenge his honor once he lost his love,
To avenge his mistress he has quitted life,
Preferring, whatever hope had ruled his soul,
His honor to Chimène, Chimène to life."
And so you'll see my death in this combat,
Far from obscuring, will enhance my fame;
This honor will survive my chosen death,
The only sacrifice which could content you.

CHIMÈNE: Since, to prevent your rushing to your death,
Your life and honor have but feeble power,
If ever I loved you, Rodrigue, in return
Defend yourself to save me from Don Sanche;
Fight now to free me from the King's decision

Which gives me to the object of my loathing.
What more shall I say? Think of your defense,
To force my duty and compel my silence;
And if your heart is still in love with me,
Emerge victorious from this combat now
Of which I am the prize. Farewell. These words,
Escaped from my lips, have made me blush with shame.
[*Exit.*]

DON RODRIGUE: Is there a foe now that I cannot conquer?
Come, Moors, Navarrans and Castillians,
And all the valiant men that Spain has nurtured,
Combine together, make a single army
To fight one so inspired. Join all your efforts
Against so sweet a hope—to reach your aim,
You still will be too few. [*Exit.*]

Scene 2—*The Infanta's house.*

(*Enter the* INFANTA.)

INFANTA: Shall I respect for pride of birth profess
Which makes my love a crime? Or lend an ear
To you, Love, whose enchanting influence
Makes me revolt against it? Poor Princess,
To which side should you owe obedience?
Rodrigue, your valor makes you doubly dear
And worthy of me, but you're not a prince.

Pitiless Fate, which severs my renown
From my desires! Is it, indeed, laid down
That to choose virtue brings one such distress?
O Heavens! How much my luckless heart must bleed,
If it cannot succeed,
Either, after its long-drawn agony
To extinguish love, or with its love agree.

I am too scrupulous; Reason may wonder

That I should scorn him; for although my birth
Reserves me for a monarch, I should live under
Your laws, Rodrigue, with honor; and your worth,
Since you have conquered kings, a crown may gain:
And does not the title, Cid, that you have won,
Show plainly over whom you ought to reign?

Though worthy, he belongs still to Chimène:
The gift I made undoes me. Her father's fate
Has made between those two such little hate
That duty prosecutes him with regret;
And so I hope not any fruit to get
From his crime or my woes, since Fate allows
Love to endure even between two foes.

(*Enter* LÉONOR.)

Why have you come, Léonor?
LÉONOR: To applaud you
On the repose your soul has gained at last.
INFANTA: Where in my torment should I find repose?
LÉONOR: If love lives upon hope and dies with it,
Rodrigue no longer can bewitch your courage,
You know the fight in which Chimène involves him:
Either he dies, or marries her. Your hope
Is dead, and you are cured.
INFANTA: Far from it yet!
LÉONOR: What can you hope for?
INFANTA: Rather say what hope
You would forbid me? For if Rodrigue fights
On these conditions, I have many means
To break the effect of them. Love, the sweet cause
Of all my cruel pains, to lovers' minds
Can teach a dozen stratagems.
LÉONOR: Could you
Do anything, after a father slain
Kindled no strife between them? For Chimène
Shows by her conduct that it is not hate
That now directs her action. She obtained

A combat, and accepted as her champion
The first who offered. She had no recourse
To noble warriors, famous for their deeds.
Don Sanche sufficed her, and deserves her choice
Since he is arming now for the first time.
She likes, in this fight, his lack of experience;
As he's without renown, she's confident;
And her compliance ought to make you see
She wants a combat which will force her duty,
Give to her Rodrigue an easy triumph,
And sanction her to seem appeased at last.

INFANTA: I've noticed this, and yet my heart adores,
As much as Chimène does, this conqueror.
But what alas! shall I resolve to do?

LÉONOR: Better to recollect of whom you were born:
Heaven owes you a king; you love a subject.

INFANTA: My love has changed its object. For no longer
Do I love Rodrigue, a mere gentleman:
No, it's no longer thus I name him now.
I love the author of these splendid deeds,
The valiant Cid, the master of two kings.
Yet I will quell my passions, not from fear
Of any blame, but so as not to upset
So beautiful a love; and if, to please me,
He were to be crowned, I still would not take back
The gift I made. And since his victory
In such a combat is assured, once more
I'll give him to Chimène. And you, Léonor,
Who see the darts with which my heart is pierced,
Come, see me finish as I have begun. [*Exeunt.*]

Scene 3—*Chimène's house.*

(*Enter* CHIMÈNE *and* ELVIRE.)

CHIMÈNE: How I suffer, Elvire, how I'm to be pitied!
I can but hope, but all is to be feared;

To prayers that fall unbidden from my lips
I dare not lend assent. I wish for nothing
Without a prompt retraction. I have made
Two rivals fight for me. The happiest issue
Will cost me tears. Whatever fate ordains,
Either my father still lies unavenged
Or else my lover's killed.

ELVIRE: I see you eased
In one way or another. Either you have
Rodrigue, or you're avenged. Whatever fate
Ordains for you, it safeguards your good name
And gives you a husband.

CHIMÈNE: The object of my hate
Or of my anger! Rodrigue's murderer,
Or else my father's! Either way I'm given
A husband steeped in blood I cherished most;
My soul revolts from both alternatives.
I fear the issue more than I fear death.
Vengeance and Love, away! You vex my spirit
And hold no sweetness for me at this price.
And you, the powerful Mover of the fate
Which now torments me, terminate this combat
Without a victory to either side,
Without a victim or a vanquisher.

ELVIRE: That would be treating you with too much harshness.
This combat brings new tortures for your soul,
If you are left demanding justice still,
Still showing deep resentment, and pursuing
Your lover's death. Madame, it would be better
If the rare valor crowning now his brow
Enforced your silence; if the law of arms
Stifled your sighs; and if the King should force you
To follow your desires.

CHIMÈNE: If he should win,
Do you imagine that I will surrender?
My duty is too strong, my loss too great;
The law of combat and the royal will
Are not enough. Although Rodrigue may conquer

Don Sanche with ease, he cannot conquer thus
Chimène's integrity: whatever a monarch
Has promised to his victory, my honor
Will raise against him a thousand other foes.

ELVIRE: Take care that Heaven, to punish your strange pride,
Does not, in the end, let anyone avenge you.
What! Would you still refuse the happiness
Of being able to keep silence now
With honor? What do you expect to get?
Will your lover's death restore your father to you?
Is one stroke of misfortune not enough?
Must you have loss on loss, grief upon grief?
Come, in this fixed caprice, you don't deserve
The lover who is destined for your husband;
And we shall see the righteous wrath of heaven
Leave you instead with Don Sanche for a husband.

CHIMÈNE: Elvire, I have been racked enough already.
Do not increase my torture with such words.
I wish to avoid them both: yet, I confess,
Rodrigue has all my prayers. Not that my passion
Inclines me to his side, but if he falls
I would be handed over to Don Sanche.
My wish is born of fear. What do I see,
Unhappy that I am? Elvire, all is over.

(*Enter* DON SANCHE.)

DON SANCHE: Obliged to lay this weapon at your feet . . .

CHIMÈNE: Stained with the blood of Rodrigue! Do you dare
To show yourself to me, after you've stolen
What I loved best! Shine out, my love, for now
You've nothing more to fear! My father's paid.
Cease to constrain yourself. A single blow
Has made my reputation safe, my soul
Brought to despair, and has set free my love.

DON SANCHE: With a calmer mind . . .

CHIMÈNE: Do you still speak to me,
Vile murderer of a hero I adore?

Go! You caught him treacherously! A warrior
Valiant as he would never have succumbed
To such an assailant. Hope nothing from me:
You have not served me; in thinking to avenge me
You've robbed me of my life.

DON SANCHE: A strange delusion!
You will not listen to me.

CHIMÈNE: Do you wish me
To hear you brag of killing him? that I
Should hear at leisure with what insolence
You paint his fall, my crime, and your great prowess?
[*Exeunt.*]

Scene 4—*The Palace.*

(*Enter* DON FERDINAND, DON DIÈGUE, DON ARIAS, DON SANCHE, DON ALONSO, CHIMÈNE *and* ELVIRE.)

CHIMÈNE: Sire, I need no more dissimulate
What all my efforts could not hide from you.
I loved him, as you know; but to avenge
My father, I have wished to put a price
Upon his dearest head. Your majesty
Has noticed how I made my passion yield
To duty. Rodrigue now, at last, is dead.
His death has changed me from a mortal foe
Into a desolate lover. I owed this vengeance
To one who gave me life, and now I owe
These tears unto my love. Don Sanche destroyed me
In taking my defense; and I'm the reward
Of the destroyer. Sire, if ever pity
Can move a king, revoke your harsh decision;
For the price of victory in which I lose
All that I love, I'll leave him all I have
If he will let me in a sacred cloister
Lament continually until I die
My father and my lover.

DON DIÈGUE: She loves him, Sire,
And thinks no longer that it is a crime
To confess a lawful love.
DON FERDINAND: You are mistaken,
Chimène, your lover is not dead. Don Sanche,
Who was vanquished, brought a false report.
DON SANCHE: No, Sire.
In spite of me, she has deceived herself.
I came from the combat to recount the issue.
That noble warrior, with whom she is in love
Said, when he had disarmed me, "Do not fear:
I'd rather leave the victory uncertain
Than shed the blood that's hazarded for Chimène;
But since my duty calls me to the King,
Describe our combat to her: carry her
Your sword on my behalf." So, Sire, I went.
This object has deceived her: she supposed
That I was victor, seeing me return,
And suddenly her wrath betrayed her love
With so much fury and impatience
I could not make her listen. As for me,
Though I am conquered, yet I count myself
As happy; and despite the infinite loss
To my loving heart, I yet love my defeat
Which crowns a perfect love.
DON FERDINAND: You need not blush,
My daughter, at so fine a love, nor seek
The means to disavow it. Laudable shame
In vain solicits you. Your good name is now
No more involved; your duty's paid; your father
Is satisfied; and it was for his sake
Rodrigue was so endangered. Now you see
That heaven disposes otherwise. You have done
So much for your father; do something now for yourself
And do not be rebellious to my orders,
Who gave you one so dearly loved for husband.

(*Enter the* INFANTA, DON RODRIGUE *and* LÉONOR.)

INFANTA: Dry your tears, Chimène, and without sadness
Receive this noble victor from the hands
Of your princess.

DON RODRIGUE: Sire, do not be offended,
If, before you, love throws me at her feet.
I do not come here to demand my conquest;
I come once more to offer you my life,
Madame; my love will never let me use
The law of combat or the King's command
To force consent. If all that has been done
Is still too little for a father, say
By what means else you will be satisfied.
Must I fight with a thousand rivals more,
Extend my exploits to the ends of the earth,
Alone assault a camp, or put to flight
A hostile army, or surpass in fame
Heroes of legend? If my crime by that
Can be washed clean at last, I dare do all,
And can achieve all; but if your proud honor,
Still inexorable, cannot be appeased
Without the culprit's death, there is no need
To arm against me the power of other men.
My life is at your feet; avenge yourself;
Your hands alone are given the right to conquer
One so invincible; then take a vengeance
Impossible to all others. But let my death
Suffice to punish me. Banish me not
From your remembrance; and since my death
Preserves your fame, preserve my memory,
And sometimes say, in pitying my fate,
"Had he not loved me, he would not be dead."

CHIMÈNE: Rise, Rodrigue. Sire, I must confess
I've said too much for me to unsay it now.
Rodrigue has virtues which I cannot hate,
And when a king commands, one should obey.
But though you have already sentenced me,
Could you allow yourself to see this marriage?

And if of my duty you exact this effort
Does it accord with all your justice, Sire?
If Rodrigue is so needful to the state
Should I be the reward for what he does,
And be delivered to the eternal shame
Of having bathed my hands in father's blood?

DON FERDINAND: Time often made legitimate what seemed
Impossible without crime. Rodrigue has won you;
You should be his. But yet, although his valor
Has conquered you today, I'd be a foe
To your good name, if I should give him now
The prize of victory. To postpone this marriage
Would not infringe the law which at some time
Must make you his. If you wish, take a year
To wipe away your tears. Rodrigue meanwhile
Must take up arms. For after having conquered
The Moors upon our coasts, upset their plans,
Repulsed their efforts, go to carry war
To their own country; lead my army there,
Ravage their land. At the very name of Cid
They tremble; they have named you as their lord,
And they will want you for their king. But yet,
Amid your great deeds still be faithful to her:
Return, if possible, more worthy yet
To have her hand; and by your mighty deeds
Make yourself so esteemed, that she will think it
Glorious to marry you.

DON RODRIGUE: To possess Chimène,
And for your service, what can you command
That I will not accomplish? Though I must be
Far from her sight, it is great happiness
Merely to hope.

DON FERDINAND: Hope in your courage, hope
In my promise. You possess your mistress' heart:
To conquer a point of honor which wars against you,
Leave it to time, your valor and your king.

The Precious Damsels

A FARCE IN ONE ACT

by MOLIÈRE

TRANSLATED BY *Morris Bishop*

The Characters

LA GRANGE, *young gentleman*
DU CROISY, *young gentleman*
GORGIBUS, *well-to-do bourgeois*
MAGDELON, *daughter of Gorgibus*
CATHOS, *niece of Gorgibus*
MAROTTE, *maidservant in Gorgibus' household*
ALMANZOR, *lackey in Gorgibus' household*
MASCARILLE, *manservant of La Grange*
JODELET, *manservant of Du Croisy*
LUCILE, CÉLIMÈNE, *neighbors*
TWO SEDAN-CHAIR BEARERS
FIDDLERS
TWO HIRED BULLIES (*may be omitted in stage presentation*)

The scene is in the house of Gorgibus, in Paris.

LA GRANGE *and* DU CROISY *are discovered.*

DU CROISY: Seigneur la Grange—

LA GRANGE: What?

DU CROISY: Look at me for a moment . . . And don't laugh.

LA GRANGE: All right. Well?

DU CROISY: What do you think of our visit? Are you happy about it?

LA GRANGE: Well, in your opinion, do you think we have any reason to be?

DU CROISY: To tell the truth, not much.

LA GRANGE: To speak for myself, I admit I was thoroughly disgusted. Has anyone ever seen two scatterbrained country girls put on such airs? Or two men treated as offhandedly as we were? They could hardly bring themselves to the point of asking us to sit down. I've never seen so many mutual confidences in the ear, so much yawning, so much eye-rubbing, so much repetition of "What time is it?" And to everything we could think of to say to them, could they find any answer except "Yes" and "No"? So won't you admit that if we'd been the scurviest people on earth, they couldn't have treated us worse than they did?

DU CROISY: It seems to me you're taking the matter very much to heart.

LA GRANGE: Certainly I take it to heart. So much so that I want to get revenge for their impertinence. I know what made them so haughty toward us. [They are precious.

DU CROISY: Precious?

LA GRANGE: Yes. The precious are people who go in for preciosity.

DU CROISY: Preciosity?

LA GRANGE: Exactly. Preciosity is the new fashion among the intellectuals. They're so pure and sensitive and dainty that they can't stand anything common or real. They can't call anything by its right name; they play a kind of literary game, to see who can make the most far-fetched allusions, according to their special code of affectation.] [1] This pre-

[1] [The passage between brackets is interpolated by the translator.]

cious fashion has not only infected Paris, it has spread into the provinces, and our ridiculous damsels have taken a good dose of it. In short, they are combinations of the precious and the coquette. I can see the sort of thing they would appreciate; and if you'll agree, we'll play a trick on them which will show up their folly, and may teach them to judge people better.

DU CROISY: How do you mean?

LA GRANGE: I have a valet named Mascarille. In the opinion of a good many people, he passes for a wit in the modern manner, for there's nothing cheaper than wit nowadays. He's a fantastic fellow, who has taken it into his head to play the gentleman of quality. He makes a specialty of elegance and refinement; he writes poetry; and he looks down on the other servants; coarse brutes, he calls them.

DU CROISY: Well, what do you expect to do with him?

LA GRANGE: What do I expect to do? The thing to do—but first let's get out of here.

(*Enter* GORGIBUS.)

GORGIBUS: Well, gentlemen, you have seen my niece and my daughter. How are things going? What is the result of your visit?

LA GRANGE: That is something you can learn better from them than from us. All we can tell you is that we thank you for the favor you have done us, and we remain your very humble servants. (*Exit* LA GRANGE *and* DU CROISY.)

GORGIBUS: Well now, what's this? They seem to be leaving in a very bad humor. I wonder what's the reason. I'd better find out. Hey there, you!

(*Enter* MAROTTE.)

MAROTTE: What do you wish, sir?

GORGIBUS: Where are the ladies?

MAROTTE: In their boudoir.

GORGIBUS: What are they doing?

MAROTTE: Making lip salve.

GORGIBUS: Too much salve. And too much lip. Tell them to

come down. (*Exit* MAROTTE) Those hussies are trying to ruin me, with their lip salve. All I see around is whites of eggs, virgin-milk, and a hundred other groceries I don't recognize. Since we have been here they have used up the fat of a dozen pigs at least; and four menservants could live on the sheep's trotters they get rid of. (*Enter* MAGDELON *and* CATHOS) Girls, you've got to stop spending so much money to grease your mugs. Now tell me, what did you do to those gentlemen, so that I just saw them go out with a very chilly air indeed? Didn't I order you to receive them as gentlemen I proposed to give you as husbands?

MAGDELON: What regard, Father, do you expect us to bestow upon the irregular proceedings of those persons?

CATHOS: And how, Uncle, could a somewhat reasonable girl make shift with their characters?

GORGIBUS: What objection can you find to them?

MAGDELON: What kind of gallantry did they display! What! To begin right off with marriage!

GORGIBUS: What do you expect them to begin with? Concubinage? Isn't their procedure one you ought to approve, as I should too? Isn't that the gentlemanly thing to do? And that sacred bond that they propose, isn't it an evidence of their honorable intentions?

MAGDELON: Father, you're so utterly bourgeois! It makes me ashamed to hear you talk that way. You ought to take a course in conversation as a fine art.

GORGIBUS: I use conversation as a fine way of saying what I mean. And I say that marriage is a holy and sacred matter, and it's only decent to begin with it.

MAGDELON: Dear me, if everyone were like you, novels would be very short! A nice thing it would be, if the Great Cyrus married his Mandane right at the beginning, or if Aronce married Clélie in the first chapter!

GORGIBUS (*to* CATHOS): What is she trying to say?

MAGDELON: Father, my cousin will tell you, just as well as I, that marriage should never occur until after the other adventures are over. A lover, in order to be acceptable, should be able to toy with noble fancies, and play the gamut of emotion, sweet and tender and impassioned. And he should woo according to the rules. First he should see the future object of his affections in church, or on the promenade, or in some public ceremony. Or else he should make a fatal visit to her house with a relative or friend; and he emerges in a trance, all melancholy. For a while he hides his passion from the loved one, but nevertheless he pays her a few calls, when some problem of gallantry is always brought up to exercise the wits of the assembly. The day of the declaration arrives; this should usually take place in a garden path, while the rest of the party has gone on. This declaration is followed by immediate anger on our part, which shows itself in our blushes; and for a time our fury banishes the lover from our presence. Then he finds some way to calm us down, and little by little he accustoms us to his description of his passion, and he draws from us that admission which causes us so much distress. Then come the adventures: the rivals who cross an affection which has been established, the persecutions of fathers, the jealousies which are conceived on some false basis, the reproaches, the despairs, the abductions and all the consequences. That's how matters are treated according to proper etiquette; those are rules of gallantry which can hardly be set aside. But to come right out at the beginning with proposing a matrimonial union, and to put all your love-making in the marriage contract, and to start the romance at the wrong end, really, Father, nothing could be more hucksterish than such a procedure, and the mere thought of it makes me sick at my stomach.

GORGIBUS: What kind of rubbish is all this? I suppose that's the highfalutin style in fashion.

CATHOS: In fact, Uncle, one could barely be righter than my cousin. How can one properly receive persons who are quite grotesque in matters of gallantry? I'll wager they have never even seen the Map of Loveland, and that the towns of Sweetnotes, Deference Minor, Truelove-Tokentown, and

Prettyverse Village are strange country to them. Don't you see that their persons breathe the dreary dullard, and that they don't make a good impression on people? To come courting without frills at the knee, with a hat naked of feathers, a head uncurled, and a coat confessing a dearth of ribbons! Good heavens, what kind of lovers are those! What paucity in vesture, what aridity of conversation! It's not to be endured, it's not to be countenanced! What's more, I noticed that their neckcloths are not made by the right furnisher, and that their galligaskins are a good half-foot too narrow.

GORGIBUS: I think they're both crazy, and I can't understand anything of this gibberish. Cathos, and you, Magdelon—

MAGDELON: Please, Father, divest yourself of these strange appellations, and address us otherwise.

GORGIBUS: What strange appellations? Aren't they your christened names?

MAGDELON: Good heavens, how vulgar you are! One thing that amazes me is that you could have fathered a girl of my intelligence. Has anyone ever spoken in literary style of Cathos or of Magdelon? Won't you admit that one of those names would be enough to ruin the finest novel on earth?

CATHOS: It is true, Uncle, that a somewhat sensitive ear suffers furiously on hearing the utterance of those vocables; and the name of Polyxena, which my cousin has chosen, and that of Aminta, which I have adopted, have a certain grace, you will surely grant.

GORGIBUS: Listen; one word will be enough. I don't intend that you shall have any other names than those which were given to you by your godfathers and godmothers. And as for those gentlemen in question, I know their families and their finances, and it is my firm desire that you dispose yourselves to receive them as husbands. I'm getting tired of having you on my hands. Taking care of two girls is coming to be too much of a job for a man of my age.

CATHOS: As for me, Uncle, all I can tell you is that I find

marriage a very shocking performance. How can one endure the idea of sleeping beside a man who is absolutely nude?

MAGDELON: Permit us only to breathe a bit in the fine society of Paris, where we have so recently arrived. Let us have time to weave the plot of our romance, and don't force the conclusion so fast.

GORGIBUS (*aside*): No doubt about it, they're completely mad. (*Aloud*) Once more, I don't understand anything of all this balderdash. I am going to be the master here; and to put an end to this sort of talk, either you'll both be married very soon, or, faith, you'll go into a nunnery. I take my oath on that. (*Exit* GORGIBUS.)

CATHOS: Good heavens, my dear, how your father's spiritual substance is buried in gross matter! How coarse his intelligence is! What darkness in his soul!

MAGDELON: What do you expect, my dear? I am ashamed for him. I can hardly persuade myself that I am really his daughter, and I think that some day an adventure will occur which will reveal that I had a more illustrious origin.

CATHOS: I can well believe it. Yes, all the evidence points that way. And as for me, when I look at myself—

(*Enter* MAROTTE.)

MAROTTE: There's a lackey here asking if you're at home. He says his master wants to come and see you.

MAGDELON: Learn, idiot, to pronounce yourself less vulgarly. Say: "Here is a necessary evil, asking if your visibility is accessible."

MAROTTE: Well, I don't understand Latin, and I haven't had your chance to learn philosophy in *The Great Cyrus*.

MAGDELON: Impudent! Really, you're insufferable. Who is the master of this lackey?

MAROTTE: He says he's the Marquis de Mascarille.

MAGDELON: Oh, my dear, a marquis! Yes, go and tell him that he can see us. (*To* CATHOS) No doubt he's one of the wits who has heard about us.

CATHOS: Oh, assuredly, my dear.

MAGDELON: We'd better receive him in this parlor, and not in our bedroom as the great ladies do. Let's just arrange our hair a little, and support our reputation. (*To* MAROTTE) Quick, come into the other room and display before us the counselor of the graces.

MAROTTE: Good land, I don't know what kind of a creature that is. You've got to talk Christian, if you want me to understand.

CATHOS: Bring us the mirror, you ignorant fool, and take care not to sully the glass by the communication of your image.

(*Exit* CATHOS, MAGDELON, *and* MAROTTE. *Enter* MASCARILLE *in a sedan chair, carried by two* BEARERS.)

MASCARILLE: Hey, bearers, hey, hey, hey! Now, now, now, now, now, now! I think these scoundrels want to destroy me by crashing against the walls and the floors.

FIRST BEARER: Well, after all, it was a narrow door. And nothing would do but we should bring you right in here.

MASCARILLE: Naturally, indeed! Would you wish, menials, that I should expose the prolixity of my plumes to the inclemencies of the pluvious season, and that I should inscribe my shoe prints in mud? Come, get your chair out of here.

SECOND BEARER: Pay us, then, please sir.

MASCARILLE: Huh?

SECOND BEARER: I say, sir, that you should give us our money, if you please.

MASCARILLE (*giving him a slap on the face*): What, rascal, ask money of a person of my quality?

SECOND BEARER: Is that the way you pay poor men? And does your quality give us anything to eat?

MASCARILLE: Ah ha! I will teach you your place! This riffraff wants to swindle me!

FIRST BEARER (*removing one of the poles from the sedan chair*): Come on, pay us—and quickly!

MASCARILLE: How's that?

FIRST BEARER: I say that I want my money right away.

MASCARILLE: He's a reasonable man.

FIRST BEARER: Hurry up!

MASCARILLE: Oh, yes, indeed. You talk very sensibly; but the other man is a knave who doesn't know what he's saying. Here. Are you satisfied?

FIRST BEARER: No, I'm not satisfied. You slapped my friend's face, and if—

MASCARILLE: Now, just take it easy. Here is for the slap. One can get anything from me if one goes about it properly. Now go, and come back for me soon to take me to the Louvre, for the King's retirement.

(*Exit* BEARERS. *Enter* MAROTTE.)

MAROTTE: Monsieur, my mistresses are coming in right away.

MASCARILLE: No need for haste; I am comfortably established here to await them.

MAROTTE: Here they are.

(*Enter* MAGDELON *and* CATHOS. *Exit* MAROTTE.)

MASCARILLE: Mesdames, you may no doubt be surprised by the audacity of my visit; but your merit brings this distress upon you, and merit has for me such a puissant charm that I speed everywhere in its pursuit.

MAGDELON: If you are in pursuit of merit, it is not upon our domains that you should hunt.

CATHOS: If merit is to be found here, you must necessarily have brought it with you.

MASCARILLE: Ah! I file objection against your statements. Renown speaks justly in reporting your worth; you will make a grand slam of the gallant world of Paris.

MAGDELON: Your amiability excites a little too far the liberality of its praises; and my cousin and I take good care not to confide our serious trust to the dulcet sound of your flattery.

CATHOS: My dear, we should have chairs set.

MAGDELON: Here, Almanzor!

(*Enter* ALMANZOR.)

ALMANZOR: Madame?

MAGDELON: Quick, propel hither the commodities of conversation.

(ALMANZOR *arranges chairs and exits.*)

MASCARILLE: But at least, is there security here for me?

CATHOS: What are you afraid of?

MASCARILLE: Some larceny of my heart, some assassination of my liberty. I see here some eyes which have the look of very naughty fellows, insulters of a man's freedom; they would treat a soul as a Barbary galley slave. What the devil is this? As one approaches them, they put themselves murderously upon their guard! Faith, I distrust them, I shall fly, or I demand a solid guarantee that they will do me no harm.

MAGDELON (*to* CATHOS): My dear, he has the frolic character.

CATHOS: I see that he is Amilcar, out of the novel *Clélie*.

MAGDELON (*to* MASCARILLE): Have no fear; our eyes have no evil designs, and your heart may sleep in assurance of their integrity.

CATHOS: But have mercy, monsieur; do not be inexorable toward this chair which has been holding out its arms to you for a good quarter-hour; content a little its desire to embrace you.

MASCARILLE (*after seating himself, combing his hair, adjusting his stockings*): Well, ladies, and how do you find Paris?

MAGDELON: Dear me, what is there to say? It would be the very antipodes of reason not to confess that Paris is the great central office of marvels, the clearing-house of good taste, wit, and gallantry.

MASCARILLE: As for me, I insist that outside of Paris there is no salvation for people of breeding.

CATHOS: That is an incontestable truth.

MASCARILLE: It's a little muddy, of course; but we have the sedan chair.

MAGDELON: It is true that the sedan chair is a sweet sanctuary against the insults of the mud and bad weather.

MASCARILLE: You receive many visits; what celebrated wit belongs to your circle?

MAGDELON: Alas! We are hardly known as yet; but we are becoming so, and we have a special friend who has promised to bring here all the gentlemen who write for the *Recueil des pièces choisies*.

CATHOS: And certain others who have been indicated to us as the final authorities on gracious living.

MASCARILLE: I am the person to arrange that. They all come to see me, and I may say that I never rise in the morning without a half-dozen of the wits in attendance.

MAGDELON: Heavens, we shall be obliged to you, with a really perfervid obligation, if you will do us that kindness. For after all, one must be acquainted with all those gentlemen, if one wants to belong to the world of elegance. They are the ones who make and break reputations in Paris, and you know well that there is a certain individual whom you merely have to know personally to acquire the reputation of being an insider, even if you have no other qualifications. But personally, what I regard as most important is that by means of these feasts of wit and soul one learns hundreds of things which are absolutely essential, the very quintessence of smartness. Thus one finds out everyday the chitchat of the gallant world, and all the quips and verses that are being passed around. We learn at just the right moment that so-and-so has composed the neatest little thing on such-and-such a subject; and a certain lady has supplied the words for a new tune; and a gentleman has written a madrigal on gaining a lady's favors; and another has composed some stanzas on an infidelity; Monsieur Blank wrote last night an epigram in verse to Mademoiselle Dash, and she sent him the reply this morning about eight; an author has a certain plot for a new book; another has reached Part Three in his new novel; and another's works have just gone to press. That is what brings you regard in society; and if you don't know that sort of thing, I wouldn't give a penny for all the wit you might have.

CATHOS: In fact, I think anyone who makes the slightest claim to smartness is quite too ridiculous if he doesn't know the most trifling little quatrain which has just been written, and for my part, I should be abominably ashamed if someone should chance to ask me if I had seen something new, and I hadn't seen it.

MASCARILLE: It is certainly shaming not to have the first sight of everything which is being turned out. But don't distress yourselves. I am thinking of establishing in your house an Academy of the Wits, and I promise you that not a scrap of verse will turn up in all Paris without your knowing it by heart before anyone else. Why, for myself, not to boast, I toss them off when I'm in the mood. You will hear quoted in the most exclusive coteries of Paris two hundred songs of mine, and the same number of sonnets, four hundred epigrams and more than a thousand limericks, not counting the enigmas and the portraits.

MAGDELON: I will admit that I'm stupendously fond of portraits; I can't think of anything smarter.

MASCARILLE: Portraits are hard; they require depth, depth. You will see some of mine which won't displease you.

CATHOS: As for me, I love enigmas definitely monstrously.

MASCARILLE: A good exercise for the brains. I popped off four this morning, which I'll give you to guess.

MAGDELON: Limericks are agreeable, when they're deftly done.

MASCARILLE: They're my specialty! I'm busy now putting the whole of Roman history into limerick form.

MAGDELON: Oh, certainly that's immoderately lovely! Reserve a copy for me, if you have it printed.

MASCARILLE: I promise you each a copy, very handsomely bound. Publication is beneath my rank; I only do it to help out the booksellers, who simply persecute me.

MAGDELON: I should think it would be a great pleasure to see oneself in print.

MASCARILLE: Yes, rather. But while I think of it, I must tell you an impromptu I did yesterday when I was visiting a friend of mine, a duchess. I'm devilishly good at impromptus.

CATHOS: The impromptu is the absolute touchstone of wit.

MASCARILLE: Then listen.

MAGDELON: We are all ears.

MASCARILLE:

Oh, oh! I was so carefree and imprudent!
I was just gazing at you, as who wouldn't?
You stole my heart, engulfing me in grief;
Stop thief! Stop thief! Stop thief! Stop thief! Stop thief!

CATHOS: Dear heaven! That's the last word in the gallant style!

MASCARILLE: Everything I do has a certain dash; there's nothing pedantic about it.

MAGDELON: Oh, it's a thousand leagues from the pedantic!

MASCARILLE: Did you notice the beginning: "Oh, oh"? In the sense of: "How extraordinary!—Oh, oh!" Like a man who suddenly becomes aware of something—"Oh, oh!" Surprise, you see—"Oh, oh!"

MAGDELON: Yes, I think that "Oh, oh!" is really prodigious.

MASCARILLE: But it seems like nothing at all.

CATHOS: Sweet heaven, what are you saying! That is the sort of thing that is completely priceless.

MAGDELON: Certainly. I would rather have written that "Oh, oh!" than a whole epic poem.

MASCARILLE: Your taste is good, egad.

MAGDELON: Well, it's not precisely bad.

MASCARILLE: Don't you rather like: "I was so carefree and imprudent"? Carefree and imprudent, taken off my guard, so to speak; a perfectly everyday turn of speech; carefree and imprudent. "I was just gazing at you," that is, innocently, respectfully, like an unhappy little sheep. "As who wouldn't?" That is, the most natural thing in the world, I observe you, I contemplate you, I gaze upon you, as who wouldn't? "You stole my heart, engulfing me in grief." How do you like "engulfing me in grief"?

CATHOS: Superb!

MASCARILLE: The two hard g's together give a suggestion of

surprise and terror. "Engulf in grief." Like a poor little mousie suddenly engulfed by a dreadful cat. "Engulfing me in grief."

MAGDELON: Nothing could possibly be finer.

MASCARILLE: "You stole my heart," that is, you robbed me, you carried it away. "Stop thief! Stop thief! Stop thief! Stop thief! Stop thief!" Wouldn't you say it was a man shouting and running after a robber to try to catch him? "Stop thief! Stop thief! Stop thief! Stop thief! Stop thief!" (*He rises, runs around stage, and collapses in his chair.*)

MAGDELON: One must admit that that is extremely witty and gallant.

MASCARILLE: I must sing you the tune I've composed for it.

CATHOS: You've studied music?

MASCARILLE: What, me? Not at all.

CATHOS: How is it possible, then—

MASCARILLE: People of quality know everything without ever having learned anything.

MAGDELON: He's perfectly right, my dear.

MASCARILLE: See if the tune suits your taste. (*Clears his throat*) La, la, la, la, la. The brutality of the season has furiously outraged the delicacy of my voice. But no matter; it's just an offhand performance. (*Sings*)

CATHOS: Oh, what passion in that tune! I don't know why I don't die of it.

MAGDELON: There is chromatic in that.

MASCARILLE: Don't you find that the thought is well rendered in the music? "Stop thief!" And then, as if you were shouting very loud: "Stop, stop, stop, stop thief!" And then finally, as if you were completely out of breath: "Stop thief!"

MAGDELON: It's the positive cream of art, the cream of the cream, or even the cream of the cream of the cream. I assure you, it's marvelous; I am enchanted with both words and music.

CATHOS: I've never heard anything quite so powerful.

MASCARILLE: Everything I do comes to me naturally; I've never studied.

MAGDELON: Nature has been your doting mother and you are her spoiled child.

MASCARILLE: Tell me, how do you pass your time?

CATHOS: Ah, we barely do.

MAGDELON: Till now, we have been enduring a ghastly starvation of amusement.

MASCARILLE: I shall be happy to take you to the theatre one of these days, if you like. As it happens, they are about to put on a new play which I should be happy to have you attend with me.

MAGDELON: That's an offer not to be refused.

MASCARILLE: But I must ask you to applaud properly, when we are there, for I have promised to help put the play over; the author came to request it just this morning. It's the custom here for the authors to come and read their new plays to us gentlemen of quality, to persuade us to approve them and give them some advance reputation. You may well suppose that when we say something, the commoners in the pit won't dare to contradict us. For my part, I am very scrupulous about it; and when I've promised some playwright, I always shout: "Beautiful! Beautiful!" before they've lit the footlights.

MAGDELON: No doubt about it, Paris is a wonderful place. Hundreds of things go on here that one doesn't know in the provinces, however intelligent one may be.

CATHOS: You needn't say another word. Now that you've informed us, we shall make it a point to cry out properly at every speech.

MASCARILLE (*to* MAGDELON): Possibly I'm mistaken, but you look to me like the kind of person who has written some little comedy.

MAGDELON: Oh, there might be something in what you say.

MASCARILLE: Aha! On my word, we must have a look at it. Just between us, I have scribbled one which I want to put on.

MAGDELON: Oho! Which troupe will you give it to?

MASCARILLE: A fine question! To the Hôtel de Bourgogne,[2] of

[2] [The official troupe, Molière's rivals.—Trans.]

course. They are the only ones who can bring out what's in a text; the others are ignoramuses who read their lines the way people speak. They don't know how to thunder out a good line of verse, and stop at the right place; and how can you tell which is the fine passage, if the actor doesn't pause at it, and thus indicate that it's time to applaud?

CATHOS: In fact, there is a way of communicating the beauties of a work to the audience; and nothing has any more value than what the performer puts into it.

MASCARILLE: How do you like my ribbons and galloons? Do you find them harmonious to my accouterments?

CATHOS: Oh, quite.

MASCARILLE: The ribbon is well chosen?

MAGDELON: Furiously well. It's pure Perdrigeon.[3]

MASCARILLE: What do you say to my knee ruffles?

MAGDELON: They strike the absolutely right note.

MASCARILLE: I can at least claim that they are a good foot wider than the common ones.

MAGDELON: I must admit that I have never seen the elegance of the habiliments carried to such a fever pitch.

MASCARILLE: Apply a moment to these gloves the approbation of your olfactory organ.

MAGDELON: They smell petrifyingly good.

CATHOS: I have never inhaled a more harmonious aroma.

MASCARILLE (*presenting his powdered wig*): And how about this?

MAGDELON: It has real character; one's sense of sublimity is deliciously moved.

MASCARILLE: You don't mention my plumes. How do you find them?

CATHOS: Terrifyingly beautiful.

MASCARILLE: Do you know that each feather costs me a golden louis? But it's my weakness; I can't resist buying the very finest there is.

MAGDELON: I assure you that we utterly sympathize with you. I am furiously delicate about everything I wear; and even

[3] [The furnisher à la mode.—Trans.]

down to my stockings, I can't bear anything which doesn't come from the right shop.

MASCARILLE (*shouts suddenly*): Ow, ow, ow! Damme, ladies, you're treating me very badly! I have good cause to complain of your actions; this is not kind of you.

CATHOS: What is it? What's the matter?

MASCARILLE: What? When you both assault my heart at the same time? To attack me from right and left? Ha, that's contrary to all the rights of man. It isn't fair; I am going to shout: "Murder! Murder!"

CATHOS (*to* MAGDELON): One must admit that he says things in a most individual style.

MAGDELON: He has a very remarkable wit.

CATHOS (*to* MASCARILLE): You're more frightened than hurt; your heart cries out before it's wounded.

MASCARILLE: The devil it does! It's wounded from head to foot.

(*Enter* MAROTTE.)

MAROTTE: Madame, there's a gentleman to see you.

MAGDELON: Who is it?

MAROTTE: The Vicomte de Jodelet.

MASCARILLE: The Vicomte de Jodelet?

MAROTTE: Yes, sir.

CATHOS: Do you know him?

MASCARILLE: Why, he's my best friend!

MAGDELON: Have him come in immediately.

(*Exit* MAROTTE.)

MASCARILLE: We haven't seen each other for some time; I'm delighted by this happy chance.

CATHOS: Here he is.

(*Enter* ALMANZOR, *introducing* JODELET.)

MASCARILLE: Ah! Vicomte!

JODELET (*embracing* MASCARILLE): Ah! Marquis!

MASCARILLE: How happy I am to see you again!

JODELET: How joyful I am to find you here!

MASCARILLE: Kiss me again, please. (*They embrace*)

MAGDELON (*to* CATHOS): Darling, we're beginning to be known; the world of fashion is finding the way to our door.

MASCARILLE: Ladies, permit me to present this gentleman to you. Upon my word, he is worthy of your acquaintance.

JODELET: It is only just that I should come to render to you what is your due; your charms exercise their seignorial rights on all sorts of people.

MAGDELON: You are carrying your civilities to the uttermost confines of flattery.

CATHOS: This day must be marked in our diaries by a red letter.

MAGDELON (*to* ALMANZOR): Come, boy, must I always tell you what to do? Don't you see that we need the augmentation of a chair?

MASCARILLE: Don't be surprised at the Vicomte's looks. He has just got out of bed from an illness which left him so pale.[4]

JODELET: That's the result of staying up so late at Court, and of all the sufferings of war service.

MASCARILLE: Do you realize, ladies, that you see in the Vicomte one of the most valiant men of our century? He is a champion soldier, a nonpareil nonesuch.

JODELET: You don't owe me any compliments, Marquis; your record is well known also.

MASCARILLE: It is true that we have met in the right spots.

JODELET: And in some pretty hot spots too.

MASCARILLE (*looking at the ladies*): Yes, but not so hot as this spot! Ha, ha, ha!

JODELET: We became acquainted in the army. The first time we saw each other, he was in command of a cavalry regiment on the Maltese galleys.

MASCARILLE: That's true. But you were in the army before I was; and I remember that I was still only a minor officer when you were in command of two thousand horses.

[4] [Following the traditions of the *commedia dell' arte*, Jodelet played his part in white-face, like a modern clown or Pierrot.—Trans.]

JODELET: War is a fine thing, but egad, the Court now rewards very poorly old servicemen like us.

MASCARILLE: That's why I'm going to hang up my sword on the hook.

CATHOS: As for me, I have an appalling weakness for men of war.

MAGDELON: I am fond of them too; but I like to have their valor seasoned with wit.

MASCARILLE: Vicomte, do you remember that half-moon fortification we took by storm at the siege of Arras?

JODELET: Half-moon? What do you mean? It was a good full moon.

MASCARILLE: I think you're right.

JODELET: Good gad, I ought to remember it. I was wounded there in the leg by a grenade; I still have the scars. (*To* CATHOS) Just feel a little there, please; you'll recognize where I got smacked.

CATHOS: It's true, it's a dreadful bump.

MASCARILLE (*to* MAGDELON): Give me your hand a minute. Feel right there, at the back of my head. Have you got it?

MAGDELON: Yes, I feel something.

MASCARILLE: That's a musket shot I caught in my last campaign.

JODELET (*unbuttoning his shirt*): And here's where a sword went right through me at the attack on Gravelines.

MASCARILLE (*putting his hand on his top breeches button*): I'm going to show you a frightful wound.

MAGDELON: It's not necessary; we can believe it without seeing it.

MASCARILLE: They are honorable wounds, which show what kind of people we are.

CATHOS: We don't doubt at all what kind of people you are.

MASCARILLE: Vicomte, have you got your carriage here?

JODELET: Why?

MASCARILLE: We could take the ladies for a ride outside the gates, and give them an entertainment.

MAGDELON: Oh, we can't go out today.

MASCARILLE: Then let's have some music in and dance.

JODELET: A noble thought!

MAGDELON: Well, we'd agree to that. But we ought to have some more people.

MASCARILLE: Holà! Champagne, Picard, Bourguignon, Cascaret, Basque, La Verdure, Lorrain, Provençal, La Violette! Where the devil are all my lackeys? I don't think there's a gentleman in all France who is worse served than I am. Those rascals are always leaving me alone.

MAGDELON: Almanzor, tell the gentleman's servants to fetch some musicians; and bring in the ladies from next door, to people the solitude of our dance. (*Exit* ALMANZOR.)

MASCARILLE: Vicomte, what's your opinion of those eyes there?

JODELET: Well, Marquis, what do *you* think?

MASCARILLE: Why, I say that our liberty will have some trouble in getting out of here with a whole skin. At least, to speak for myself, I'm all of aquiver, and my heart hangs only by a single thread.

MAGDELON (*to* CATHOS): How natural is everything he says! He puts things so agreeably!

CATHOS: It's true that he makes a furious expenditure of wit.

MASCARILLE: To show that I'm sincere, I'm going to make an impromptu on that theme. (*He meditates.*)

CATHOS: Oh, I implore you with all my heart's devotion, let us have something done especially for us.

JODELET: I should like to do the same, but I'm a little incommoded in the poetic vein, because of all the literary bleedings I've suffered in the last few days.

MASCARILLE: Now, what the devil is this? I can always do the first line very nicely, but I have a lot of trouble with the others. Gad, I'm being hurried too much. I'll make you an impromptu at my leisure, and I think you'll find it very fine indeed.

JODELET: He really has a devilish wit.

MAGDELON: And so gallant, and so neatly put!

MASCARILLE: Vicomte, tell me, will you, is it long since you've seen the Countess?

JODELET: It's more than three weeks since I paid her a visit.

MASCARILLE: Do you know that the Duke came to see me this morning? He wanted to take me to the country to go stag hunting.

MAGDELON: Here are our friends now. (*Enter* LUCILE, CÉLIMÈNE, ALMANZOR, FIDDLERS) Bless me, my dears, we must ask your pardon for disturbing you. These gentlemen had the fancy to give life and soul to the feet. So we sent for you to fill the void of our gathering.

LUCILE: We are much obliged to you, certainly.

MASCARILLE: This is just an improvised affair; but one of these days we'll give you a proper ball. Are the fiddlers here?

ALMANZOR: Yes, sir; here they are.

CATHOS: Come, my dears; take your places.

MASCARILLE (*dancing alone*): La, la, la, la, la, la, la.

MAGDELON (*to* CATHOS): He has really an elegant figure.

CATHOS: He's just the dancing type.

MASCARILLE (*taking* MAGDELON'S *arm*): My freedom takes a chance, by venturing to dance. Aha, the coranto! Keep the time, musicians, keep the time! Oh, what ignorant fools! No one can dance with them. Can't you play in time? La, la, la, la, la, la, la, la. Steady, you village fiddlers!

JODELET (*dancing*): Hey there, don't play so fast; I'm just out of a sickbed.

(*Enter* DU CROISY *and* LA GRANGE.)

LA GRANGE: Aha, you scoundrels, what are you doing here? We've been looking for you for three hours. (*He beats* MASCARILLE *with his cane.*)

MASCARILLE: Ow, ow, ow! You didn't tell me there would be a stick in it.

JODELET (*beaten by* DU CROISY): Ow, ow, ow!

LA GRANGE (*to* MASCARILLE): It's a fine thing for you, you blackguard, to try to play the man of importance.

DU CROISY: This will teach you to know your place.

(*Exit* DU CROISY *and* LA GRANGE.)

MAGDELON: What does this mean?

JODELET: It's a wager.

CATHOS: What! To let yourself be beaten that way?

MASCARILLE: Egad, I didn't want to let myself go. I have a very violent character, and I might have got really angry.

MAGDELON: To endure such an insult in our presence!

MASCARILLE: A trifle, a trifle! Let's finish the dance. We've known each other for a long time. With old friends you don't let a little thing like that upset you.

(*Enter* DU CROISY *and* LA GRANGE.)

LA GRANGE: On my word, you rogues, you won't make fools of us, I assure you. Come in, you men.

(*Enter two sturdy* BULLIES.)

MAGDELON: What kind of impudence is this, to come and disturb us in our house?

DU CROISY: What, ladies, we shall permit our lackeys to be better received than we were? We shall allow them to court you at our cost, and even offer you a dance?

MAGDELON: Your lackeys?

LA GRANGE: Yes, our lackeys. And it isn't honest and decent for you to spoil them the way you're doing.

MAGDELON: Oh, heaven! What insolence!

LA GRANGE: But they won't have the advantage of using our garments to bedazzle you. If you want to love them, it will have to be for their native charms. Come on, strip them, and be quick.

JODELET: Farewell to our finery!

MASCARILLE: Now the marquisate and the viscounty are humbled in the dust.

DU CROISY: Aha, you rascals, you wanted to follow in our footsteps! You'll have to go somewhere else for the equipment to charm your beauties, I can assure you.

LA GRANGE: It's too much, to try to take our places, and especially with our own clothes.

MASCARILLE: Ah, Fortune, what is thy inconstancy!

DU CROISY: Come on, take everything off them.[5]

LA GRANGE: Take away all those clothes; hurry. (*Exit the* BULLIES) Now, ladies, in their present state, you can continue your love passages with them as much as you please. We will leave you full liberty to do so, and my friend and I protest that we shall not be jealous at all.

(*Exit* LA GRANGE *and* DU CROISY.)

CATHOS: Oh, what a horror!

MAGDELON: I'm sick with shame!

FIDDLER (*to* MASCARILLE): What's all this, anyhow? Who's going to pay us?

MASCARILLE: Ask Monsieur le Vicomte.

FIDDLER (*to* JODELET): Who's going to give us our money?

JODELET: Ask Monsieur le Marquis.

(*Enter* GORGIBUS.)

GORGIBUS: Why, you little hussies, you've got us into a lovely mess, apparently! I've just heard some fine things about you from those gentlemen who have just gone out!

MAGDELON: Oh, Father, they've played us a cruel and ugly trick!

GORGIBUS: Yes, it's cruel and ugly, but it's the result of your impertinence, you shameful girls! They resented the way you treated them; and now, to my misfortune, I have to swallow their insult.

MAGDELON: Oh, I swear that we shall have our revenge, or I'll die of mortification! (*To* MASCARILLE *and* JODELET, *who are kneeling in supplication*) And you, you villains, do you dare to stay here after your insolent actions?

MASCARILLE: What a way to treat a marquis! What society has come to! The slightest little misadventure makes our dear ones scorn us! Come on, old comrade, let's seek our fortune somewhere else. I see clearly that here only the vain appearances are prized, and there is no esteem for

[5] [The traditional stage business requires a slow, reluctant disrobing. Jodelet removes a series of waistcoats, and appears, wigless, in a cook's white cap and apron. Mascarille wears a lackey's smock.—Trans.]

naked virtue. (*Exit* MASCARILLE *and* JODELET.)

FIDDLER: Monsieur, we expect you to pay us for our music, since they didn't.

GORGIBUS: Yes, yes, I'll pay you; and this is how. (*Beats them*) And you, you rascally wenches, I don't know what keeps me from doing the same to you. We'll be a laughingstock to everybody; that's what you've brought on us by your fantasticalities. Go hide your faces, wenches; hide them for good. And you who are the cause of their follies, you crack-brained fancies, pernicious amusements of idle minds, novels, verses, songs and sonnets, may the devil take the lot of you!

Tartuffe

by MOLIÈRE

TRANSLATED BY *Morris Bishop*

The Characters

MADAME PERNELLE, *mother of Orgon*

ORGON

ELMIRE, *Orgon's wife*

DAMIS, *son of Orgon, stepson of Elmire*

MARIANE, *daughter of Orgon and stepdaughter of Elmire*

VALÈRE

CLÉANTE, *brother-in-law of Orgon, brother of Elmire*

TARTUFFE

DORINE, *companion of Mariane*

MONSIEUR LOYAL, *bailiff*

A POLICE OFFICER

FLIPOTE, *Madame Pernelle's servant*

The setting throughout is the salon of Orgon's house, in Paris. The furnishings are those of a well-to-do bourgeois.

Act I

MADAME PERNELLE, FLIPOTE, ELMIRE, MARIANE, DORINE, DAMIS, CLÉANTE.

MME PERNELLE: Come on, Flipote, come on; I've had enough.
ELMIRE: Mother, you walk so fast I can't keep up.
MME PERNELLE: Don't try to keep up, then. Ha! Daughter-in-law!
Little I care if you're polite with me.
ELMIRE: I want to be so with my husband's mother.
Why must you go? I hope you're not offended.
MME PERNELLE: Why? I can't stand the way that things are going!
In my son's house they pay no heed to me.
I am not edified; not edified.
I give you good advice. Who pays attention?
Everyone speaks his mind, none shows respect.
This place is Bedlam; everyone is king here.
DORINE: If—
MME PERNELLE: You, my dear, you're just a paid companion,
A forward hussy, who talks a lot too much.
You have to give your views on everything.
DAMIS: But—
MME PERNELLE: You are a fool. F-O-O-L spells fool.
Your grandmother, she ought to know a fool.
And I have told your father a hundred times
You're impudent, your character is bad;
And what he'll get from you, my boy, is trouble.
MARIANE: I think—
MME PERNELLE: You think! The fool's little sister thinks!
Butter won't melt in that prim mouth of yours.
Still waters, they are deep—and dangerous.
And something hides behind that mousy manner.
ELMIRE: But, Mother—
MME PERNELLE: Dear Elmire, I will be frank.
I find your attitude unfortunate.

Your task should be to set a good example.
Their own dead mother did so, better than you.
I disapprove of your extravagance;
You get yourself all rigged up like a princess.
A wife, my dear, needs no such finery,
If she would please her husband's eyes alone.

CLÉANTE: But, madame, after all—

MME PERNELLE: You are her brother.
You have my reverence, esteem, and love.
But if I were my son, her happy husband,
I'd beg of you never to call again.
The principles I hear you recommend
Are not the sort that decent folk observe.
I'm speaking frankly; that's the way I am;
And when I feel a thing, I cannot hide it.

DAMIS: There's nothing wrong about Monsieur Tartuffe?

MME PERNELLE: He is a worthy man with principles;
And I admit that I am irritated
To hear him criticized by fools like you.

DAMIS: You want me to permit a canting critic
To come and play the tyrant in our home?
We can't indulge in innocent amusement
Unless that gentleman gives his consent?

DORINE: If one believes him and his principles,
Everything that we do becomes a crime.
He checks on everything, he's so sincere.

MME PERNELLE: And what he checks on is most properly checked.
He wants to lead you on the road to heaven.
My son is well inspired to make you love him.

DAMIS: Grandmother, look; Father can do his utmost;
Nothing on earth can make me love the fellow.
Anything else I'd say would be a lie.
I simply cannot stand him and his actions.
I can see trouble coming; I can see
I'll have a set-to with that holy fraud.

DORINE: It seems to me perfectly scandalous

That this outsider should take over things.
He came to us a beggar, with no shoes,
And all his clothes were worth about a dollar.
But that's forgotten, now he's found his place;
He has the final veto; he's the boss.

MME PERNELLE: Mercy upon us! Things would be much better
If all his pious rules were put in force.

DORINE: He is a saint in your imagination.
In fact, he's nothing but a hypocrite.

MME PERNELLE: What silly talk is this!

DORINE: I wouldn't trust him
Out of my sight; his servant Laurent either.

MME PERNELLE: The servant I don't know; but for the master,
I guarantee that he's a man of virtue.
And you dislike him, you cold-shoulder him
Merely because he tells the truth about you.
The one thing that he really hates is sin,
And heaven's advantage is his only motive.

DORINE: Yes, but why is it that for some time now
He won't allow us any visitors?
What is so shocking in a friendly call,
That he should make a frightful fuss about it?
And shall I tell you what I really think?
I think that he is jealous of Madame.
(*She indicates* ELMIRE.)

MME PERNELLE: Be quiet, you! Be careful what you say!
He's not the only one who blames these visits.
All the commotion that these callers make,
Their carriages forever at the door,
The noisy gangs of lackeys, hanging around,
Have caused a lot of comment from the neighbors.
Oh, I will grant that nothing serious happens,
But people talk, and people shouldn't talk.

CLÉANTE: You want to put a stop to conversation?
Wouldn't it be somewhat regrettable
If we should have to give up our best friends,

Just because fools may say some foolish things?
Even supposing we should bar the door,
Do you think people then would cease to talk?
There is no wall so high it shuts out slander.
So let's not give a thought to silly gossip,
And let us try to live in innocence,
And let the talkers talk just as they please.

DORINE: Our neighbor Daphne and her little husband
Are doubtless those who speak so ill of us.
Those whose behavior is ridiculous
Always are first to see the faults of others.
They never fail to catch the faintest hint
That mutual attachments may exist.
And then how glad they are to spread the news,
Suggesting—oh, what horrors they suggest!
And others' acts, colored to suit their tastes,
They put to use to authorize their own.
They think that some resemblance will appear
To mask their own intrigues with innocence;
They hope thus to confuse the public censure
And make it fall on good and ill alike.

MME PERNELLE: All these fine words do not affect the case.
Orante, for instance, leads a model life.
She works for heaven alone; and people say
That she condemns the customs of this house.

DORINE: There is a fine example! That good woman!
She lives austerely now, that's true enough;
But age has put this ardor in her soul,
And makes her play the prude, despite herself.
As long as men would pay their court to her,
She made her graces work for her advantage.
But her allurements ceasing to allure,
She quits society, which quitted her,
And with a veil of virtue tries to hide
The dimming of her antiquated charms.
That is the classic fate of old coquettes;
They hate to see their gallants disappear.

Unhappy and abandoned, they can see
No other recourse than the trade of prude.
And these good women with severity
Make universal censure, pardon nothing.
Loudly they blame the lives of everyone,
Not out of charity, but out of envy,
Which can't endure that any woman share
In pleasures time has thieved away from them.

MME PERNELLE (*to* ELMIRE):

That is the kind of nonsense that you like;
Thus in your house we have to hold our tongues
So that my lady here can hold the floor.
But I've a little speech to make myself,
And here it is: My son did very wisely
In welcoming that pious gentleman;
And heaven sent him here advisedly
To guide your spirits, strayed from the true path.
And you should heed him, for your souls' salvation.
What he reproves has needed his reproof.
These parties and these balls, these conversations,
Are all inventions of the Evil One.
There one may hear no edifying speeches,
But only idle words and songs and chatter,
Often at some poor fellow man's expense.
There you find masters in the art of slander.
Even the man of sense may be upset
By the loose talk one hears in such assemblies,
All a great buzz of gossip and of rumor.
As a great preacher said the other day,
These gatherings are towers of Babylon,
For people merely babble on, he said.
And then in illustration of his point—
(*Points to* CLÉANTE.)
And now monsieur is snickering already!
Go join the funny men who make you laugh!
My dear Elmire, good-by; I've said enough.
This household has come down in my opinion.

'Twill be a blue moon ere I come again.
(*Giving* FLIPOTE *a box on the ear*)
Wake up, woolgatherer! Wake up, rattlehead!
God's mercy! I will beat those brains of yours!
On your way, trollop!
(*Exit all except* CLÉANTE *and* DORINE.)

CLÉANTE: I wouldn't see her out
For fear I'd get another dressing-down.
For really that good woman—

DORINE: It's too bad
The lady didn't hear you call her good.
She'd tell you you are kind to term her good,
But she's not old enough yet to be good.

CLÉANTE: Didn't she get excited about nothing!
And isn't she crazy about her Tartuffe!

DORINE: In fact, that son of hers is twice as bad.
If you could see him, you'd be really shocked.
He played a fine part in the civil wars,
Was faithful to the King through thick and thin;
But now he acts as if he'd lost his wits,
Since he has been bewitched by his Tartuffe.
He calls him brother, actually loves him
More than his mother, son, daughter, and wife,
Confides his secrets to Tartuffe alone,
And makes him sole director of his actions;
Hugs him and pats him tenderly; he couldn't
Show more affection for a darling bride;
Gives him the place of honor at his table,
And beams to see him eat enough for six.
He saves the best bits for Tartuffe alone,
And cries "God bless you!" when the fellow belches.
He's mad about the man, his pet, his hero,
And quotes him, apropos of everything,
And makes a miracle of every action,
An oracle of every slightest word.
And Tartuffe knows a good thing when he sees it,
Puts on an act, the better to fool his dupe;

His holy manner pays him off in cash,
While he makes bold to criticize us all.
Even that boy who serves him as a lackey
Takes it upon himself to give us lessons,
And lectures us with angry, popping eyes,
And throws away our ribbons, rouge, and patches.
The rascal tore to bits a neckerchief
We'd put to press in some big holy book,
Saying we made a criminal connection
Between the devil's toys and holiness!

(*Enter* ELMIRE, MARIANE, DAMIS.)

ELMIRE: Lucky for you you didn't come and hear
The speech she made us, standing in the doorway.
I saw my husband, but he didn't see me.
I think I'll wait for him in the upstairs parlor.
(*Exit* ELMIRE *and* MARIANE.)
CLÉANTE: Not to waste time, I'll wait to see him here.
I merely want to greet him and be gone.
DAMIS: Bring up the question of my sister's marriage.
I've an idea Tartuffe is against it.
He's swaying Father, making difficulties.
You know I'm personally interested.
As Valère and my sister are in love,
I'm more than fond myself of Valère's sister.
And if I had to—
DORINE: He's coming.
(*Exit* DAMIS. *Enter* ORGON.)
ORGON: Good morning, brother.
CLÉANTE: I was just leaving. I'm glad to see you back.
And did you find the country all in bloom?
ORGON: Dorine . . . Just wait a minute, please, Cléante,
Until I have a chance to inform myself
About the household news during my absence.
(*To* DORINE)
Everything's been all right, the past few days?
How's everyone? What has been going on?

DORINE: Two days ago, your lady had a fever,
And a bad headache, really terrible.
ORGON: And Tartuffe?
DORINE: Tartuffe? Oh, he's doing fine,
So fat and red-faced, such a healthy color.
ORGON: Poor fellow!
DORINE: She had some nausea in the evening,
And couldn't touch a single thing at supper.
Her headache still was a real torture to her.
ORGON: And Tartuffe?
DORINE: Ate his supper in her presence,
And piously devoured two partridges,
Also a hash of half a leg of mutton.
ORGON: Poor fellow!
DORINE: During all the following night
She did not shut her eyes a single moment.
It was so very warm she could not sleep;
We had to sit beside her until morning.
ORGON: And Tartuffe?
DORINE: Oh, Tartuffe was sleepy enough.
He went right after dinner to his room,
Immediately he got in his warm bed,
And peacefully slept until the following day.
ORGON: Poor fellow!
DORINE: She listened to our arguments,
And had the doctor give her a good bleeding,
And after that she felt a great deal better.
ORGON: And Tartuffe?
DORINE: Why, he cheered up very nicely.
To fortify his spirit against trouble
And to make up for Madame's loss of blood,
He took at lunch four glasses full of wine.
ORGON: Poor fellow!
DORINE: Now both are doing very well.
I'll tell Madame the sympathetic interest
You've taken in the news of her recovery. (*Exit* DORINE.)
CLÉANTE: She's laughing in your face, my dear Orgon;
And while I wouldn't want to make you angry,

I'm frank to say she has good reason to.
I can't conceive such an infatuation.
This fellow must cast some uncanny spell
Which paralyzes all your common sense.
After you've rescued him from poverty,
To think you've gone so far—

ORGON: Enough, Cléante.
You do not know the man you're talking of.

CLÉANTE: Well, I don't know him personally, it's true,
But I know well what kind of man he is.

ORGON: Brother-in-law, you would be charmed to know him.
You would be simply overwhelmed with pleasure.
He's a man who . . . a man who . . . well, he's a man!
Follow his teachings, you gain peace of mind,
You learn to see the world as so much filth.
My talks with him have changed me utterly;
He's taught me to despise worldly attachments,
He frees my soul from earthly love and friendship;
If brother and children, mother and wife should die,
It wouldn't bother me as much as that!
(*Snaps his fingers.*)

CLÉANTE: These sentiments are what I call humane.

ORGON: If you'd been present when we made acquaintance,
You'd have become his friend, the same as I.
He used to come to our church every day,
And kneel near me, with such a gentle air!
And everyone in church would notice him
Because of the fervent way in which he prayed.
He sighed so deep, he made such cries of transport!
And every now and then he'd kiss the floor!
When I was going out, he'd run ahead
To offer me holy water at the door.
His servant lad, no less devout than he,
Told me about his life, his poverty.
I made him presents; but with modesty,
He always tried to give me back a part.
"This is too much!" he'd tell me. "Twice too much!
I don't deserve to have you pity me!"

And when I would refuse to take them back,
He'd give them to the poor! I saw him do it!
'Twas heaven that made me bring him to my house;
And since that time, everything prospers here.
He censures everything, and for my honor
He takes an active interest in my wife,
Warns me when people look too kindly at her—
He's twice as jealous of her as I could be.
You can't imagine his religious scruples!
The merest trifle is a sin to him;
Nothing's too insignificant to shock him.
Why, he accused himself the other day
Of capturing a flea while he was praying,
And pinching it to death with too much anger!

CLÉANTE: Good Lord, my dear Orgon, I think you're crazy!
Or are you trying to make a fool of me?
What do you think that all this nonsense means?

ORGON: Cléante, this sounds to me like irreligion!
You've had some tendency to that already;
And as I've warned you a good dozen times,
You'll get yourself in trouble some fine day.

CLÉANTE: I've heard that kind of talk from others like you.
They want to make the whole world blind like them.
It's irreligion just to have open eyes!
If you're not taken in by mummery,
They say you've no respect for sacred things.
You cannot scare me with that sort of language.
I know what I say, and heaven can see my heart.
We aren't befooled by such performances;
There's false devotion like false bravery.
And as you see upon the field of honor
The really brave are not the noisiest ones,
The truly pious, whom we should imitate,
Are not the ones who show off their devotion.
Isn't there some distinction to be made
Between hypocrisy and piety?
It seems you want to treat them both alike,
Honor the mask as much as the true face,

Make artifice equal sincerity,
Confuse the outward semblance with the truth,
Esteem the phantom equally with the person,
Take counterfeit money on a par with gold.
Really, humanity is most peculiar!
Men won't remain in the mean middle way;
The boundaries of reason are too narrow.
They force their character beyond its limits,
And often spoil even most noble aims
By exaggeration, carrying things too far.
All this, Orgon, is only said in passing.

ORGON: Cléante, you are no doubt a reverend doctor.
All of man's wisdom has been lodged in you.
You are the world's one wise, enlightened sage,
The oracle, the Cato of our times,
And all mankind, compared with you, are fools.

CLÉANTE: No, Orgon, I am not a reverend doctor,
And the world's wisdom is not lodged in me.
But there is one thing that I do well know:
To tell the difference between true and false.
And as I see no kind of character
More honorable than true devotion is,
Nothing more noble and more beautiful
Than fervent, genuine, holy piety,
So I find nothing on earth more odious
Than the false show of whited sepulchres,
These charlatans, these public pietists
Whose sacrilegious and perfidious manners
Deliberately betray and parody
All that men hold most hallowed and most sacred.
These are the people who for mean advantage
Make piety their trade and merchandise,
And try to buy credit and offices,
Rolling their eyes and mouthing holy words.
Their pilgrim's progress takes the road to heaven
As a short, easy way to worldly fortune.
We see them pray with one hand out for alms;
They preach of solitude, but stay at court.

And with their holy zeal they keep their vices;
They're vengeful, faithless, treacherous, and tricky,
And to destroy an enemy, they cover
Their savage hate with heaven's interest.
And when they hate, they're the more dangerous,
Because they take up weapons we revere,
Because their fury, to general applause,
Takes an anointed sword to stab our backs.
The type that I describe is all too common.
But the true pietists can be recognized.
Take Ariston, for instance, Périandre,
Oronte, Alcidamas, or Polydore.
No one's suspicious of their genuineness.
Such people don't go trumpeting their virtue,
They don't put on a nauseating show,
For their devotion's human, reasonable.
They do not censure all the acts of men—
There's too much pride in taking on that role.
They leave the high talk to their imitators,
And by their actions set us an example.
They don't see evil everywhere abounding;
Indeed, they're lenient toward their fellow men.
They don't form pressure groups to push intrigues;
To lead a good life is their only aim.
They don't pursue the sinner with their hate;
The sin and not the sinner is their target.
They don't espouse the interests of heaven
With greater zeal than heaven does itself.
That is the kind of people I admire;
They are the models we should imitate;
And, to be frank, your man's not one of them.
Although I know you praise him in good faith,
I think you're taken in by false appearance.

ORGON: Cléante, you've now entirely finished?

CLÉANTE: Yes.

ORGON: I am your humble servant.
(*Starts to leave.*)

CLÉANTE: Just a moment.

Let's deal with something else. You have consented
That young Valère should have your daughter's hand.

ORGON: Yes.

CLÉANTE: And what's more, you'd even set the day.

ORGON: That is correct.

CLÉANTE: Then why is it postponed?

ORGON: I don't know why.

CLÉANTE: You have another idea?

ORGON: Perhaps.

CLÉANTE: You hint you'd go back on your word.

ORGON: I won't say that.

CLÉANTE: There is some obstacle
To keep you from fulfilling your engagement?

ORGON: Maybe.

CLÉANTE: Why must you beat around the bush?
Valère has asked me to inquire about it.

ORGON: How fortunate!

CLÉANTE: What shall I tell him, then?

ORGON: Whatever you like.

CLÉANTE: But it is necessary
To know your plans. So what are they?

ORGON: To follow
The will of heaven.

CLÉANTE: I want to get this clear.
You've given Valère your word. You'll keep your word?

ORGON: Good-by. (*Exit* ORGON.)

CLÉANTE: I fear that courtship's in for trouble;
And I must tell Valère the look of things.

Act II

ORGON, MARIANE.

ORGON: Mariane!

MARIANE: Father?

ORGON: Come here. I want to speak
In confidence.

(*He peers into a cupboard.*)

MARIANE: What are you looking for?

ORGON: I want to see if there's an eavesdropper there,
For that's the kind of place they choose to hide in.
No, it's all right. Now, Mariane, my dear,
You've always had a gentle character,
And I have always been most fond of you.

MARIANE: I have been very grateful for your love.

ORGON: Excellent, daughter. To deserve my affection
You should be ready to accept my judgments.

MARIANE: I've always done so, and I'm proud of it.

ORGON: Splendid. Now tell me, what do you think of Tartuffe?

MARIANE: What do I think?

ORGON: Yes. Don't speak hastily.

MARIANE: Dear me! I think whatever you think I should.

(DORINE *enters unnoticed.*)

ORGON: Well said. Now this is what you ought to think.
He is a man of most unusual merit;
He moves your heart, and you'd be overjoyed
To have me pick him out to be your husband.
Eh?
(MARIANE *starts back in surprise.*)

MARIANE: Eh?

ORGON: What?

MARIANE: What did you say?

ORGON: What?

MARIANE: Did I hear rightly?

ORGON: What's this?

MARIANE: Who is it you say that moves my heart?
Who is it that it would make me overjoyed
To have you fix upon to be my husband?

ORGON: Tartuffe.

MARIANE: Oh, no, no, no, it's impossible.
Why do you want to make me say what's false?

ORGON: I say it because I want to make it true.

I have decided on it, that's enough.

MARIANE: Father, you really mean—

ORGON: Yes, it's my purpose
To make Tartuffe a member of our family.
He'll be your husband, I'm resolved on that.
And your desires—
(*He turns, and perceives* DORINE.)
What are you doing here?
Your curiosity is certainly excessive
To make you listen to our private talk.

DORINE: I'd heard the story—I suppose it started
Out of pure guesswork or some chance remark—
That this peculiar marriage was afoot;
But I've been saying it's all poppycock.

ORGON: You mean you find it unbelievable?

DORINE: So much so that I don't believe you now.

ORGON: I know how I can bring you to believe it.

DORINE: Yes, you're just being funny. I know *you*.

ORGON: I'm telling you exactly what will happen.

DORINE: Rubbish!

ORGON: My good girl, it's not rubbish at all.

DORINE (*to* MARIANE):
Do not believe a word your father says.
He's joking.

ORGON: I tell you—

DORINE: No, whatever you do,
Nobody can believe it.

ORGON: I can't hold in—

DORINE: All right, then, I'll believe you, if I must.
But how a sensible-looking man like you,
With a big beard in the middle of his face,
Can be so simple-minded—

ORGON: Listen to me.
You have been taking certain liberties here
Which I don't like at all, I tell you frankly.

DORINE: Now, let's not get excited, sir, I beg you.
Is your idea just to look absurd?

A bigot has no business with your daughter;
He has a lot of other things to think of.
What good does such a marriage do to you?
How comes it that you, with your property,
Should choose a beggar son-in-law—

ORGON: Be quiet!
That's just the reason why we should revere him!
His poverty's a worthy poverty,
Which properly sets him above rank and wealth.
He's let his worldly goods all slip away,
Because he'd no concern for temporal things,
Because he loved eternal goods alone.
But my financial aid will help him rise
Out of his troubles, regain his property,
Estates well known in his home territory.
He is a landed squire, a gentleman.

DORINE: Yes, so he says. His vanity about it
Is unbecoming with his piety.
When you take up a holy, innocent life,
You shouldn't boast about your name and rank.
Devotion should imply humility,
Which doesn't fit with smugness and ambition.
Why be so proud? . . . But you don't like this talk.
Let's treat his person, not his noble blood.
Doesn't it trouble you that a man like him
Should be possessor of a girl like her?
Shouldn't you think about the decencies,
Foresee the consequence of such a union?
You're putting a girl's virtue to the test
By forcing her to a distasteful marriage;
And her desire to be a faithful wife
Depends upon the qualities of the husband.
The men who wear the horns are just the ones
Who force their wives to be—what they become.
It's hard indeed for a woman to be faithful
To certain husbands cast in a certain mold.
A father who gives a girl to a man she hates

Must be responsible for her missteps.
So think how dangerous your project is!
ORGON: And so you want to teach me about life!
DORINE: You could do worse than follow my advice.
ORGON: Daughter, we'll waste no time with all this nonsense.
I know what's best for you; I am your father.
It's true that I had pledged you to Valère,
But now I hear that he plays cards for money;
Further, I fear he's somewhat a freethinker.
I do not see him frequently in church.
DORINE: You think he ought to go there just when you do,
Like those who only want to catch your attention?
ORGON: I didn't ask your views upon the matter.
(*To* MARIANE)
The other man has made his peace with heaven,
And that's the greatest wealth a man can have.
This marriage will be rich in every blessing,
And filled with pleasures and with satisfactions.
You will be faithful, in your mutual joys,
Just like a pair of little turtle doves.
There'll never be an argument between you;
You'll make of him whatever you want to make.
DORINE: All that she'll make of him is a horned monster.
ORGON: What talk is this?
DORINE: I say he has the build for it.
The stars have doomed him, and his natural fate
Will be more powerful than your daughter's virtue.
ORGON: Stop interrupting me, and hold your tongue,
And don't go meddling in what's none of your business.
DORINE: I'm only speaking, sir, for your own good.
(*She interrupts* ORGON *whenever he turns to speak to his daughter.*)
ORGON: That's all too kind of you; and so, be silent.
DORINE: If I didn't love you—
ORGON: I don't want to be loved.
DORINE: I want to love you, sir, in spite of yourself.
ORGON: Ha!

DORINE: Cherishing your honor, I can't bear
The mockeries you'd lay yourself open to.
ORGON: You won't shut up?
DORINE: My conscientious duty
Is not to permit you to make such an alliance.
ORGON: Will you shut up, you snake! Your impudence—
DORINE: Why, you're so holy, and you fly in a rage!
ORGON: You drive me crazy with your balderdash,
And so I order you to keep your mouth shut.
DORINE: All right. But even when silent, I can think.
ORGON: Think if you like; but take good care you don't
Utter a word, or else—
(*Threatens* DORINE *with a gesture. Turns to* MARIANE.)
As a sensible man,
I've thought the matter out.
DORINE: It drives me mad
Not to be able to speak.
(ORGON *turns to her; she falls silent.*)
ORGON: Although no dandy,
Tartuffe has looks—
DORINE: All right, if you like them hard.
ORGON: And even if you had no sympathy
For his other gifts—
DORINE: Oh, what a lucky girl!
If I were she, I would make sure no man
Would marry me by force and escape scot-free;
And I would prove, soon after the ceremony,
That a woman always has her vengeance ready.
ORGON (*to* DORINE):
So, you won't pay attention to my orders?
DORINE: What's your objection? I'm not talking to you.
ORGON: Then what are you doing?
DORINE: Talking to myself.
ORGON: Excellent. So, to punish her insolence,
I'll have to give her a good slap in the face.
(*Raises his hand and poises it for a blow, but whenever he looks at* DORINE, *she stands still and mute.*)

Daughter, you ought to think well of my project . . .
Believe the husband . . . whom I've chosen for you . . .
(*To* DORINE)
Why don't you talk to yourself?

DORINE: I've nothing to say.

ORGON: Just say one little word!

DORINE: I don't feel like it.

ORGON: I was all ready for you.

DORINE: I'm not so dumb.

ORGON (*turns to* MARIANE):
In short, Mariane, you owe obedience,
And you must show respect for my opinion.

DORINE (*fleeing*):
You'd never make me agree to such a husband.
(ORGON *tries to slap her; she escapes, and exits.*)

ORGON: That forward girl of yours, Mariane, is a pest,
And she provokes me to the sin of anger.
I'm in no state to carry on our talk;
Her insolent speech has got me all excited,
And I must take a walk to calm myself.
(*Exit* ORGON. DORINE *re-enters cautiously.*)

DORINE: What, Mariane, you've lost your power of speech?
And do I have to play your part for you?
You'll let him make this asinine proposal,
And not combat it with a single word?

MARIANE: What can I do against his absolute power?

DORINE: Anything, in the face of such a threat.

MARIANE: And what?

DORINE: Tell him a heart can't love by proxy;
The marriage is for your sake, not for his;
And since you are the person who's concerned,
The husband ought to please you and not him;
And since he finds Tartuffe so fascinating,
He is the one who ought to marry him.

MARIANE: I know; but Father is so masterful
I've never had the courage to oppose him.

DORINE: Look here; Valère has made his formal suit;

Now let me ask you: Do you love him, or don't you?
MARIANE: Oh, you're unjust, Dorine! You know I love him!
You have no reason even to ask the question!
Haven't I poured it out a hundred times,
And don't you know the greatness of my love?
DORINE: I never know if one is quite sincere,
If your great love is really genuine.
MARIANE: You do me a great wrong in doubting it.
I thought my feelings were sufficiently clear.
DORINE: In short, you love him?
MARIANE: Yes, and passionately.
DORINE: And it would seem that he loves you no less?
MARIANE: I think so.
DORINE: And you both are equally eager
To be united in marriage?
MARIANE: Certainly.
DORINE: About this other proposal, what's your plan?
MARIANE: To kill myself, if I am driven to it.
DORINE: Splendid! I hadn't thought of that way out.
To escape from trouble, you only have to die.
A marvelous remedy . . . It makes me furious,
Whenever I listen to that kind of talk.
MARIANE: Good heavens, what a temper you get into!
You don't much sympathize with others' sorrows.
DORINE: I don't much sympathize with those who drivel,
And then go limp, like you, when the test comes.
MARIANE: What can I do? I'm naturally timid—
DORINE: But love demands a firm, courageous heart.
MARIANE: I have been constant, answering Valère's love.
But he must ask, and gain, Father's consent.
DORINE: But if your father is a perfect crank,
Who's so infatuated with Tartuffe
He disavows the marriage he agreed to,
Is that a thing to blame your suitor for?
MARIANE: If I refuse Tartuffe with open scorn,
Won't I reveal how deeply I'm in love?
Brilliant though Valère is, shall I abandon

For him my modesty, my daughterly duty?
Do you want me to display my love to the world?
DORINE: No, I want nothing at all. I see you wish
To be Madame Tartuffe; and now I think of it,
I'm wrong in weaning you from this alliance.
Why should I argue against your inclinations?
The match would seem an advantageous one.
Monsieur Tartuffe! He's not a nobody!
Monsieur Tartuffe is not the kind who needs
To stand on his head to get applause and money.
One would be lucky indeed to be his wife.
Why, everyone is glorifying him!
He's noble—in his own home town! And handsome!
His ears are rosy red, like his complexion!
You will be all too happy with such a husband.
MARIANE: Yes, but—
DORINE: What ecstasy will fill your soul,
When you are wife to that good-looking man!
MARIANE: Stop, if you please, this agonizing talk,
And give me counsel how to escape the marriage.
I've made my mind up; I'll do anything.
DORINE: No, a good daughter should obey her father,
Though he should choose a monkey for her mate.
You've a fine future; what are you grumbling for?
You'll have a coach to perambulate his city,
Which you'll find rich in uncles, aunts, and cousins
Whom you will be delighted to entertain.
You'll be received in high society,
You'll call upon the Lord High Mayoress,
And on the Lord High Tax-Collectoress,
Who'll seat you honorably on a kitchen chair.
And you can hope for a ball at carnival time,
An orchestra consisting of two bagpipes,
And sometimes a marionette show—with a monkey!
However, if your husband—
MARIANE: You're killing me!
Stop it, and help me with some good advice.

DORINE: You must excuse me.
MARIANE: Oh, dear Dorine, please!
DORINE: To punish you, the marriage must go through.
MARIANE: Dorine!
DORINE: No!
MARIANE: If I state my opposition—
DORINE: Tartuffe's your man. You must put up with him.
MARIANE: I have confided everything to you.
So now—
DORINE: No. You will be tartufficated.
MARIANE: Since my unhappy destiny can't move you,
I must surrender now to my despair.
And from despair my heart will take advice.
I know the infallible remedy for my woes.
DORINE: Here, here, come back. I'll put aside my anger.
I must take pity upon you after all.
MARIANE: If they insist on making a martyr of me,
I tell you, Dorine, that I shall simply die.
DORINE: Don't worry. If we're clever enough, we can
Prevent it . . . But here's your lover, your Valère.

(*Enter* VALÈRE. *He speaks at first jestingly.*)

VALÈRE: Mademoiselle, a story's going round
That's new to me. Very fine news, no doubt.
MARIANE: What's that?
VALÈRE: That you're to marry Tartuffe.
MARIANE: Truly,
My father has this idea in his head.
VALÈRE: Your father, mademoiselle—
MARIANE: Has changed his purpose.
And he has just been making this proposal.
VALÈRE: Seriously?
MARIANE: Yes, seriously indeed.
He has come out in favor of this marriage.
VALÈRE: And what is your opinion on the matter,
Mademoiselle?
MARIANE: I don't know.

VALÈRE: Frank, at least.
You don't know?
MARIANE: No.
VALÈRE: No?
MARIANE: What is your advice?
VALÈRE: Why, my advice is to accept this husband.
MARIANE: That's your advice?
VALÈRE: Yes.
MARIANE: Really?
VALÈRE: Certainly.
It is an opportunity not to be scorned.
MARIANE: Well, I am very glad to have your counsel.
VALÈRE: I think you'll follow it without much trouble.
MARIANE: With no more trouble than you had in giving it.
VALÈRE: I gave the advice only to give you pleasure.
MARIANE: And I shall follow it to give *you* pleasure.
DORINE (*aside*): We'll soon find out how this is going to end.
VALÈRE: So this is how you love me? You deceived me
When you—
MARIANE: I beg you not to talk of that.
You told me outright that I ought to accept
The man who is designated for my husband;
And I say that's what I intend to do,
Since now you give me that excellent advice.
VALÈRE: Don't try to excuse yourself by quoting me;
You had already formed your resolution,
And now you're seizing on a frivolous pretext
To authorize yourself to break your word.
MARIANE: Well said; it's true.
VALÈRE: Certainly. And your heart
Has never felt any real love for me.
MARIANE: Oh, dear! Why, you may think so, if you wish.
VALÈRE: Yes, if I wish! You think you've wounded me,
But maybe I have other plans in mind.
I know where I can get a better welcome.
MARIANE: I don't doubt that. Anyone would admire
Your character.

VALÈRE: Let's leave my character out.
It's not so wonderful; indeed, you prove it.
But there's another girl who may be kinder;
She won't be ashamed to take me on the rebound,
And gladly she'll console me for losing you.
MARIANE: The loss is not so great. The consolation
Ought to come easily in this shift of partners.
VALÈRE: I'll do my very best, you may be sure.
Nobody likes to know he's been forgotten.
In such a case, the best is to forget,
And if you can't forget, pretend to do so.
It is unpardonably weak, I think,
To display love for one who abandons us.
MARIANE: That is a very lofty sentiment.
VALÈRE: You're right. It should be generally approved.
What! You would like to have me keep forever
My love for you unchanging in my heart,
See you go happily to another's arms,
And seek no solace for my cast-off love?
MARIANE: Why, not at all! That's just what I desire!
I wish that it were all arranged already!
VALÈRE: You'd like that?
MARIANE: Yes.
VALÈRE: I've borne insults enough!
I'll try immediately to satisfy you.
(*Starts to leave and returns, as in succeeding speeches.*)
MARIANE: Good.
VALÈRE: Remember at least that you're the one
Who is driving me to this expedient.
MARIANE: Yes.
VALÈRE: And remember that my purpose is
To follow your example.
MARIANE: If you like.
VALÈRE: Enough. Your wishes will be carried out.
MARIANE: Fine!
VALÈRE: So this is the last time that you'll see me.
MARIANE: Excellent!

VALÈRE (*starts to exit; at the door, turns*):
Uh?
MARIANE: What?
VALÈRE: Did I hear you call me?
MARIANE: You must be dreaming.
VALÈRE: Well, I'm on my way.
I bid you farewell.
MARIANE: Adieu, sir.
DORINE: As for me,
I think you both are addled in the brain.
I've let you squabble to your heart's content
To find out where you'd land yourselves at last.
Monsieur Valère!
(DORINE *tries to take* VALÈRE *by the arm, but he makes a show of resistance.*)
VALÈRE: What do you want, Dorine?
DORINE: Come here!
VALÈRE: No, no, she's put me in a fury.
I'm doing what she wanted, don't restrain me.
DORINE: Stop!
VALÈRE: No, the matter's settled, you can see.
DORINE: Aha!
MARIANE: My presence seems to irritate him;
The best thing is for me to leave him alone.
(DORINE *leaves* VALÈRE *and runs to* MARIANE.)
DORINE: Where are you going?
MARIANE: Let me alone!
DORINE: Come back!
MARIANE: There's no use trying to hold me back, Dorine.
VALÈRE: Clearly it tortures her to look at me.
I'd better free her from that painful sight.
DORINE (*leaving* MARIANE *and running to* VALÈRE):
What the deuce! You'll do nothing of the sort!
Stop all this nonsense! Both of you come here!
(*She pulls at them, one with each hand.*)
VALÈRE: What's your idea?
MARIANE: What do you want to do?

DORINE: Make peace between you and get you out of trouble.
(*To* VALÈRE)
You must be crazy to get in such a quarrel.
VALÈRE: Didn't you hear the way she talked to me?
DORINE (*to* MARIANE):
You must be crazy too, to get so angry.
MARIANE: Didn't you see the way he treated me?
DORINE (*to* VALÈRE):
You're crazy, both of you. I can bear witness
The only thing she wants is to be yours.
(*To* MARIANE)
He loves you only, and his one desire
Is marriage with you, I'll stake my life on that.
MARIANE (*to* VALÈRE):
Then why did you give me your horrible advice?
VALÈRE (*to* MARIANE):
And why ask my advice on such a subject?
DORINE: I said you were both crazy. Give me your hands.
(*To* VALÈRE)
Yours, now.
VALÈRE (*giving* DORINE *his hand*):
Why give you my hand?
DORINE (*to* MARIANE):
Now give me yours.
MARIANE (*giving* DORINE *her hand*):
What is the sense of this?
DORINE: Come on, step forward.
You're both in love more than you realize.
VALÈRE (*to* MARIANE):
Yes, but don't do things so reluctantly,
And give a man at least a friendly look.
(MARIANE *looks at* VALÈRE, *and smiles feebly.*)
DORINE: The fact is, lovers are extremely crazy!
VALÈRE (*to* MARIANE): Haven't I reason to complain of you?
Tell me sincerely, wasn't it unkind
To amuse yourself by hurting me so much?
MARIANE: But you yourself, aren't you the most ungrateful—

DORINE: Let's leave this argument to another time,
And think of fending off that fatal marriage.
MARIANE: But have you any idea how to do so?
DORINE: There are a lot of things that we can do.
Your father's talking nonsense, he's not serious.
But the best thing for you is to pretend
To gently yield to his fantasticality
So that, in case of crisis, you can easily
Keep on postponing the wedding ceremony.
You can cure many things by gaining time.
First you will take as your excuse some illness,
Which will strike suddenly and cause delays;
And then you'll meet an omen of misfortune.
You'll pass, perhaps, a funeral in the street,
Or break a mirror, or dream of muddy water.
The great thing is that nobody can bind you
To anyone without your saying yes.
But out of prudence, it would be advisable
That you two shouldn't be caught talking together.
(*To* VALÈRE)
Now go, and use the influence of your friends
To help you get the girl who was promised you.
And we shall make her brother work for us;
And her stepmother, she'll be on our side.
Good-by.
VALÈRE (*to* MARIANE): Though we'll all do the most we can,
My greatest hope and confidence lie in you.
MARIANE: I can't be sure what Father may decide,
But I shall never be anyone's bride but yours.
VALÈRE: You make me very happy! In spite of all—
DORINE: Lovers are never tired; they talk forever.
Come on; get going.
VALÈRE (*takes a step toward exit, and returns*):
Finally—
DORINE: Talk, talk, talk!
(*Pushes each of them by the shoulder.*)
You go out this way; you go out the other.

Act III

DAMIS, DORINE.

DAMIS: Now let a bolt of lightning strike me dead,
Call me a scoundrel, anything you please,
If any talk of duty will hold me back,
If I don't take some action to settle things.
DORINE: Just take it easy, calm yourself a little.
Your father has merely talked about the matter.
People don't execute all they propose;
There's many a slip between the cup and the lip.
DAMIS: I've got to stop that swine's conspiracies;
I've got to tell him a few simple facts.
DORINE: I tell you, take it easy; let your stepmother
Handle the fellow, as she does your father.
She has some influence on Tartuffe's mind.
He acts in a very obliging way to her;
Maybe he has a kind of weakness for her.
Lord knows I hope so! That would be convenient!
For your sake she will have to interview him,
Learn what his feelings are, point out to him
What dreadful troubles he will bring about
If he encourages Orgon in his purpose.
His valet says he's praying; I couldn't see him.
But he'll be coming down in a moment or two.
So go out, please; let me arrange the matter.
DAMIS: I can be present during the interview.
DORINE: No, they must be alone.
DAMIS: I will keep quiet.
DORINE: Nonsense! I know how you can get excited,
And that's the way to ruin everything.
Go on!
DAMIS: I want to see, and I won't get angry.
DORINE: Oh, what a nuisance you are! He's coming! Get out!
(DORINE *pushes* DAMIS *out. Enter* TARTUFFE. *He observes* DORINE *and calls off-stage.*)

TARTUFFE: Put my hair shirt away and my flagellator,
Laurent; and pray for heaven's continual grace.
If anyone wants me, say I'm off to the prison
To give away the charity given me.
DORINE (*aside*): Eyewash and affectation, if you ask me!
TARTUFFE: What do you want?
DORINE: To tell you—
TARTUFFE (*drawing out a handkerchief*): Oh, dear heaven!
Before you speak, please take this handkerchief.
DORINE: What?
TARTUFFE: Cover that bosom which I must not see.
Such sights as that are hurtful to the spirit,
And they may well awaken guilty thoughts.
DORINE: You must be very sensitive to temptation.
Flesh makes a great impression on your senses!
Of course, I don't know how you're stimulated,
But I am not so readily aroused.
If I should see you naked from head to foot,
I wouldn't be tempted by all the skin you've got.
TARTUFFE: Please be a little modest in your speech,
Or I must leave the room immediately.
DORINE: No, no, it's I who will go and leave you in peace.
But there is something that I have to tell you.
Madame Elmire is coming to the parlor,
And she would like to have a word with you.
TARTUFFE: Oh, very gladly.
DORINE (*aside*): How he softens down!
Bless me, I think that I was right about him.
TARTUFFE: She's coming soon?
DORINE: I think I hear her now.
Yes, here she is. I'll leave you two together.
(*Exit* DORINE. *Enter* ELMIRE.)
TARTUFFE: May heaven, by its high, omnipotent mercy,
Forever grant you health of soul and body,
And bless your days according to the desire
Of one who is humblest of heaven's worshipers!
ELMIRE: I'm deeply grateful for your pious wish.

Let us sit down, to be more comfortable.
TARTUFFE: I hope you have recovered from your illness?
ELMIRE: It's better, thank you; the fever left me soon.
TARTUFFE: My prayers are all too insignificant
To have brought this grace upon you from on high;
But every supplication I have made
Has had as object your recovery.
ELMIRE: Your pious zeal took all too much upon it.
TARTUFFE: Your precious health concerned me very deeply,
And to restore it gladly I'd give my own.
ELMIRE: You're carrying Christian charity too far;
But I'm indebted to you for your kindness.
TARTUFFE: What I have done is less than you deserve.

(Enter DAMIS *cautiously, behind backs of* TARTUFFE *and* ELMIRE; *he hides in the cupboard previously mentioned.)*

ELMIRE: I wanted to speak privately to you.
I'm glad we have this chance to be unobserved.
TARTUFFE: I am glad too. It's very sweet to me,
Madame, to find myself alone with you.
It is an opportunity I've prayed for
Without success, until this happy moment.
ELMIRE: I too have wished a chance for intimate talk,
When you might speak from the heart, without disguise.
TARTUFFE: And what I wish is, as a singular grace,
To lay my soul utterly bare before you,
And vow to you that all of my objections
To the visitors who come to pay you homage
Do not arise from any hostility,
But rather from the extravagance of my zeal,
From my emotion—
ELMIRE: I gladly take it so.
I'm sure my welfare gives you this concern.
TARTUFFE *(squeezing her fingertips)*:
Indeed, madame, indeed; such is my ardor—

ELMIRE: Ouch! You are hurting me!

TARTUFFE: Excess of zeal!
I'd no idea of hurting you at all.
I'd rather . . .
(*Puts his hand on her knee.*)

ELMIRE: Your hand—what, pray, is it doing there?

TARTUFFE: Just feeling the material; so soft!

ELMIRE: Well, please stop feeling it. I'm very ticklish.
(*She pushes her chair aside;* TARTUFFE *brings his chair close.*)

TARTUFFE: Really, this lace is marvelously done!
The modern needlework is truly astounding.
There's never before been anything to match it.

ELMIRE: Quite so. But let us talk about our business.
I hear my husband wants to break his word
And marry to you his daughter. Is that true?

TARTUFFE: He's hinted at it. But to tell the truth,
That's not the happiness I languish for.
It's elsewhere that I see the alluring charms
Of the felicity that I desire.

ELMIRE: I see; you do not love the things of earth.

TARTUFFE: The heart in my bosom is not made of stone.

ELMIRE: I think that all your longings turn to heaven,
That nothing upon this earth tempts your desires.

TARTUFFE: The love which draws us to eternal beauty
Does not exclude the love of temporal things.
And easily our senses may be charmed
By the perfect vessels heaven has fabricated.
Its glory is reflected in such creatures
As you, who show its rarest marvels forth.
Upon your face are heavenly beauties lavished
To dazzle the eyes, to fill the heart with transport.
O perfect beauty! I could not look upon you
Without admiring in you Nature's author,
And without feeling ardent love in my heart
For this fair portrait of divinity!
At first I trembled, lest my secret flame

Should be a stratagem of the Evil One;
Even, I was resolved to flee your presence,
A possible obstacle to my salvation.
But finally I realized, my fair one,
That there need be no guilt in such a passion,
That I can make it chime with modesty;
And so I let my heart follow its bent.
I know it is a great audacity
For me to dare to offer you this heart;
But my affection seeks all from your bounty,
And nothing from my own weak enterprise.
In you is all my hope, my good, my peace;
On you depends my punishment or my bliss;
By your decree alone may I be happy,
If you are willing; unhappy, if that's your will.

ELMIRE: This is a gallant declaration indeed,
But I must say I find it rather surprising.
I think you should have steeled your emotions better,
Considering what such a purpose means.
A pious man like you, so widely known—

TARTUFFE: Ah, pious though I be, I'm still a man.
And when one glimpses your celestial beauties,
The heart is captured, and it cannot argue.
I know such words from me may seem surprising,
But after all, madame, I'm not an angel.
If you condemn the avowal I make to you,
You must accuse your own bewitching charms.
Since I first saw their more than earthly splendor,
You were the sovereign of my secret soul,
And the ineffable sweetness of your glance
Broke the resistance of my struggling heart.
You conquered all, my fasting, prayers, and tears;
And all my vows were made to you alone.
My eyes have told you this, so have my sighs;
And now, for greater clarity, my words.
And if you look with a compassionate spirit
Upon the woes of your unworthy slave,

If you consent to bring me consolation,
To condescend to my unworthiness,
I'll vow to you, O lovely miracle,
Immeasurable worship and devotion.
And in my hands your honor runs no risk,
Nor need it fear any disgrace or scandal.
These young court gallants women dote upon
Are careless in their acts and vain of speech.
They like to boast about their amorous triumphs;
There are no favors that they don't divulge;
Their inconsiderate tongues betray their trust,
Dishonoring the altar where they worship.
Men of my stamp, however, are discreet;
With us one is always sure of secrecy.
The care we take of our own reputations
Is a guarantee to the person we adore.
She who accepts our heart acquires in us
Love without scandal, pleasure without fear.

ELMIRE: I'm fascinated; and your rhetoric
Explains itself in very lucid terms.
Aren't you afraid that I may be in the mood
To tell my husband about your gallant longings,
And that this information may disturb
The warm affection that he holds for you?

TARTUFFE: I know that you are far too merciful,
That you will pardon my temerity;
Pity for human weakness will excuse
The violence of a love which may offend you.
Look in your mirror, you will recognize
A man's not blind, he's only flesh and blood.

ELMIRE: Another woman might take it otherwise,
But I will show that I can be discreet.
I'll not repeat the matter to my husband,
But in return I want one thing of you:
That's to urge openly, with no quibbling talk,
The marriage of Valère and Mariane,
And to renounce the unreasonable claim

By which you'd win her who is pledged to another.
And—

DAMIS (*emerging from the cupboard*):
No, madame, no! This news must be reported!
I was concealed there, I could hear everything!
And heaven's favor must have led me there
To confound the pride of a treacherous evildoer,
To open a way for me to avenge myself
On his hypocrisy and insolence,
To undeceive my father, and lay bare
The soul of a scoundrel who talks to you of love!

ELMIRE: No, Damis; it's enough if he mends his ways,
Deserving the pardon which I offer him.
I've promised it; don't make me break my word.
It's not my character to make a scene.
A woman laughs at such absurdities,
And doesn't trouble her husband's ears about them.

DAMIS: You have your reasons to take matters thus,
And I've my reasons to do otherwise.
It is ridiculous to try to spare him.
His sanctimonious impudence too long
Has got the better of my just resentment;
Too long he's roused up trouble in our home;
And far too long the rogue has ruled my father,
And blocked my courtship as he has Valère's.
It's time that Father should be told the truth,
And heaven has given me the means to do so.
To heaven I owe this opportunity;
It's far too favorable to be neglected.
Why, I'd deserve to have it snatched away,
If I held it in my hand and didn't use it.

ELMIRE: Damis—

DAMIS: Please, I must do what I think best.
I've never been so happy as I am now!
There's no use trying to force me to surrender
The pleasure of holding vengeance in my hand!
I'm going to settle things immediately—

And here's my opportunity in person.

(*Enter* ORGON.)

Father, we're going to celebrate your coming
With a tasty bit of news which will surprise you.
You are well paid for all your kindnesses!
Monsieur has a special form of gratitude.
He's just revealed his zeal for your well-being,
Which aims at nothing less than your dishonor.
I have surprised him making to madame
The insulting avowal of a guilty love.
Her character is gentle; generously
She earnestly desired to keep it secret.
But I cannot condone such impudence.
To keep you in the dark would be an outrage.

ELMIRE: I think a wife ought never to disturb
A husband's peace with silly tales like these;
They have no application to her honor,
And it's enough that we defend ourselves.
That's what I think. Damis, you'd have said nothing,
If I had had some influence over you. (*Exit* ELMIRE.)

ORGON: Oh, heavens, is this strange story credible?

TARTUFFE: Yes, brother; I am a wicked, guilty man,
A wretched sinner full of iniquity,
The greatest scoundrel who has ever lived.
Each moment of my life has been polluted,
It is a mass of crime and filthiness.
I see that heaven, for my punishment,
Chooses this circumstance to mortify me.
However great the misdeed I am charged with,
I will not pridefully defend myself.
Believe their words, and give your anger rein,
And drive me from the house like a criminal.
No matter what may be my portion of shame,
I have deserved to suffer far, far more.

ORGON (*to* DAMIS):
Traitor! And do you dare, by lying words,

To try to tarnish his virtue's purity?
DAMIS: What! All this hypocritic blubbering
Will make you disbelieve—
ORGON: Silence, you pest!
TARTUFFE: Ah, let him speak! How wrongly you accuse him!
You would do better to believe his words.
Why, in this case, be favorable to me?
How do you know of what I am capable?
How can you trust, dear brother, my appearance?
Does my behavior prove me better in fact?
No, no, you let my outward semblance cheat you.
Alas, I am far from being what men think!
I'm taken commonly for an upright man,
But the truth is that I am nothing worth. (*To* DAMIS)
Speak, my dear boy, and call me infamous,
Perfidious, worthless, thief and murderer,
Load me with names still more detestable;
I do not contradict, for I have deserved them.
(*Kneels*)
I long to suffer their shame upon my knees,
As retribution for my criminal life.
ORGON (*to* TARTUFFE): Dear brother, it's too much. (*To* DAMIS) Your heart's not moved,
Traitor?
DAMIS: His talk can fool you to this point?
ORGON: Silence, scoundrel! (*To* TARTUFFE) Brother, I beg you, stand.
(*To* DAMIS) Rascal!
DAMIS: He can—
ORGON: Silence!
DAMIS: I will go mad!
ORGON: Just say a word, and I will break your head!
TARTUFFE: Be not enangered, brother, in God's name.
For I would rather bear most grievous pain
Than have him suffer the slightest scratch for me.
ORGON (*to* DAMIS):
Ingrate!

TARTUFFE: Leave him in peace. If I must kneel
To ask you for his pardon—
ORGON (*to* TARTUFFE): Alas, you're joking!
(*To* DAMIS)
Observe his goodness!
DAMIS: Then—
ORGON: Peace!
DAMIS: What, I—
ORGON: Enough!
I can see well the motive of your attack.
You hate him, all of you; I see my wife,
Children, and servants baying after him.
You're using every impudent device
To oust this holy person from my home.
But the more efforts you make to banish him,
The greater efforts I'll make to keep him here.
And now I'll hasten to give him my daughter's hand
To abase the pride of the entire family.
DAMIS: You think that you will force her to marry him?
ORGON: Yes, and to spite you, on this very evening.
Oh, I defy you all! And I will teach you
You'll have to obey me! I'm the master here.
Now, take your words back, ruffian! On the spot
Cast yourself at his feet to ask his pardon!
DAMIS: What! From this scoundrel, by whose trickeries—
ORGON: Ah, you resist, you knave! And you insult him!
Give me a stick, a stick! (*To* TARTUFFE) Don't hold me back!
(*To* DAMIS) Now you get out of this house this very minute,
And never dare to enter it again!
DAMIS: All right, I'll go, but—
ORGON: Quick, get out of here!
Reptile, I'll take your name out of my will,
And for good measure you can have my curse!
(*Exit* DAMIS.)
Think of offending so a holy man!

TARTUFFE: May heaven pardon him the pain he gives me!
(*To* ORGON) Ah, could you know how grievous it is to see
My character blackened in my brother's eyes—
ORGON: Alas!
TARTUFFE: The thought of this ingratitude
Makes my soul suffer such a cruel torture . . .
The horror it inspires . . . My heart is torn
So that I cannot speak! I'll die of it!
ORGON (*runs weeping to the door whence he has driven* DAMIS): Villain! I'm sorry I withheld my hand,
And didn't knock you down upon the spot!
Brother, compose yourself; don't be distressed.
TARTUFFE: Let's have no more of these afflicting quarrels.
I see I bring dissensions to your home;
I think it best, dear brother, that I leave it.
ORGON: You're joking!
TARTUFFE: Here I'm hated, and I see
That one would bring my rectitude in question.
ORGON: What of it? Do you think I listen to them?
TARTUFFE: Ah, they'll continue surely their campaign.
These stories you repudiate today
Perhaps another time will be believed.
ORGON: Oh, never, brother, never.
TARTUFFE: Brother, a wife
Can easily beguile a husband's mind.
ORGON: No, no!
TARTUFFE: I'll leave the house upon the instant,
And thus remove all reason to attack me.
ORGON: No, you'll remain; my life depends upon it.
TARTUFFE: Well, I'll remain, to mortify my spirit.
Still, if you wished it—
ORGON: Oh!
TARTUFFE: We'll say no more.
I see how I must now conduct myself.
Honor is delicate, and as your friend
I'll avoid cause for gossip and suspicion,
And flee the presence of your wife; I'll never—

ORGON: No, you'll attend her, to defy them all.
My greatest pleasure is to spite the world.
I want you to be seen with her constantly.
And that's not all; the better to affront them
I want to have no other heir than you.
And so I'll take immediately the steps
To make you sole inheritor of my wealth.
A good friend, whom I make my son-in-law,
Is dearer to me than my wife and children.
Will you accept what I propose to you?
TARTUFFE: May heaven's will be done in everything!
ORGON: Poor fellow! Let's draw up the document,
And let the jealous drown in their own bile!

Act IV

CLÉANTE, TARTUFFE.

CLÉANTE: The matter's common talk. You may believe me,
The scandalous tale is not to your advantage.
And I am glad I chanced to find you, sir,
To tell you my opinion in a word.
I won't attempt to weigh the rights and wrongs,
I will assume the unpleasant story's true.
Granted that Damis acted badly toward you,
And that his accusation was unfounded,
Should not a Christian pardon the offense,
Extinguishing thus Damis' desire for vengeance?
And should you let this quarrel be the cause
Of the exile of a son from his father's house?
Let me repeat to you, in perfect frankness,
That everybody's scandalized about it.
And if you take my advice, you will make peace
And not let things be carried to extremes;
You'll sacrifice your bitterness to God,

And bring the son back to his father's favor.
TARTUFFE: Alas, for my part, I would happily do so.
I harbor no resentment, sir, against him.
I pardon him freely, blame him not at all;
I long with all my heart to do him good.
But this is not in heaven's interest.
If he returns here, I must leave the house.
After his unimaginable action
We can't associate without disgrace.
God knows what people would conclude about it;
They would accuse me of sheer calculation.
Knowing my guilt, they'd say, I was pretending
Feelings of charity for my accuser.
They'd say I fear him and want to humor him
In order to persuade him to keep silence.
CLÉANTE: You try to give me plausible excuses,
But all your arguments are too far-fetched.
Why take heaven's interest upon yourself?
Does heaven need you to punish malefactors?
No, no; let God take care of his own vengeance;
He has prescribed forgiveness for offenses.
Don't be concerned about the world's reactions
When you are following heaven's almighty orders.
Will you let worry about what people say
Wipe out the credit of doing a good deed?
No, no; let's rather do what God commands,
And let's not trouble with other considerations.
TARTUFFE: I've told you that I pardon him in my heart;
Thus I obey God's holy ordinances.
But after the scandalous insults of today,
God does not order me to live with him.
CLÉANTE: And does God order you to lend yourself
To the father's act, prompted by pure caprice,
And to accept the gift of property
To which you have no legal right at all?
TARTUFFE: No one who knows me well can have the thought
That I am prompted by self-interest.

All this world's goods have little charm for me,
I am not dazzled by their deceptive glitter.
If I decide to accept from the father's hands
This gift of his benevolence, the reason
Is only, I tell you truly, that I fear
That all this wealth may fall in wicked hands,
That its possessors may be men who make
A criminal usage of it in the world,
Who will not use it, as my purpose is,
For heaven's glory and for my neighbor's good.
CLÉANTE: Your fears, my good sir, are sophistical.
They may give rise to suits by legal heirs.
Let Damis be inheritor of his wealth
At his own risk, without your interference.
Reflect, it's better that he should misuse it
Than that you be accused of cheating him.
I am astounded that you could have heard
This proposition made without being shocked.
For are there any maxims of true piety
Which teach the robbing of legitimate heirs?
If God has put in your heart an adamant
Objection to your living with Damis,
Would not the best thing be for you to leave
Decently and with honor, and not permit
The son of the house to be forbidden the door,
Against all common sense, and for your sake?
Believe me, sir, your character would look
Extremely strange—
TARTUFFE: Sir, it is half-past three;
And it is time for my pious exercises.
You will excuse me if I leave you now. (*Exit* TARTUFFE.)
CLÉANTE: Oh!

(*Enter* ELMIRE, MARIANE, DORINE.)

DORINE: Sir, I beg you, won't you help to save her?
For she is suffering from a cruel grief.
The pledge of marriage that her father has made

Plunges her in continual despair.
He's coming now; please, let's unite our efforts
And try to upset, either by force or trick,
That fatal project which undoes us all.

(*Enter* ORGON.)

ORGON: Ah! I'm delighted to see you all assembled!
(*To* MARIANE) There's something nice for you in this contract here!
And certainly you know what that implies.

MARIANE (*kneeling*): Father, I call on heaven, which knows my grief!
By everything that can affect your heart,
Relax a little the rights of fatherhood,
And set me free from this obedience.
Do not reduce me, by your harsh command,
To cry to heaven against my bounden duty.
Alas, don't make a long calamity
Of the life which you, Father, have given me.
Though you forbid me to wed the one I love,
In spite of all the fond hopes I had cherished,
At least—I beg your mercy on my knees—
Spare me the anguish of wedding one I hate,
And do not force me to some desperate act
By using all your powers upon my person.

ORGON (*aside*): Courage, my heart! Down with this human weakness!

MARIANE: I'm not distressed by your affection for him;
Openly show it; give him your property;
And if that's not enough, give him mine too.
I'm perfectly willing; I'll hand it over to you.
But do not give him, pray, my self, my person!
And let me in the austerity of a convent
Consume the unhappy days allotted me.

ORGON: Aha! You're one of those who seek a convent
As soon as a father crosses them in love!
Get up! The more your heart recoils from him,

All the more meritorious is the yielding.
So mortify your senses by this marriage,
And let's have no more nonsense out of you!

DORINE: But what—

ORGON: Be silent! Speak when you're spoken to!
I won't allow you to utter a single word!

CLÉANTE: If you'll permit me to offer some advice—

ORGON: Cléante, your advice is perfectly marvelous,
So sensible I prize it very highly;
But it's my privilege not to follow it.

ELMIRE (*to* ORGON): Seeing what's happening, I'm almost speechless.
I am amazed by your infatuation.
You must be totally bewitched by him
To doubt our word about today's occurrence.

ORGON: My precious, I believe the evidence.
I know how fond you are of my rascal son.
Clearly you were afraid to disavow
The scheme he tried to work on that poor fellow.
You were too calm, in short, to be quite convincing.
You'd have looked otherwise if really moved.

ELMIRE: And should a woman's honor be so stirred
If someone makes an amorous proposal?
And does the mere suggestion then require
A fiery glance and fierce, abusive words?
Why, all I do is laugh at such advances,
And I don't like to bring them into notice.
I think that we should show our virtue calmly;
I don't agree with those excited prudes
Whose honor is equipped with teeth and claws,
Ready to scratch your face at the slightest word.
Heaven preserve me from such purity!
For Virtue needs no diabolic look;
I've noticed that a haughty, chilly No
As a rebuff is mightily effective.

ORGON: You needn't try to throw me off the track.

ELMIRE: Your gullibility amazes me!

I wonder if your blind faith would be shaken
If I could make you witness of the truth.

ORGON: Witness?

ELMIRE: Yes.

ORGON: Nonsense!

ELMIRE: What if I found a way
To show you the fact under your very eyes?

ORGON: Fairy tales!

ELMIRE: What a man! I wish you'd answer.
I don't suggest that you believe our words.
But let's suppose that we could hide you here
Where you could clearly see and hear everything,
Then what would you say about your worthy friend?

ORGON: I'd say in that case . . . I'd say nothing at all,
For it can't be.

ELMIRE: You've been too long in error,
And you've accused me far too long of falsehood.
Now for my satisfaction, on the spot
I'll make you witness that we tell the truth.

ORGON: I'll take you up on that. We'll see your tricks;
We'll see what you can do to keep your promise.

ELMIRE (*to* DORINE): Send him in here.

DORINE: He's clever as a fox;
Perhaps it won't be easy to decoy him.

ELMIRE: No, one is easily fooled by one's belovèd,
And self-conceit will end in self-deception.
Have him come down. (*To* CLÉANTE *and* MARIANE)
And you two, please go out.

(*Exit* DORINE, CLÉANTE, *and* MARIANE.)

(*To* ORGON) Pull up this table. Now get under it.

ORGON: What?

ELMIRE: You will have to be concealed, of course.

ORGON: But why beneath this table?

ELMIRE: Good heavens, don't argue!
I have my plan; you'll see how it comes out.
Under the table, I say; and when you're there,
Make sure that nobody can see or hear you.

ORGON: I'm very indulgent to you, I confess.
I want to see how you get out of this.
(*Crawls under table, which is draped with a cloth hanging nearly to floor.*)

ELMIRE: I doubt if you'll have any reproach to make.
But I am going to deal with a ticklish subject,
So please don't let yourself be scandalized.
Whatever I say must be permissible;
It's only to convince you, as I promised.
Since I am forced to it, I'll have to use
Blandishing words to tempt him to unmask,
And smile upon his impudent desires,
And let him be audacious as he likes.
As it's for your sake, and for his confusion,
That I'll pretend to yield to his appeals,
I'll stop as soon as you are quite convinced;
Things will go only so far as you may wish.
Your task will be to check his bold advances
When you think matters have gone far enough,
And you must spare your wife, and not expose her
To more than you need to disillusion you.
Your interests are concerned; you are the master—
He's coming! Keep quiet! Don't let yourself be seen!

(*Enter* TARTUFFE.)

TARTUFFE: I understand you wished to speak to me.

ELMIRE: Yes, I've a secret to reveal to you.
But first, please shut that door before I speak;
And take a look around for fear of surprise.
(TARTUFFE *shuts door and looks in cupboard.*)
We certainly don't want a repetition
Of what took place a little while ago.
That was a disagreeable surprise,
And Damis put me into a panic for you.
You saw that I did everything I could
To cross his purpose and to calm him down.
It's true that I was thrown in such confusion

It didn't occur to me to deny his words.
But heaven be praised, the result was all the better,
And everything is on a surer footing.
Your reputation is proof against all storms;
And now my husband cannot be suspicious.
In order to show a confident face to slander,
He wants us to be constantly together.
So now I'm able, without fear of blame,
To be alone with you here—and with the door shut.
And so I am at liberty to reveal
My feelings—but perhaps I go too far.

TARTUFFE: This talk is somewhat hard to understand,
Madame. You seem to have changed considerably.

ELMIRE: Why, if you're angry that I once rebuffed you,
Little you understand a woman's heart!
You don't know what it's trying to convey,
When it defends itself so languidly!
Our modesty must always make a struggle
Against the emotions which may rise in us.
Even though overmastered by our feelings,
We always find it shameful to admit them.
At first we fight against them; but our manner
Ought to make evident the heart's surrender.
For honor's sake we must oppose our longings,
And our denials promise everything.
I am afraid I'm speaking all too frankly,
And showing small regard for modesty;
But since I've come into the open, tell me,
Would I have struggled to hold Damis back?
And would I, please, so graciously, so long,
Have listened to the offer of your heart?
Would I have taken the matter as I did,
If I had not found pleasure in your offer?
And when I tried on my own part to force you
To refuse the marriage which had been announced,
What was the import of my urgency,
If not my personal interest in you,

And my distress for fear the projected union
Would divide a heart I wanted to keep entire?

TARUFFE: Surely, madame, it gives me joy extreme
To hear such words from thy belovèd lips!
Their honey pours into my senses, makes
Undreamed-of sweetness flood through all my veins!
My highest aim is that of pleasing you;
My heart finds its beatitude in your love;
And yet this heart now begs the liberty
To dare to doubt its own felicity.
For I could think your words a mere device
To force me to break off a marriage arranged.
And to explain myself with perfect clearness,
I shall not put my trust in your sweet words,
Until the tangible favors which I long for
Will guarantee your words' sincerity,
And in my soul implant a constant faith
In the dear bounties which you would bestow.

ELMIRE (*coughs to warn her husband*): What do you mean?
You want to go so fast
And push love to its climax all in a moment?
I've forced myself to make a fond admission;
However, that is not enough for you.
You won't be satisfied unless you gain
The final favors at the very beginning?

TARTUFFE: The less one merits, the less one dares to hope;
And talk gives little assurance to our longing.
One easily mistrusts a promise of bliss;
One has to enjoy it before one can believe it.
Knowing how little I deserve your bounty,
I doubt the happiness I dare aspire to.
And I shall not believe a word, madame,
Until you crown my ardent love with facts.

ELMIRE: Dear me! Your love is acting like a tyrant!
It puts me in an awkward situation!
It seems to set a fury in men's hearts,
With such a violence it seeks its goal!

Can I not raise my hands against your onslaught?
Will you not give me even time to breathe?
And is it decent to be so exacting,
To give no quarter when you ask surrender?
And thus, by your insistence, to abuse
The inclination a person may have for you?

TARTUFFE: If you receive my homage with compassion,
Why, pray, withhold the tangible testimony?

ELMIRE: But how can I consent, without offending
Heaven, according to your constant theme?

TARTUFFE: If it is only heaven that stands in the way,
It's easy for me to remove such obstacles,
And that need not restrain your heart's desire.

ELMIRE: And yet they frighten us so with heaven's decrees!

TARTUFFE: I can soon banish such ridiculous fear,
Madame; there is an art of removing scruples.
It's true that heaven forbids some satisfactions,
But there are possible ways to understandings.
To suit our various needs, there is a science
Of loosening the bonds of human conscience,
And rectifying the evil of an action
By means of the purity of our intention.
Madame, I shall instruct you in these secrets,
If you will put your confidence in me.
Content my longings, do not be afraid;
All the responsibility is mine . . .
(ELMIRE *coughs.*)
You have a nasty cough.

ELMIRE: It tortures me.

TARTUFFE: Perhaps you'd care to accept a licorice cough drop?

ELMIRE: It's a persistent cold, and I'm afraid
That all the cough drops in the world won't help it.

TARTUFFE: Very distressing.

ELMIRE: More than I can say.

TARTUFFE: Well, anyway, I can dispel your scruples.
You are assured that I will keep the secret.
Evil does not exist until it's published;

It's worldly scandal that creates the offense;
And sin in silence is not sin at all.

ELMIRE (*coughs*): In short, I see that I shall have to yield,
Make up my mind to grant you everything.
Otherwise, I suppose, I can't convince
One who is asking irrefutable proof.
Certainly I dislike to go so far,
I take the step against my better judgment;
But since I'm mercilessly driven to it,
Since no one listens to my arguments,
Since absolute conviction is demanded,
I must decide to satisfy all doubts.
And if there's any offense in my consenting,
The one who forces me must take the blame;
Certainly I am not responsible.

TARTUFFE: I take it on myself, madame. The matter—

ELMIRE: But first, open the door a little, please;
See if my husband isn't in the hall.

TARTUFFE: What sense is there in worrying about him?
He is the type that you can lead by the nose,
The type to glory in our intimacies.
He can see anything now and not believe it.

ELMIRE: It makes no difference. Please, I'd feel much safer
If you would take a careful look around.

(*Exit* TARTUFFE. ORGON *emerges from under the table.*)

ORGON: Oh, what a bad, abominable man!
I am astounded! I just can't understand it.

ELMIRE: What, coming out so soon? Don't be absurd!
Crawl in again, nothing has happened yet!
Why don't you wait till the end to make quite sure,
So you won't have to trust to mere conjectures?

ORGON: Nothing more wicked has ever come out of hell!

ELMIRE: You shouldn't be in a hurry to believe things,
So why not let yourself be quite convinced?
Just take your time; maybe you're still mistaken . . .

(*As* TARTUFFE *returns,* ELMIRE *makes* ORGON *crouch behind her.*)

TARTUFFE: Everything's working out, madame, for the best.
I've had a look into the neighboring rooms.
There's no one there. And now, to my delight—

ORGON (*springing forth*):
Hold on a minute! Don't get so excited,
And let your passions run away with you!
Aha! You holy man, you wanted to fool me!
How rapidly you yielded to temptation!
Wedding my daughter and lusting for my wife!
I've long suspected things were not aboveboard;
I always thought that you would change your style.
But now the proof is carried far enough.
I'm satisfied, and this is all I need.

ELMIRE (*to* TARTUFFE): It's not my nature to have done all this,
But I've been forced to treat you in this manner.

TARTUFFE (*to* ORGON):
What, you can think—

ORGON: Come on, don't make a fuss.
Get out of here without another word.

TARTUFFE: I only wanted—

ORGON: There's no time for talk.
But now, this very second, leave the house!

TARTUFFE: You are the one to leave! Don't be so proud!
I will remind you, the house belongs to me!
I'll show you that it's useless to resort
To such poor shifts to pick a quarrel with me!
You're in a bad position to insult me,
For I have means to break and punish imposture,
To avenge offended heaven, and make repent
Those who dare say that I must leave the house!

(*Exit* TARTUFFE.)

ELMIRE: What is he talking about? What can he mean?

ORGON: Faith, I am worried. It's no laughing matter.

ELMIRE: What is it?

ORGON: His talk has shown me my mistake.
I am disturbed about that deed of gift.

ELMIRE: A deed of gift?
ORGON: Yes; it's been signed already.
But there's another thing which bothers me.
ELMIRE: What's that?
ORGON: I'll tell you; but first I want to see
If there's a certain strongbox still upstairs.

Act V

Enter ORGON *and* CLÉANTE.

CLÉANTE: Where are you hurrying to?
ORGON: How do I know?
CLÉANTE: I think we ought to have a consultation
To see what can be done about the affair.
ORGON: It is the strongbox that alarms me most,
More than the other matters all together.
CLÉANTE: So the mysterious strongbox is important?
ORGON: My poor friend Argas gave it me in trust,
Pledging me to the utmost secrecy.
When he was exiled, he came first to me;
He said his life and all his property
May hang upon the contents of these papers.
CLÉANTE: Then why did you entrust them to another?
ORGON: My motive was to keep my conscience easy.
I told that scoundrel all about the matter,
And then his arguments persuaded me
To let him keep the strongbox in his hands,
So that, in case of any investigation,
I'd have a pretext to deny the facts,
And thus my conscience, in security,
Could take an oath contrary to the truth.
CLÉANTE: It looks to me as if you're in for it.
The deed of gift, the transfer of the strongbox—
I have to tell you frankly what I think—
Were inconsiderate, to say the least.

With these as evidence, he can involve you deeply.
Since he has such a weapon in his hands,
You were imprudent to push him to extremes;
You should have looked for some more subtle method.

ORGON: What! Under all his outward show of fervor,
To hide a treacherous heart, an evil soul!
To think I picked him up, a penniless beggar!
All right, I now renounce all worthy men.
Henceforth I'll have a terrible horror of them;
I'm going to be a devil to them all!

CLÉANTE: Now there you go again, getting excited!
You can't be moderate in anything.
You never seem to find the sensible course;
From one excess you fall into the other.
You see your error, and you recognize
That you were taken in by pious fraud;
But now, to correct yourself, what reason is there
That you should fall into a greater error,
And lump the character of all worthy men
With the character of a perfidious rascal?
Because a blackguard boldly takes you in,
Impersonating an austere believer,
You would conclude that everyone's like him,
And that no true believer now exists?
Let the freethinkers draw those false conclusions.
Distinguish virtue from its outward seeming,
Never give your esteem too hastily,
Keep to the reasonable middle way.
Try not to give your honor to impostors,
But don't insult genuine piety.
And if you must choose one extreme or the other,
Let your fault be excessive leniency.

(*Enter* DAMIS.)

DAMIS: Is it true, father, that a rogue threatens you,
Forgetting all the favors he's received,
And that he's now presumptuous enough

To use your benefits as arms against you?
ORGON: I'm deeply grieved to say, my son, it's true.
DAMIS: Give me the word, I'll go and cut his ears off!
One shouldn't waver before his insolence.
I'll undertake to set you free of him;
I'll fix him so he'll never bother us!
CLÉANTE: That's a young man's solution, certainly.
Compose yourself and don't get so excited.
Under the government we have today,
Violence is no way to settle matters.

(*Enter* MME PERNELLE, MARIANE, ELMIRE, DORINE.)

MME PERNELLE: What are these goings-on I hear about?
ORGON: Strange things indeed I've seen with my own eyes,
And a strange reward for all my kindnesses!
I rescue a man out of his poverty,
Give him a home, treat him like my own brother,
And every day I load him with benefits,
I give him my daughter and all my property;
At the same time, the faithless, infamous scoundrel
Foully proposes to seduce my wife!
And still not satisfied with this base purpose,
He dares to use against me my own favors,
And tries to ruin me by using the hold
I've given him, out of my foolish kindness,
To throw me out of my own property,
And bring me down to the state in which I found him!
DORINE: Poor fellow!
MME PERNELLE: My son, I can't believe
He could have wished to do such an evil thing.
ORGON: What!
MME PERNELLE: Men of principle are always envied.
ORGON: Mother, please tell me exactly what you mean.
MME PERNELLE: I mean that people here are very peculiar,
And I know well how everybody hates him.
ORGON: And what has hatred got to do with it?

MME PERNELLE: When you were a boy, I told you a thousand times
Virtue is always unpopular in this world;
The envious, they will die, but envy won't.
ORGON: What has all that to do with the present case?
MME PERNELLE: Surely, people have made up stories about him.
ORGON: I told you that I saw everything myself!
MME PERNELLE: The malice of slanderers is most excessive.
ORGON: You'll make me sin through anger, Mother! I tell you
I saw his attempt at crime with my own eyes!
MME PERNELLE: Many a tongue is ready to spread slander,
And nothing in this world is proof against it.
ORGON: What you are saying makes no sense at all.
I saw him, I say, with my own eyes I saw him!
I saw him try to do it! Now do I have to
Yell in your ears a hundred times: "I saw him"?
MME PERNELLE: Mercy! Appearances are often deceptive;
You cannot always judge by what you see.
ORGON: You'll drive me crazy!
MME PERNELLE: False suspicions are common,
And good is often ill interpreted.
ORGON: I should interpret then as a charity
The attempt to kiss my wife?
MME PERNELLE: To accuse a man,
You have to have a full and sufficient reason;
You ought to wait until you're sure of things.
ORGON: And how the devil can I be any surer?
I should have waited until, before my eyes,
He'd . . . No, you pretty nearly made me say it.
MME PERNELLE: His soul is filled with a too holy zeal.
I simply can't conceive the possibility
He could have attempted the things that people say.
ORGON: Good heavens, you put me into such a fury,
I don't know what I'd say, if you weren't my mother!
DORINE: It's only fair, good sir; you wouldn't believe us,
And now you find they won't believe you either.

CLÉANTE: We're losing precious time in idle talk.
We ought to plan our actions, and not sleep
In view of the threats that scoundrel has expressed.
DAMIS: What! Do you really think he'd have the nerve—
ELMIRE: Oh, I don't think that he'd take legal action,
For his ingratitude would be all too clear.
CLÉANTE: Don't be too sure. No doubt he has devices
To get a show of reason on his side.
For less than this a powerful organization
Has got men into a very nasty mess.
And I repeat that since he holds such weapons,
You never ought to have driven him so far.
ORGON: All right, but what could I do? At his insolence
I simply couldn't hold my anger in.
CLÉANTE: I wish with all my heart we could patch up
Some kind of outward peace between you two.
ELMIRE: If I had known he held such trumps in hand,
I wouldn't have given him such provocation.
(MONSIEUR LOYAL *appears at door.* DORINE *goes to meet him.*)
ORGON (*to* DORINE): What does that fellow want? Find out and tell me.
I'm in no state to deal with callers now.
M. LOYAL: How do you do, dear sister? Will you arrange
For me to speak to the gentleman?
DORINE: He's engaged.
I doubt if he can talk to anyone now.
M. LOYAL: I shouldn't like to intrude upon him here,
But I don't think my business will upset him.
I'm sure he'll find my news most interesting.
DORINE: Your name?
M. LOYAL: Just tell him that Monsieur Tartuffe
Has sent me, with a most obliging message.
DORINE (*to* ORGON): He is a messenger—and quite soft-spoken—
From our Tartuffe. He says he has some news
That you'll be glad to hear.

CLÉANTE: You'd better see
Who this man is and what he has to say.
ORGON: Maybe he's coming to patch the business up.
How do you think I ought to act to him?
CLÉANTE: You mustn't show how deeply you're offended;
And if he offers peace, you'd better heed him.
M. LOYAL: Greetings, good sir! May heaven smite your foes,
And shower its blessings on you in abundance!
ORGON (*to* CLÉANTE): A civil opening! As I foresaw,
This is a hint of reconciliation.
M. LOYAL: Your family was always dear to me,
And frequently I served your honored father.
ORGON: I am ashamed, sir, and I ask your pardon;
I cannot place you or recall your name.
M. LOYAL: My name is Loyal; I'm from Normandy[1]
And I'm a process server by profession.
For forty years I've had the happiness
Praise God, to hold that honorable office.
And so I come, sir, with your kind permission,
To serve upon you this judicial writ.
ORGON: What! You came here—
M. LOYAL: Now, no excitement, please.
It's just a little notice of eviction.
You and your family must quit the house,
Remove your furniture, make place for others,
Without delay, deferment, or reprieve.
ORGON: What, leave this house!
M. LOYAL: If you will be so good.
The house belongs, as you are well aware,
To good Monsieur Tartuffe, beyond dispute.
He is possessed of all your property
By virtue of a contract which I bear.
It's in due form, it cannot be protested.
DAMIS: I am amazed to hear such impudence!
M. LOYAL: Young sir, I have no business here with you,
But with your father, a reasonable man,

[1] [A byword for pettifoggery.—Trans.]

Who knows the duties of a court officer,
And wouldn't think of contravening justice.
ORGON: But—
M. LOYAL: Yes, I know that not for a million francs
Would you propose to defy authority,
And that, like a gentleman, you will permit
The execution of my orders here.
DAMIS: You might well get a sound and wholesome caning
On your black jacket, Monsieur Process Server.
M. LOYAL (*to* ORGON): Sir, bid your son be silent or retire.
I should regret to put in my report
Menaces of assault and battery.
DORINE (*aside*): His name is Loyal? I should say Disloyal.
M. LOYAL: I have a great respect for upright men,
And I agreed to serve this writ on you
Just to oblige you and to give you pleasure,
To keep the service from the hands of others
Who would not feel my admiration for you,
And would not act with my consideration.
ORGON: What could be worse than ordering a man
To quit his home?
M. LOYAL: But I am giving you time.
I will suspend, monsieur, until tomorrow
The execution of the legal writ.
I'll merely come with a dozen of my men
To spend the night, without publicity.
And for form's sake I'll ask you, please, to bring me
The keys of the house before you go to bed.
We'll take care not to trouble your repose,
Nor suffer any impropriety.
Tomorrow morning early you'll remove
Your personal possessions from the house.
My men will help you; I picked sturdy ones
To serve you in putting everything outside.
No one, I think, could act more fairly with you.
And as I'm treating you with great indulgence,
I'll ask you for your kind co-operation

In not impeding my duties' execution.
ORGON (*aside*): How happily I'd give this very moment
My last remaining hundred golden louis
For the pleasure of landing on that ugly snout
The most enormous punch in history!
CLÉANTE (*aside to* ORGON):
Easy, don't spoil things.
DAMIS: At his insolence
I can't hold in; I've got an itching fist.
DORINE: That noble back of yours, Monsieur Loyal,
Seems to demand a few good cudgel blows.
M. LOYAL: Such words, my dear, may call for penal action.
The law makes no distinction as to sex.
CLÉANTE: Let's have no more of this, sir. That's enough.
Give us that paper, please, and leave the house.
M. LOYAL: *Au revoir*, gentlemen. God keep you in joy!
ORGON: May he confound you, and the man who sent you!
(*Exit* M. LOYAL.)
Well, Mother, you see if I was right or not;
And by this summons you can judge of the rest.
MME PERNELLE: I'm flabbergasted, I'm struck all of a heap!
DORINE: Oh, really! Aren't you doing wrong to blame him?
Clearly his purposes are for your good!
He's showing how he loves his fellow man;
He knows that often wealth corrupts the soul.
Out of pure charity, he would remove
The slightest obstacle to your salvation.
ORGON: Shut up, shut up! How often must I say it?
CLÉANTE: Let's think about the proper course to take.
ELMIRE: Go tell the world of his audacity!
His action makes the contract null and void.
Public opinion will be so aroused
By his black treason that he can't succeed.

(*Enter* VALÈRE.)

VALÈRE: I'm sorry, sir, to bring you any distress,
But I'm obliged to by the pressing danger.

An old and excellent friend of mine, who knows
How I'm affected by all that touches you,
Out of regard for me has violated
The secrecy he owes to state affairs.
The news he sends me makes it very clear
That you can save yourself only by flight.
The scoundrel who befooled you for so long
Has made an accusation to the King,
And to support his charges has delivered
The strongbox of an outlaw of the state,
Which you, he says, have criminally hidden,
Flouting the duty of a loyal subject.
I don't know much about the crime alleged,
But orders to arrest you have been issued.
Tartuffe himself is charged to accompany
The officer who is to take you prisoner.

CLÉANTE: Thus he gets armed support, to aid his purpose
To take possession of your property.

ORGON: Oh what a wicked creature that man is!

VALÈRE: Any delay is fatal; so I've brought
My carriage to the door to whisk you off,
And a thousand louis for the emergency.
So don't lose time; this is a knock-down blow;
The only way to dodge it is to flee.
I'll guarantee you a sure hiding place,
And I'll accompany you until the end.

ORGON: Oh, I owe everything to your kindly actions!
I'll leave my thanks until a better time;
I pray that heaven may grant me the occasion
Some day, to recognize your generous service.
Good-by, my friends; be sure to—

CLÉANTE: Hurry, hurry!
Dear brother, we will take care of everything.

(ORGON *and* VALÈRE *start to run off. Enter* POLICE OFFICER *and* TARTUFFE.)

TARTUFFE: Here, here, good sir! Don't run away so fast!
A lodging's ready for you close at hand.

By the King's orders you're a prisoner!
ORGON: Scoundrel, you kept this wicked deed till last!
And thus, you rascal, you complete my ruin!
This is the crown of all your villainies!
TARTUFFE: I shall not be embittered by your insults.
I have been taught by heaven to suffer all.
CLÉANTE: So this is holy moderation, is it?
DAMIS: Shameful to make of heaven his accomplice!
TARTUFFE: You cannot move me by a show of anger,
For all I think of is to do my duty.
MARIANE: Much glory you will draw from this affair,
And surely you'll derive much honor from it.
TARTUFFE: An action can be only glorious
When it's commanded by the royal power.
ORGON: Have you remembered that my helping hand
Was all that rescued you from beggary?
TARTUFFE: True, I may be beholden for some aid,
But my first duty is to serve the King.
This sacred, just, and all-compelling duty
Extinguishes all gratitude in my heart.
To its compulsion I would sacrifice
My friends, my relatives, my wife—myself!
ELMIRE: Impostor!
DORINE: How he treacherously makes
A cloak and shield of all that we revere!
CLÉANTE: But if this noble zeal which animates you
Is quite as perfect as you say it is,
How comes it that it waited to appear
Till you were caught addressing Orgon's wife?
And why did you denounce him only when,
For honor's sake, he had to throw you out?
I won't allege—though it might have held you back—
His gift to you of all his property;
But since you treat him now as a guilty man,
Why did you stoop to accepting all his money?
TARTUFFE (*to* POLICE OFFICER): Deliver me, sir, from all these railing words,

And execute your orders, if you please.
OFFICER: Yes, I've delayed too long in doing so.
Aptly enough, you ask for it yourself.
So here's the execution: follow me
To the prison cell that's ready for your lodging.
TARTUFFE: What, me, sir?
OFFICER: You, sir, yes.
TARTUFFE: But why to prison?
OFFICER: It's not to you I owe an explanation.
(*To* ORGON) You've had a nasty scare; but calm yourself.
Our present King is enemy of fraud,
His eyes can penetrate his subjects' hearts;
The art of charlatans cannot delude him.
And his great spirit, wise in the ways of men,
Watches his kingdom with discerning eyes.
No one can take him easily by surprise,
And his firm reason yields to no excess.
To worthy men he gives immortal glory,
And yet his zeal for virtue is not blind.
His love for genuine faith does not eclipse
The horror one should feel for false devotion.
Tartuffe was not the sort to hoodwink him
Who has avoided many a subtler snare.
Immediately he saw in its true color
The base conniving of that evil mind.
This man, accusing you, betrayed himself;
And, by the retribution of high justice,
The King identified him as a rogue
Already famous under another name,
And with a criminal record to his credit
Lengthy enough to fill a score of volumes.
In short, His Majesty abhorred this man's
Mean and ungrateful treachery toward you.
With this crime added to the ample list,
The King commanded me to accompany him,
Only to see what impudence would dare,
And force Tartuffe to make you reparation.

Now in your presence I shall seize the papers
Of which the scoundrel has possessed himself.
The King declares the contract null and void
Which made Tartuffe a gift of all your wealth,
And finally he pardons that offense
In which the exile of a friend involved you.
Thus he rewards your past fidelity,
Which, in the civil wars, upheld his rights;
And thus he proves his heart ever remembers
To recompense a subject's worthy action.
He shows that merit's not unrecognized,
That he is mindful more of good than evil.

DORINE: May heaven be praised!

MME PERNELLE: Now I can breathe again!

ELMIRE: All's well then!

MARIANE: Who would have dared foretell it!

ORGON (*to* TARTUFFE):
So now we've got you, villain—

CLÉANTE: Brother, stop.
Don't stoop to any unworthy exultation,
But leave a wretched man to his wretched fate;
You need not add to the pangs of his remorse.
Hope rather that his heart may now be touched
To heed the call of virtue; that he may
Detest his vice and thus correct his life,
And move the justice of our King to mercy;
While you shall kneel before the royal bounty,
And pay its due to the King's clemency.

ORGON: Well said, indeed. So let us, at his feet,
Joyfully thank him for his heartfelt kindness.
And after this first duty has been done,
There is a second claiming our concern;
So by a happy marriage we shall crown
The noble-hearted ardor of Valère.

The Would-Be Gentleman

A COMEDY-BALLET

by MOLIÈRE

TRANSLATED BY *Morris Bishop*

The Characters

MONSIEUR JOURDAIN, *bourgeois*

MADAME JOURDAIN, *his wife*

LUCILE, *his daughter*

CLÉONTE, *in love with Lucile*

DORIMÈNE, *a marquise*

DORANTE, *a count*

NICOLE, *servant of Monsieur Jourdain*

COVIELLE, *manservant of Cléonte*

A MUSIC MASTER

THE MUSIC MASTER'S PUPIL

A DANCING MASTER

A FENCING MASTER

A PHILOSOPHY MASTER

A MERCHANT TAILOR

A JOURNEYMAN TAILOR

TWO LACKEYS, *several* SINGERS, INSTRUMENTALISTS, DANCERS, COOKS, TAILOR'S APPRENTICES, *and other characters in the ballets.*

The scene is in Paris, in Monsieur Jourdain's house.

Act I

After the overture, the curtain rises. The MUSIC MASTER'S PUPIL *is working at a table. He may rise, strike some notes on a harpsichord, and return to his composition. He hums his tune, trying both the men's and women's parts.*

Enter the MUSIC MASTER, *three* SINGERS, *and two* VIOLINISTS.

MUSIC MASTER (*to his musicians*): All right, come in here, and take a rest until he comes.

(*Enter from the opposite side the* DANCING MASTER *and four* DANCERS.)

DANCING MASTER (*to his* DANCERS): Come in this way.

MUSIC MASTER (*to* PUPIL): All done?

PUPIL: Yes.

MUSIC MASTER: Let me see it a minute. (*Inspects composition*) That will do nicely.

DANCING MASTER: Is it something new?

MUSIC MASTER: Yes; it's the music for a serenade I've had him working on here, while we're waiting for our man to get up.

DANCING MASTER: May I take a look?

MUSIC MASTER: You will hear it, with the words, when he comes. He won't be long.

DANCING MASTER: We're certainly occupied now, both of us.

MUSIC MASTER: That's right. We've both found the man we've been looking for. This Monsieur Jourdain is a very nice property, with his visions of nobility and gallantry. In the interests of your art of dance and mine of music, we could well wish there were many more like him.

DANCING MASTER: Well, not exactly like him. I could wish he had more appreciation of the things we do for him.

MUSIC MASTER: It's true he doesn't know much about them. But he pays well; and that's what our arts need more than anything else right now.

DANCING MASTER: Well, personally, I admit I enjoy a little recognition. Applause really stimulates me. And I find it an actual torture to perform for idiots, and to bear their uncouth comments on our creations. There is genuine pleasure, confess it, in working for people who can recognize the fine points of our art, and reward us for our work with heart-warming approval. Yes, the best payment we can receive is to see our work appreciated, and welcomed with the applause which does us honor. There is no better return for all our labor and fatigue; and enlightened praise gives exquisite delight.

MUSIC MASTER: I agree; I enjoy such praise as much as you do. Certainly nothing gratifies us like that kind of applause. But you can't live on applause; praise alone won't pay the rent. We need something a bit more solid; the best hand people can give us is a hand with cash in it. True enough, our man has no cultivation; he gets everything all wrong, and he is sure to applaud the wrong thing; but his money purifies his bad taste. His fat purse is full of critical insight; his approval is convertible into cash; and this ignorant commoner is a lot more useful to us, as you are well aware, than that noble amateur of the arts who introduced us to him.

DANCING MASTER: There is some truth in what you're saying. But I think you dwell on money a little too much. Material advantage is so base a thing that a man of character should never show any concern for it.

MUSIC MASTER: Still, you seem to accept the money our man hands you.

DANCING MASTER: By all means; but I don't make my happiness depend upon it; and I could wish that with all his wealth he had some tincture of good taste.

MUSIC MASTER: Naturally I should like that too. That's what we're both laboring to bring about, as best we can. But at any rate, he is helping us to get a reputation; he will underwrite the things that others will applaud for him.

DANCING MASTER: Here he is now.

(*Enter* MONSIEUR JOURDAIN *and two* LACKEYS. MONSIEUR JOURDAIN *wears a gorgeous striped dressing gown, lined with green and orange.*)

M. JOURDAIN: Well, sirs, how's things? You're going to show me your little thingamajig?

DANCING MASTER: What? What little thingamajig?

M. JOURDAIN: Why, the—what d'you call it? Your prologue or dialogue of song and dance.

DANCING MASTER: Ha, ha!

MUSIC MASTER: We are quite ready, sir.

M. JOURDAIN: I've held you up a little. But the fact is I'm dressing today in court style; and my tailor sent me some silk stockings I thought I'd never get on.

MUSIC MASTER: We are here only to await your leisure.

M. JOURDAIN: I'll ask you both not to leave until they've brought my coat, so you can see it.

DANCING MASTER: Whatever you wish.

M. JOURDAIN: You'll see me turned out properly from head to foot.

MUSIC MASTER: We don't doubt it.

M. JOURDAIN: I've just had this dressing gown made.

DANCING MASTER: It is very handsome.

M. JOURDAIN: My tailor told me that people of quality are like this in the morning.

MUSIC MASTER: It looks very well on you.

M. JOURDAIN: Lackeys! Hey, my two lackeys!

FIRST LACKEY: What do you wish, sir?

M. JOURDAIN: Nothing. I just wanted to see if you hear me all right. (*To the two* MASTERS) What do you think of my servants' liveries?

DANCING MASTER: Magnificent.

M. JOURDAIN (*opens his dressing gown, displaying tight red velvet breeches and a short green velvet jacket*): And here's a little sports costume to do my exercises in, in the morning.

MUSIC MASTER: Very smart.

M. JOURDAIN: Lackey!

FIRST LACKEY: Yes, sir?

M. JOURDAIN: Other lackey!

SECOND LACKEY: Yes, sir?

M. JOURDAIN: Here, hold my gown. (*He removes his gown*) How do you like me this way?

DANCING MASTER: Splendid. It couldn't be more perfect.

M. JOURDAIN: Now let's have your little business.

MUSIC MASTER: First, I should like to have you hear a composition which this young man here has just done for the serenade you ordered. He is one of my pupils; he is very gifted for this sort of thing.

M. JOURDAIN: Yes; but you shouldn't have had it done by a pupil. You aren't too good to do the job yourself.

MUSIC MASTER: Don't let the word "pupil" put you off, sir. Such pupils as this know as much as the greatest masters; and the melody is as lovely as it can be. Just listen.

M. JOURDAIN: Give me my dressing gown so I can listen better . . . Wait a minute, I think it will be better without the dressing gown . . . No, give it back to me. It'll be better that way.

A WOMAN SINGER:

> Ah, grievous is my woe, I languish night and day
> Since thy imperious eye has brought me 'neath thy sway;
> If thus thou deal'st, my fair, with one who loves thee so,
> Ah, what must be the fate of one who is thy foe?

M. JOURDAIN: That song seems to me rather dismal. It puts you to sleep. I wish you could brighten it up a little here and there.

MUSIC MASTER: It is necessary, sir, that the music fit the words.

M. JOURDAIN: I learned a very pretty one a little while ago. Wait a minute . . . now . . . how did it go?

DANCING MASTER: Really, I don't know.

M. JOURDAIN: Something about a sheep.

DANCING MASTER: A sheep?

M. JOURDAIN: Yes. Aha! (*He sings*)

> I thought my dear Jeannette

Was just a little lamb;
I thought my dear Jeannette
Was sweet as currant jam.
Oh, dear, oh, dear, oh, dear!
I must have made a bungle!
She's crueler, it's clear,
Than a tiger in the jungle!

Isn't that pretty?

MUSIC MASTER: Extremely pretty.

DANCING MASTER: And you sing it well.

M. JOURDAIN: And I never studied music!

MUSIC MASTER: You ought to learn music, sir, as you are learning the dance. The two arts have a very close connection.

DANCING MASTER: And they open a man's mind to things of beauty.

M. JOURDAIN: Do people of quality study music too?

MUSIC MASTER: Oh, yes, sir.

M. JOURDAIN: Well, then, I'll study it. But I don't know how I'll find the time; for not to mention the fencing master who's giving me lessons, I have hired a philosophy professor; he's to begin this morning.

MUSIC MASTER: Philosophy is very fine; but music, sir, music—

DANCING MASTER: Music and the dance; music and the dance, that's all you really need.

MUSIC MASTER: There is nothing so useful in a state as music.

DANCING MASTER: There is nothing so necessary to men as the dance.

MUSIC MASTER: Without music, a state can hardly persist.

DANCING MASTER: Without the dance, a man is totally helpless.

MUSIC MASTER: All the disorders and wars in the world come about because men haven't learned music.

DANCING MASTER: All men's misfortunes, and the appalling disasters of history, the blunders of statesmen and the errors of great generals, they have all occurred for lack of knowledge of dancing.

M. JOURDAIN: How is that?

MUSIC MASTER: Doesn't war come from discords among men?

M. JOURDAIN: That's true.

MUSIC MASTER: And if everybody should learn music, wouldn't that be a way to harmonize everything, and to bring universal peace to the world?

M. JOURDAIN: You're right.

DANCING MASTER: When a man has made some blunder, whether in his family affairs, or in government, or in generalship, don't we always say: "So-and-so has made a false step in such a matter"?

M. JOURDAIN: Yes, we say that.

DANCING MASTER: And taking a false step, can that result from anything else than not knowing how to dance?

M. JOURDAIN: That's true. You're both right!

DANCING MASTER: It's just to show you the excellence and utility of dancing and music.

M. JOURDAIN: I understand that now.

MUSIC MASTER: Do you want to see our productions?

M. JOURDAIN: Yes.

MUSIC MASTER: I have already told you, this is a little effort of mine to delineate the various emotions that music can express.

M. JOURDAIN: Very good.

MUSIC MASTER (*to the* SINGERS): Step forward, please. (*To* MONSIEUR JOURDAIN) You must imagine that they are dressed as shepherds.

M. JOURDAIN: Why are they always shepherds? All I ever see around is shepherds.

MUSIC MASTER: When one wants to make people speak in music, one must always put them in a pastoral setting. That's what we call verisimilitude. Singing has always been the specialty of shepherds and shepherdesses. It is hardly natural, in a dramatic dialogue, that princes or commoners should sing their emotions.

M. JOURDAIN: All right, all right. Let's hear it.

WOMAN SINGER:

A heart that tyrant love's dictation captures
Is filled with turbulence incessantly.
They say that languishing and sighs are raptures,
But still our dearest boon is liberty!

FIRST MALE SINGER:
Nought is so sweet as tender ardors thronging
To make twin hearts blend in a lover's kiss.
There is no happiness without love's longing;
Take love from life, you cancel all its bliss.

SECOND MALE SINGER:
It would be sweet to enter love's domain,
If one could find in love true steadfastness;
But oh, alas! Oh, cruelty and pain!
How can one find a faithful shepherdess?
The sex is fickle and inconstant; hence
One must renounce for aye love's blandishments!

FIRST MALE SINGER:
Dear love is revealed—

WOMAN SINGER:
How delightful to yield—

SECOND MALE SINGER:
But love is a cheat!

FIRST MALE SINGER:
My darling, my sweet!

WOMAN SINGER (*to* SECOND MALE SINGER):
Dear love, I adjure you—

SECOND MALE SINGER:
I cannot endure you!

FIRST MALE SINGER (*to* SECOND MALE SINGER):
Ah, learn to love, forget your peevishness!

WOMAN SINGER:
And I shall gladly tell you where you'll see
A faithful shepherdess!

SECOND MALE SINGER:
Where to discover such a prodigy?

WOMAN SINGER (*to* SECOND MALE SINGER):
Just in defense of womankind,

I offer here my heart to you!

SECOND MALE SINGER:

Sweet shepherdess, and shall I find
That it will be forever true?

WOMAN SINGER:

Let us essay, and make a test
Which of us two can love the best!

SECOND MALE SINGER:

And may the one accursèd be
Who first shall fail in constancy!

THE THREE SINGERS:

The power that kindles deathless fires
Now let us all pay tribute to!
How sweet it is when love inspires
Two hearts that ever shall be true!

M. JOURDAIN: Is that all?

MUSIC MASTER: Yes.

M. JOURDAIN: A neat job. Very neat. There were some remarks in it that weren't bad.

DANCING MASTER: Now, as my part of the performance, here is a little effort to display the most beautiful postures and evolutions with which a dance may be varied.

M. JOURDAIN: More shepherds?

DANCING MASTER: They are anything you please.

(*Four* DANCERS *execute various steps and evolutions at the* DANCING MASTER'*s order. This is the first* Interlude, *marking the division of the play into acts.*)

Act II

The action is continuous. After the Interlude, *the dancers retire, leaving* MONSIEUR JOURDAIN, *the* MUSIC MASTER, *the* DANCING MASTER, *and the two* LACKEYS.

M. JOURDAIN: No nonsense about that! Those boys cut some fine capers.

MUSIC MASTER: When the dance is combined with the music, it will be much more effective. You will find very gallant the little ballet we have organized for you.

M. JOURDAIN: Have it ready soon, anyhow. The person I've ordered all this for is to do me the honor of coming to dinner today.

DANCING MASTER: It's all ready.

MUSIC MASTER: Incidentally, sir, you should go farther. A person like you, doing things in a big way, and with a taste for the finer things of life, should have a musicale at home every Wednesday or Thursday.

M. JOURDAIN: Do people of quality have that?

MUSIC MASTER: Yes, sir.

M. JOURDAIN: I'll have it, then. It will be nice, will it?

MUSIC MASTER: Certainly. You will need three voices: a soprano, a counter-tenor, and a basso; they will be accompanied by a bass viol, a theorbo or archlute, and a harpsichord for the sustained bass, with two violins to play the refrains.

M. JOURDAIN: You ought to put in an accordion too. The accordion is an instrument I like; it's harmonious.

MUSIC MASTER: Just let us arrange things.

M. JOURDAIN: Anyway, don't forget to send me some singers by and by, to sing at the dinner.

MUSIC MASTER: You will have everything you need.

M. JOURDAIN: And especially, be sure the ballet is nice.

MUSIC MASTER: You will be pleased, I am sure; especially with certain minuets you will see.

M. JOURDAIN: The minuet! That's my dance! You should see me dance the minuet! Come on, dancing master!

DANCING MASTER: A hat for the gentleman, please! (MONSIEUR JOURDAIN *seizes a lackey's hat, claps it on over his nightcap, removing it to make the sweeping bows required by the dance; the* DANCING MASTER *sings the music, and also his instructions*) La, la, la; La, la, la, la, la, la. La, la, la, repeat. La, la, la; La, la. Keep in tune—if you please. La, la, la, la. Right leg stiff, la, la, la. Don't move shoulders—quite so much. La, la, la, la, la; La, la, la, la, la. Both your arms—

are they crippled? La la, la, la, la. Lift your head—turn toe out. La, la, la. Stand up straight.

M. JOURDAIN (*with an intonation between "I'm done in!" and "How's that?"*): Uh!

MUSIC MASTER: Splendid! Splendid!

M. JOURDAIN: This reminds me. Teach me how to make a bow to salute a marquise. I'm going to need it soon.

DANCING MASTER: A bow to salute a marquise?

M. JOURDAIN: Yes. A marquise named Dorimène.

DANCING MASTER: Give me your hand.

M. JOURDAIN: No, you do it alone. I'll get the idea.

DANCING MASTER: If you want to make a very respectful salute, you must first make a bow stepping backward, then advance toward the lady with three forward bows, and at the last you bow down to the level of her knees.

M. JOURDAIN: Show me . . . Good.

(*Enter a* LACKEY.)

LACKEY: Monsieur, here is your fencing master who's come.

M. JOURDAIN: Tell him to come in and give me my lesson. (*Exit* LACKEY) I want you two to watch how I do it.

(*Enter* FENCING MASTER. *He salutes and hands* MONSIEUR JOURDAIN *a foil.*)

FENCING MASTER: Now, sir; first make your bow . . . Body straight . . . Weight a little more on the left thigh. Legs not so wide apart. Feet on the same line. Your wrist in line with your forward hip. The point of your weapon on the level of your shoulder. The arm not quite so straight out. The left hand at the level of the eye. Left shoulder drawn back a little more. Head up. Put on a confident look . . . Advance . . . Keep the body tense. Engage my foil in quart, and carry through . . . One, two . . . Recover . . . Thrust again, keeping feet in same position . . . Backward jump . . . When you make your thrust, sir, the sword should start before the foot, and you must keep your body protected . . . One, two . . . Now, touch my sword in tierce, and carry through . . . Advance . . . Body firm . . . Advance . . . Thrust from that position. One, two . . . Recover . . . Thrust . . . Backward jump . . . On guard, sir, on guard! (*Penetrating* MONSIEUR JOURDAIN'*s guard, he pinks his breast.*)

M. JOURDAIN: Uh?

MUSIC MASTER: You're doing marvelously.

FENCING MASTER: As I have already told you, the whole secret of swordplay consists in two things: to give; and not to receive. And as I proved the other day, with demonstrative logic, it is impossible for you to receive, if you know how to divert your enemy's weapon from the line of your body; and that depends only on a simple twist of the wrist, either inward or outward.

M. JOURDAIN: So a person who may not be very brave can be sure of killing his man, and not getting killed?

FENCING MASTER: Exactly. Didn't you see the demonstration?

M. JOURDAIN: Yes.

FENCING MASTER: Thus we can see how highly we swordsmen should be esteemed in a state, and how far the science of fencing is superior to the useless branches of knowledge, like dancing, music, and—

DANCING MASTER: Wait a minute, swordsman; please speak of the dance with respect.

MUSIC MASTER: And learn, I beg of you, to treat music with proper consideration.

FENCING MASTER: You're a funny pair, trying to compare your subjects with mine!

MUSIC MASTER: Look at the great man, will you?

DANCING MASTER: He's a comic sight, with his padded chest protector!

FENCING MASTER: My little dancing master, I'll show you some new steps. And you, my little musician, I'll make you sing—but small!

DANCING MASTER: My good blacksmith, I'll teach you your trade!

M. JOURDAIN (*to the* DANCING MASTER): Are you crazy, to pick a fight with him, who knows all about tierce and quart, and can kill a man by demonstrative logic?

DANCING MASTER: Little I care for his demonstrative logic, and his tierce and quart.

M. JOURDAIN: Take it easy, I tell you.

FENCING MASTER (*to* DANCING MASTER): What, you impertinent puppy!

M. JOURDAIN: Now, now, fencing master.

DANCING MASTER: What, you big cart horse!

M. JOURDAIN: Now, now, dancing master.

FENCING MASTER: If I let myself go—

M. JOURDAIN: Easy, easy there!

DANCING MASTER: If I lay a finger on you—

M. JOURDAIN: Gently, gently!

FENCING MASTER: I'll beat you to a pulp!

M. JOURDAIN: Please!

DANCING MASTER: I'll trim you down to size!

M. JOURDAIN: I beg and pray you!

MUSIC MASTER: We'll teach him how to talk!

M. JOURDAIN: Dear God! Stop, stop! (*Enter* PHILOSOPHY MASTER) Hello, Monsieur Philosopher, you arrive in the nick of time with your philosophy. Come and make peace among these people.

PHILOSOPHY MASTER: What is it? What is the matter, good sirs?

M. JOURDAIN: They have got angry about the standing of their professions, to the point of calling each other names and starting to fight.

PHILOSOPHY MASTER: Dear, dear! My friends, should you let yourselves get so excited? Haven't you read the learned treatise Seneca composed upon anger? Is anything more base and shameful than that passion, which turns man into a wild beast? Should not reason be the mistress of all our actions?

DANCING MASTER: Why, sir, he goes and insults us both, sneering at my trade, the dance; and at music, which is *his* profession!

PHILOSOPHY MASTER: A wise man is superior to any insult he may hear. The proper reply one should make to all affronts is moderation and patience.

FENCING MASTER: They have both had the audacity to compare their professions to mine.

PHILOSOPHY MASTER: Should such a thing move you? Men should not dispute about vainglory and precedence; what truly distinguishes men one from another is wisdom and virtue.

DANCING MASTER: I am simply telling him that dancing is a science which can hardly be sufficiently honored.

MUSIC MASTER: And I was saying that music is a science revered throughout history.

FENCING MASTER: And I was pointing out that the science of arms is the most beautiful and necessary of all sciences.

PHILOSOPHY MASTER: And what, then, is the place of philosophy? I find all three of you very impudent, to speak before me with this arrogance, and to give brazenly the name of science to things which one should not even honor with the title of craft, and which can be grouped only under the denomination of wretched trades of gladiator, minstrel, and posturer!

FENCING MASTER: Get out, you pig of a philosopher!

MUSIC MASTER: Get out, you half-wit highbrow!

DANCING MASTER: Get out, you crackpot professor!

PHILOSOPHY MASTER: What, you yokels!

(*He throws himself upon them; the other three unite to beat him.*)

M. JOURDAIN: Philosopher, sir!

PHILOSOPHY MASTER: The insolent scoundrels! The rascals!

M. JOURDAIN: Philosopher, sir!

FENCING MASTER: Devil take the swine!

M. JOURDAIN: Dear sirs!

PHILOSOPHY MASTER: Impudent rogues!

M. JOURDAIN: Philosopher, sir!

DANCING MASTER: To hell with the jackass!

M. JOURDAIN: My friends!

PHILOSOPHY MASTER: Blackguards!

M. JOURDAIN: Philosopher, sir!

MUSIC MASTER: Damn him and his insolence!

M. JOURDAIN: My dear sirs!

PHILOSOPHY MASTER: Villains! Beggars! Traitors! Impostors!

M. JOURDAIN: Philosopher, sir! Dear sirs! Philosopher, sir! My friends! Philosopher, sir! (*Exit the four* MASTERS, *fighting*) Oh, fight all you like. There's nothing I can do about it, and I won't get my dressing gown dirty trying to separate you. I'd be crazy to get into that mess; I might get a nasty bang.

(*Enter* PHILOSOPHY MASTER, *tidying his clothing.*)

PHILOSOPHY MASTER: And now let's have our lesson.

M. JOURDAIN: Ah, sir, I'm sorry for the blows you've received.

PHILOSOPHY MASTER: That's nothing. A philosopher knows how to take things as they come; and I am going to compose a satire against them, in the style of Juvenal, which will settle their hash. We'll drop the matter. What do you want to learn?

M. JOURDAIN: Everything I can, for I am crazy to be a scholar. It makes me furious that my father and mother didn't make me study all the branches of knowledge when I was young.

PHILOSOPHY MASTER: That is a very laudable sentiment. *Nam sine doctrina vita est quasi mortis imago.* You understand that; you know Latin, of course.

M. JORDAIN: Yes; but let's pretend I don't know it. Explain to me what that means.

PHILOSOPHY MASTER: That means: "Without knowledge, life is almost an image of death."

M. JOURDAIN: That Latin is right.

PHILOSOPHY MASTER: Don't you have some basic elements, some beginnings in the fields of study?

M. JOURDAIN: Oh, yes; I know how to read and write.

PHILOSOPHY MASTER: Now where would you like to begin? Would you like to have me teach you logic?

M. JOURDAIN: Just what is that logic?

PHILOSOPHY MASTER: Logic teaches the three operations of the mind.

M. JOURDAIN: What are these three operations of the mind?

PHILOSOPHY MASTER: The first, the second, and the third. The first is true conception by means of the universals. The second is true judgment by means of categories; and the third, the true drawing of logical consequences by means of the figures Barbara, Celarent, Darii, Ferio, Baralipton, and so forth.

M. JOURDAIN: Those words sound kind of repulsive. I don't like that logic. Let's learn something prettier.

PHILOSOPHY MASTER: Would you like to learn ethics?

M. JOURDAIN: Ethics?

PHILOSOPHY MASTER: Yes.

M. JOURDAIN: What do they do?

PHILOSOPHY MASTER: Ethics treats of the nature of happiness, teaches men to moderate their passions, and—

M. JOURDAIN: No, none of that. I have a devilish excitable nature; no ethics for me. When I want to get mad, I want to get good and mad.

PHILOSOPHY MASTER: Would you like to learn physics?

M. JOURDAIN: Physics? Why not leave them to the doctors?

PHILOSOPHY MASTER: Physics is the science which explains the principles of the natural world and the properties of matter. It treats the nature of the elements, of the metals, of minerals, stones, plants, and animals, and teaches us the causes of meteors, rainbows, shooting stars, comets, lightning, thunder and thunderbolts, rain, snow, hail, winds and whirlwinds.

M. JOURDAIN: There's too much rowdydow in that; too much rumpus and ruckus.

PHILOSOPHY MASTER: Well, then, what do you want me to teach you?

M. JOURDAIN: Teach me spelling.

PHILOSOPHY MASTER: Gladly.

M. JOURDAIN: And afterwards, you can teach me the almanac,

so I'll know when there's a moon and when there isn't.

PHILOSOPHY MASTER: Very well. To follow your idea and to treat this subject from a philosophical point of view, one must proceed according to the natural order of things, by an exact understanding of the nature of the letters, and of the different manner of pronouncing them. I shall first inform you that the letters are divided into vowels, from the Latin meaning "vocal," so called because they express the voiced sounds; and into consonants, meaning "with-sounding," so called because they "sound with" the vowels, and merely mark the various articulations of the voiced sounds. There are five vowels, or voiced sounds: A, E, I, O, U.

M. JOURDAIN: I understand all that.

PHILOSOPHY MASTER: The vowel A, pronounced *ah,* is formed by opening the mouth wide: *Ah.*

M. JOURDAIN: *Ah, ah.* Yes, yes.

PHILOSOPHY MASTER: The vowel E, pronounced *euh,* is formed by bringing the lower jaw closer to the upper jaw: *Euh. Ah, euh.*

M. JOURDAIN: *Ah, euh; ah, euh.* Bless my soul, yes! Oh, how beautiful that is!

PHILOSOPHY MASTER: The vowel I, pronounced *Ee,* is made by bringing the jaws still closer together, and by widening the mouth, or extending its corners toward the ears: *Ee. Ah, euh, ee.*

M. JOURDAIN: *Ah, euh, ee, ee, ee.* That's true! Hurrah for science!

PHILOSOPHY MASTER: The vowel O is formed by opening the jaws again, and by bringing the corners of the mouth closer together: *Oh.*

M. JOURDAIN: *Oh, oh.* Nothing could be truer! *Ah, euh, ee, oh, ee, oh.* That's wonderful! *Ee, oh, ee, oh!* [1]

PHILOSOPHY MASTER: The opening of the mouth makes, as it happens, a small circle which represents an O.

M. JOURDAIN: *Oh, oh, oh.* You're right: *oh.* Oh, what a fine thing it is to know something!

[1] [Traditionally, the actor here imitates an ass braying.—Trans.]

PHILOSOPHY MASTER: The vowel U [2] is formed by bringing the teeth close together, without their quite touching, and by thrusting out the lips, thus making a small aperture: *U.*

M. JOURDAIN: *U, u.* It couldn't be truer! *U!*

PHILOSOPHY MASTER: The lips are extended as if you are pouting; hence it comes that if you want to make this sound at someone, expressing contempt, all you say to him is *U.*[3]

M. JOURDAIN: *U, u.* That's right! Oh, why didn't I study sooner, to learn all that?

PHILOSOPHY MASTER: Tomorrow we shall take up the other letters, the consonants.

M. JOURDAIN: Are they as remarkable as these vowels?

PHILOSOPHY MASTER: Certainly. The consonant D, for example, is pronounced by touching the tip of the tongue to the hard palate, just above the teeth: *Da.*

M. JOURDAIN: *Da, da.* Yes. Oh, how wonderful, wonderful!

PHILOSOPHY MASTER: The F is pronounced by applying the upper teeth to the lower lip: *Fa.*

M. JOURDAIN: *Fa, fa.* It's the truth! Oh, Father and Mother, how I blame you!

PHILOSOPHY MASTER: And the R, by placing the tip of the tongue against the upper palate, so that it is brushed by the air, forcefully expelled, and yields to it, and returns constantly to the same position, making a kind of vibration: *Rra.*

M. JOURDAIN: *R, r, ra; R, rr, rrra.* That's right! Oh, what a clever man you are! And how much time I've lost! *Rrrrra.*

PHILOSOPHY MASTER: I shall explain to you all these important facts in detail.

M. JOURDAIN: Please do. And by the way, I must take you into my confidence. I am in love with a person of very high rank, and I should like to have your help in writing something in a little note I want to drop at her feet.

PHILOSOPHY MASTER: I shall be delighted.

M. JOURDAIN: It will be in the gallant style, yes?

[2] [The French U, like a German ü.—Trans.]
[3] [The sound is used by the French for booing.—Trans.]

PHILOSOPHY MASTER: Certainly. Is it poetry you want to write her?

M. JOURDAIN: No, no; no poetry.

PHILOSOPHY MASTER: You want only prose?

M. JOURDAIN: No; I don't want either poetry or prose.

PHILOSOPHY MASTER: Well, it has to be either one or the other.

M. JOURDAIN: Why?

PHILOSOPHY MASTER. For the reason, sir, that we have no means of expression other than prose and poetry.

M. JOURDAIN: There's nothing but prose or poetry?

PHILOSOPHY MASTER: Quite so, sir. All that is not prose is poetry; and all that is not poetry is prose.

M. JOURDAIN: And when a man talks, what's that?

PHILOSOPHY MASTER: Prose.

M. JOURDAIN: What? When I say: "Nicole, bring me my slippers and give me my nightcap," that's prose?

PHILOSOPHY MASTER: Yes, sir.

M. JOURDAIN: Well, I'll be hanged! For more than forty years I've been talking prose without any idea of it; I'm very much obliged to you for telling me that. So, I'd like to put in a letter: "Beautiful Marquise, your lovely eyes make me die of love." But I'd like to have it put in the gallant style; neatly turned, you know.

PHILOSOPHY MASTER: Put it, then, that the rays of her eyes reduce your heart to ashes; that for her sake you suffer night and day the tortures of—

M. JOURDAIN: No, no, no. I don't want all that. I just want what I told you: "Beautiful Marquise, your lovely eyes make me die of love."

PHILOSOPHY MASTER: Well, you ought to stretch it out a little.

M. JOURDAIN: No, I tell you. I just want only those words in the letter; but elegantly put, properly arranged. So I'm asking you to tell me, out of curiosity, the different ways you could write them.

PHILOSOPHY MASTER: Well, firstly, you could put them the way you said: "Beautiful Marquise, your lovely eyes make me die of love." Or else: "Of love, beautiful Marquise, your beautiful eyes make me die." Or else: "Your eyes, lovely, of love, Marquise beautiful, make die me." Or else: "Die, beautiful Marquise, of love your lovely eyes me make." Or else: "Me your lovely eyes of love make die, beautiful Marquise."

M. JOURDAIN: But of all those ways, which one is the best?

PHILOSOPHY MASTER: The one you said: "Beautiful Marquise, your lovely eyes make me die of love."

M. JOURDAIN: And nevertheless I have never studied; I did that straight off! I thank you with all my heart; please come again tomorrow early.

PHILOSOPHY MASTER: I won't fail to.

(*Exit* PHILOSOPHY MASTER.)

M. JOURDAIN (*to his* LACKEYS): Look here, hasn't my new suit come yet?

SECOND LACKEY: No, sir.

M. JOURDAIN: That damned tailor makes me wait until a day when I have so much to do! He makes me furious. May the quartan fever take that hangbird tailor! To the devil with the tailor! May the galloping plague seize the tailor! If I had him here now, that infernal tailor, that dog of a tailor, that pig of a tailor, I'd . . . (*Enter* MERCHANT TAILOR *and his* APPRENTICE, *carrying* M. JOURDAIN'*s suit*) Oh, here you are! I was on the point of getting angry with you.

MERCHANT TAILOR: I couldn't come sooner; I have had twenty journeymen working on your coat.

M. JOURDAIN: The silk stockings you sent me were so tight that I had a terrible time getting them on, and already there are a couple of stitches broken.

MERCHANT TAILOR: They will get looser.

M. JOURDAIN: Yes, if all the stitches break. And what's more, you made me some shoes which hurt frightfully.

MERCHANT TAILOR: Not at all, sir.

M. JOURDAIN: What do you mean, not at all?

MERCHANT TAILOR: They don't hurt you.

M. JOURDAIN: I tell you they do hurt me!

MERCHANT TAILOR: You just imagine it.

M. JOURDAIN: I imagine it because I feel it. What kind of talk is that?

MERCHANT TAILOR: Now look, here is the finest coat in all the court, the most harmoniously matched. It is a great achievement to have invented a formal coat which is not black. I defy the most eminent tailors to equal it in a dozen tries.

M. JOURDAIN: What's this? You've got the flowers upside down.

MERCHANT TAILOR: You didn't tell me you wanted them right side up.

M. JOURDAIN: Did I have to tell you that?

MERCHANT TAILOR: Yes, indeed. All the people of quality wear them this way.

M. JOURDAIN: People of quality wear the flowers upside down?

MERCHANT TAILOR: Yes, sir.

M. JOURDAIN: Oh, well, it's all right then.

MERCHANT TAILOR: If you prefer, I'll turn them right side up.

M. JOURDAIN: No, no.

MERCHANT TAILOR: You have only to say so.

M. JOURDAIN: No, I tell you. You did all right . . . Do you think the costume will look well on me?

MERCHANT TAILOR: What a question! I defy any artist to paint a finer ensemble. I have a workman who, for assembling a wide trouser, is the greatest genius on earth; and another who, for confecting a doublet, is the hero of our age.

M. JOURDAIN: The peruke and the plumes, are they all right?

MERCHANT TAILOR: Perfect.

M. JOURDAIN (*noticing the* TAILOR'*s coat*): Ah, master tailor, there is some material from the last coat you made me! I recognize it perfectly.

MERCHANT TAILOR: The fact is, the material seemed to me so beautiful that I made a coat for myself from it.

M. JOURDAIN: Yes, but you shouldn't have made it with my material.

MASTER TAILOR: Do you want to try on your coat?

M. JOURDAIN: Yes; give it to me.

MERCHANT TAILOR: Wait a moment. That's not the way to do it. I have brought some men to dress you to music; that kind of costume has to be put on with ceremony. Holà! Come in, you men. (*Enter four* JOURNEYMEN TAILORS) Put this coat on the gentleman, in the way you do for persons of quality.

(*Two* TAILORS *remove* MONSIEUR JOURDAIN'*s breeches, two others remove his jacket. They try on his new coat.* MONSIEUR JOURDAIN *promenades among them for their inspection. All takes place to the music of the entire orchestra.*)

A TAILOR: Gentleman, sir, will you give a little tip to the workmen?

M. JOURDAIN: What did you call me?

TAILOR: Gentleman, sir.

M. JOURDAIN: Gentleman, sir! That's what comes from dressing like a person of quality. If you go around always dressed as a commoner, no one will say to you: "Gentleman, sir!" Here; that's for "gentleman, sir."

TAILOR: Monsignor, we are very much obliged to you.

M. JOURDAIN: Monsignor! Oh, oh, Monsignor! Wait a bit, my friend; "Monsignor" deserves a little something. Here; that's a present from Monsignor.

TAILOR: Monsignor, we shall all drink to the health of Your Grace.

M. JOURDAIN: Your Grace! Oh, oh, oh! Wait; don't go away. "Your Grace"—to me! Faith, if he goes as far as Royal Highness he'll have my whole purse! . . . Here; that's for My Grace.

TAILOR: Monsignor, we thank you very humbly for your generosity.

M. JOURDAIN: A good thing he stopped there. I was going to give him the whole business.

(*The four* JOURNEYMEN TAILORS *express their joy in a dance, which forms the second* Interlude.)

Act III

The MERCHANT TAILOR *and his assistants exit, leaving* MONSIEUR JOURDAIN *and his two* LACKEYS *on the stage.*

M. JOURDAIN: Follow me, while I take a little walk to show my new suit around town. And especially, both of you be sure to walk directly behind me, so that everybody can see that you belong to me.

LACKEYS: Yes, sir.

M. JOURDAIN: Get Nicole for me. I want to give her some orders. No, don't move. Here she is now. (*Enter* NICOLE) Nicole!

NICOLE: Yes, what is it?

M. JOURDAIN: Listen to me.

NICOLE: He, he, he, he, he!

M. JOURDAIN: What is there to laugh at?

NICOLE: He, he, he, he, he, he!

M. JOURDAIN: What does the rascal mean?

NICOLE: He, he, he! How funny you look! He, he, he!

M. JOURDAIN: What's the matter?

NICOLE: Oh, oh, good Lord! He, he, he, he, he!

M. JOURDAIN: You scamp! Are you trying to make fun of me?

NICOLE: Oh, no, sir. I'd hate to do that. He, he, he, he, he, he!

M. JOURDAIN: I'll land one on your nose, if you laugh any more.

NICOLE: Monsieur, I can't help it. He, he, he, he, he, he!

M. JOURDAIN: You won't stop?

NICOLE: Monsieur, I beg your pardon. But you look so funny, I can't keep from laughing. He, he, he!

M. JOURDAIN: I never saw such impudence.

NICOLE: You're so comical like that. He, he!

M. JOURDAIN: I'm going to—

NICOLE: I beg you to excuse me. He, he, he, he!

M. JOURDAIN: Look here, if you laugh once more, I swear I'll apply to your cheek the biggest slap that has ever been slapped.

NICOLE: It's all over, sir. I won't laugh any more.

M. JOURDAIN: Make sure you don't. Now, I want you to clean up, in preparation for—

NICOLE: He, he!

M. JOURDAIN: To clean up properly—

NICOLE: He, he!

M. JOURDAIN: I say I want you to clean up the parlor, and—

NICOLE: He, he!

M. JOURDAIN: What, again!

NICOLE: Look here, sir, I'd rather have you beat me and let me laugh myself out. That will do me more good. He, he, he, he, he!

M. JOURDAIN: You'll drive me crazy!

NICOLE: Please, monsieur, I beg you to let me laugh. He, he, he!

M. JOURDAIN: If I catch you—

NICOLE: Monsieu-eur, I'll blow-ow-ow up, if I don't laugh. He, he, he!

M. JOURDAIN: Has anyone ever seen such a hussy! She comes and laughs insolently in my face, instead of obeying my orders!

NICOLE: What do you want me to do, sir?

M. JOURDAIN: I want you, you rogue, to see to getting the house ready for the company that is due to come soon.

NICOLE: Well, my sakes, I've lost all fancy to laugh. Your company always makes such a mess around here that the mere mention of it is enough to put me out of humor.

M. JOURDAIN: So, for your convenience, I ought to shut my door to everybody?

NICOLE: At least, you ought to shut it to certain people.

(*Enter* MADAME JOURDAIN.)

MME JOURDAIN: Aha, here's something new! Tell me, my good husband, what's this getup of yours? Are you crazy, to go and rig yourself out that way? Do you want people to mock you everywhere?

M. JOURDAIN: My good wife, only the fools, male and female, will mock me.

MME JOURDAIN: Well, they haven't waited for this occasion to start. Your behavior has been making everybody laugh for quite some time.

M. JOURDAIN: Everybody! What do you mean by everybody, if you please?

MME JOURDAIN: I mean everybody who knows what's what, and who has got more sense than you. For my part, I am scandalized by the kind of life you are leading. I vow I don't recognize our own house. You'd say it was carnival time here every day; and to make sure of it, from early morning on there's nothing but a great row of fiddlers and singers, enough to disturb the whole neighborhood.

NICOLE: Madame is quite right. I can never keep the house clean any more, with all that gang of people you bring in here. They've got big feet which go and hunt for mud in every quarter of the city, in order to bring it back here. And poor Françoise is worn almost to a shadow, scrubbing the floors that your fine folks dirty up regularly every day.

M. JOURDAIN: Now, now, Nicole, you've got to be quite a speech-maker for a peasant servant girl.

MME JOURDAIN: Nicole is quite right; she's got more sense than you. I'd like to know what you think you're doing with a dancing teacher, at your age.

NICOLE: And with a great big bully of a fighter, who stamps so he shakes the whole house, and loosens up all the tiles on the parlor floor.

M. JOURDAIN: Shut up, servant; and shut up, wife.

MME JOURDAIN: You want to learn how to dance, for when you won't be able to walk?

NICOLE: You want to kill somebody?

M. JOURDAIN: Shut up, I tell you! You are both ignorant fools; you don't know the prerogatives of all that.

MME JOURDAIN: You ought to think rather of marrying off your daughter. She's of an age to have a husband now.

M. JOURDAIN: I'll think of marrying my daughter when a proper match for her appears. But I also want to think of learning the finer things of life.

NICOLE: I've also heard, madame, that to top it off he took on a philosophy teacher today.

M. JOURDAIN: Quite right. I want to sharpen my wits, and be able to discuss things among intelligent people.

MME JOURDAIN: One of these days you'll be going to school to get yourself whipped, at your age.

M. JOURDAIN: Why not? I wish to heaven I could be whipped now, in front of everybody, if I could know what one learns in school.

NICOLE: Yes, my faith! Much good that would do you!

M. JOURDAIN: It would indeed.

MME JOURDAIN: A lot of use that would be for running your house.

M. JOURDAIN: You're right, it would. You both talk like simpletons, and I'm ashamed of your ignorance. (*To* MADAME JOURDAIN) For example, do you know what you're saying now?

MME JOURDAIN: Yes, I know that what I am saying is very well said, and you ought to think of changing your way of life.

M. JOURDAIN: I'm not talking of that. I ask you, what are the words that you are saying now?

MME JOURDAIN: They are very sensible words, and that's what your conduct is not.

M. JOURDAIN: I'm not talking of that, I tell you. I ask you; what I'm speaking to you, what I'm saying to you now, what is it?

MME JOURDAIN: Stuff and nonsense.

M. JOURDAIN: No, no, not at all. What we are both saying, the language we are talking now?

MME JOURDAIN: Well?

M. JOURDAIN: What is that called?

MME JOURDAIN: That is called whatever you've a mind to call it.

M. JOURDAIN: It is called prose, ignorant woman!

MME JOURDAIN: Prose?

M. JOURDAIN: Yes, prose. Everything which is prose is not

poetry; and everything which is not poetry is not prose. Ha, that's what comes of studying! (*To* NICOLE) And you, do you know what you have to do to make an U?

NICOLE: How's that?

M. JOURDAIN: Yes. What do you do when you make an U?

NICOLE: What?

M. JOURDAIN: Just say U, for example.

NICOLE: All right, U.

M. JOURDAIN: Now what are you doing?

NICOLE: I'm saying U.

M. JOURDAIN: Yes, but when you say U, what are you doing?

NICOLE: I'm doing what you tell me.

M. JOURDAIN: Oh, what a dreadful thing it is to have to deal with idiots! You thrust your lips outward, and you bring the upper jaw down close to the lower jaw: U. You see, U. I pout: U.

NICOLE: Yes, that's right pretty.

MME JOURDAIN: Wonderful!

M. JOURDAIN: It's quite different, if you'd seen O, and Da, da, and Fa, fa.

MME JOURDAIN: What's all this rubbish?

NICOLE: What does all that cure you of?

M. JOURDAIN: It makes me sick to see such ignorant women.

MME JOURDAIN: You ought to kick all those fellows out, with their moonshine.

NICOLE: And especially that big gawk of a fencing master, who fills the whole house with dust.

M. JOURDAIN: Yes, that fencing master worries you a lot. I'll show you how stupid you are, right away. (*He has a* LACKEY *bring him the foils, takes one, and hands one to* NICOLE) Take this. Logical demonstration, the line of the body. When you thrust in quart, this is all you have to do. And when you thrust in tierce, that's what you do. In this way, you can never get killed. Isn't it fine, to be assured of the result, when you're fighting with someone? There now, just make a thrust, to try it out.

NICOLE: All right. (*She makes several lunges, pricking* MONSIEUR JOURDAIN.)

M. JOURDAIN: Hold on! Hey, easy there! The devil take the wench!

NICOLE: You told me to thrust.

M. JOURDAIN: Yes, but you thrust in tierce before thrusting in quart; and you wouldn't wait for me to parry.

MME JOURDAIN: You're crazy, my poor husband, with your fancy ideas. It's all happened since you took into your head to hang around with the nobility.

M. JOURDAIN: When I hang around with the nobility, I show my good judgment. It's a lot finer thing than to hang around with your bourgeoisie.

MME JOURDAIN: Really now! There's a lot to be gained by associating with your nobles! You've done some nice business with that Monsieur le Comte you're so fascinated with.

M. JOURDAIN: Quiet! Think what you're saying. Are you aware, wife, that when you mention him, you don't know who he really is? He is a person of greater importance than you think, a lord who is highly considered at court. He speaks to the King just the way I am speaking to you. Isn't it a very honorable thing for people to see a person of such quality come to my house so often, calling me his dear friend, and treating me as if I were his equal? He has done me some kindnesses you would never guess; and in front of everybody he shows me such special regards that I am embarrassed myself.

MME JOURDAIN: Yes, he does you kindnesses, and he shows you special regards; but he borrows your money.

M. JOURDAIN: Well, isn't it an honor for me to lend money to a man of that rank? And can I do any less for a lord who calls me his dear friend?

MME JOURDAIN: And this lord, what does he do for you?

M. JOURDAIN: He does things that would astonish people, if they were known.

MME JOURDAIN: What things, for instance?

M. JOURDAIN: Enough; I won't explain. Let it suffice that if

I have lent him money, he will repay me well, and that soon.

MME JOURDAIN: Yes; you can expect it any minute.

M. JOURDAIN: Certainly; didn't he tell me so?

MME JOURDAIN: Yes, yes; he won't fail to do nothing of the sort.

M. JOURDAIN: He gave me his word as a gentleman.

MME JOURDAIN: Nonsense!

M. JOURDAIN: You are very obstinate, wife. I tell you he'll keep his word. I'm sure of it.

MME JOURDAIN: And I tell you he won't; and all the attentions he shows you are just to take you in.

M. JOURDAIN: Shut up; here he is.

MME JOURDAIN: That's the last straw. Perhaps he's coming to get another loan from you. The sight of him takes away my appetite.

M. JOURDAIN: Shut up, I tell you.

(*Enter* DORANTE.)

DORANTE: My dear friend Monsieur Jourdain, and how are you?

M. JOURDAIN: Very well, sir, at your humble service.

DORANTE: And Madame Jourdain here, how is she doing?

MME JOURDAIN: Madame Jourdain is doing the best she can.

DORANTE: Well, well, Monsieur Jourdain! How elegantly you're gotten up!

M. JOURDAIN: Well, you see.

DORANTE: You look very brave in that suit; we have no young sprigs at court better turned out than you are.

M. JOURDAIN: He, he!

MME JOURDAIN (*aside*): He scratches him where he itches.

DORANTE: Turn around. It's really stylish.

MME JOURDAIN (*aside*): Yes; as silly behind as in front.

DORANTE: 'Pon my word, Monsieur Jourdain, I have been extraordinarily anxious to see you. I have a higher opinion of you than of absolutely anyone else. I was talking about you this very morning in the King's bedchamber.

M. JOURDAIN: You do me too much honor, sir. (*To* MADAME JOURDAIN) In the King's bedchamber!

DORANTE: Come, come; put on your hat.

M. JOURDAIN: Monsieur, I know the respect I owe you.

DORANTE: Good Lord, put it on! Let's have no ceremony between us, please.

M. JOURDAIN: Monsieur . . .

DORANTE: Cover, I tell you, Monsieur Jourdain; you are my friend.

M. JOURDAIN: Monsieur, I am your humble servant.

DORANTE: I won't cover, if you don't.

M. JOURDAIN (*covering*): I'd rather be unmannerly than troublesome.

DORANTE: I am your debtor, as you know.

MME JOURDAIN (*aside*): Yes, we know it only too well.

DORANTE: You have generously lent me money on several occasions, and you have obliged me with the best grace in the world, most assuredly.

M. JOURDAIN: You're joking, sir.

DORANTE: But I make a point of repaying all loans, and recognizing the kindnesses that are done me.

M. JOURDAIN: I don't doubt it, sir.

DORANTE: I want to clean matters up between us. I've come so we can go over our accounts together.

M. JOURDAIN (*to* MADAME JOURDAIN): See how unjust you were!

DORANTE: I am the kind of fellow who likes to pay off his debts as soon as possible.

M. JOURDAIN (*to* MADAME JOURDAIN): I told you so!

DORANTE: Let's see how much I owe you.

M. JOURDAIN (*to* MADAME JOURDAIN): You and your ridiculous suspicions!

DORANTE: Do you remember exactly how much you lent me?

M. JOURDAIN: I think so. I made a little memorandum. Here it is. On one occasion, given to you, two hundred louis.

DORANTE: That's right.

M. JOURDAIN: Another time, one hundred twenty.

DORANTE: Yes.

M. JOURDAIN: And another time, a hundred and forty.

DORANTE: You're right.

M. JOURDAIN: These three items add up to four hundred and sixty louis, which makes five thousand and sixty francs.

DORANTE: The accounting is excellent. Five thousand and sixty francs.

M. JOURDAIN: One thousand eight hundred and thirty-two francs to your feather supplier.

DORANTE: Exactly.

M. JOURDAIN: Two thousand seven hundred and eighty francs to your tailor.

DORANTE: True enough.

M. JOURDAIN: Four thousand three hundred seventy-nine francs twelve sous and eight farthings to your haberdasher.

DORANTE: Excellent. Twelve sous eight farthings. Very exact accounting.

M. JOURDAIN: And one thousand seven hundred forty-eight francs seven sous and four farthings to your saddler.

DORANTE: That's all correct. How much does it come to?

M. JOURDAIN: Sum total, fifteen thousand eight hundred francs.

DORANTE: The sum total is quite correct: fifteen thousand eight hundred francs. Now add two hundred pistoles you can give me now; that will make exactly eighteen thousand francs, which I will pay you at the earliest possible moment.

MME JOURDAIN (*to* MONSIEUR JOURDAIN): Well, didn't I guess it?

M. JOURDAIN (*to* MADAME JOURDAIN): Silence!

DORANTE: Would it be inconvenient for you to give me that amount?

M. JOURDAIN: No, no.

MME JOURDAIN (*to* MONSIEUR JOURDAIN): That fellow is milking you like a cow.

M. JOURDAIN (*to* MADAME JOURDAIN): Shut up!

DORANTE: If it's inconvenient, I can get it somewhere else.

M. JOURDAIN: No, indeed.

MME JOURDAIN (*to* MONSIEUR JOURDAIN): He won't be satisfied until he's ruined you.

M. JOURDAIN (*to* MADAME JOURDAIN): Shut up, I tell you!

DORANTE: If it embarrasses you, you have only to say so.

M. JOURDAIN: Not at all, sir.

MME JOURDAIN (*to* MONSIEUR JOURDAIN): He's nothing but a crook.

M. JOURDAIN (*to* MADAME JOURDAIN): Will you shut up?

MME JOURDAIN (*to* MONSIEUR JOURDAIN): He'll suck you dry, down to your last penny.

M. JOURDAIN (*to* MADAME JOURDAIN): I tell you to shut your mouth!

DORANTE: There are plenty of people who would be delighted to lend it to me; but since you're my best friend, I thought I would be doing you an injury if I asked anyone else.

M. JOURDAIN: You do me too much honor, my dear sir. I'll go and fetch what you want.

MME JOURDAIN (*to* MONSIEUR JOURDAIN): What! You're going to give it to him?

M. JOURDAIN (*to* MADAME JOURDAIN): What can I do? Do you expect me to refuse a man of such rank, who talked of me this very morning in the King's bedchamber?

MME JOURDAIN (*to* MONSIEUR JOURDAIN): Go on, you're just an easy mark! (*Exit* MONSIEUR JOURDAIN.)

DORANTE: You seem cast down about something. What is the matter, Madame Jourdain?

MME JOURDAIN: I've cut my eyeteeth; I wasn't born yesterday.

DORANTE: And your charming daughter, I don't see her. Where is she?

MME JOURDAIN: My charming daughter is all right where she is.

DORANTE: How is she getting along?

MME JOURDAIN: She is getting along on her two legs.

DORANTE: Wouldn't you like to bring her some day to see the

command performance of the ballet and comedy before the King?

MME JOURDAIN: Oh, yes, we certainly need a good laugh; a good laugh is certainly what we need.

DORANTE: I think, Madame Jourdain, you must have had many admirers in your youth; you must have been so pretty and of such a charming humor.

MME JOURDAIN: Good land, sir, is Madame Jourdain doddering already? She's got one foot in the grave, maybe?

DORANTE: 'Pon my soul, Madame Jourdain, I ask your pardon. I didn't realize you're still young; I'm so unobservant. I beg you to excuse my impoliteness.

(*Enter* MONSIEUR JOURDAIN.)

M. JOURDAIN: Here are two hundred louis exactly.

DORANTE: I assure you, Monsieur Jourdain, that I am very much at your service; I am most eager to do you some good turn at court.

M. JOURDAIN: I am very deeply obliged to you.

DORANTE: If Madame Jourdain wants to see the performance before His Majesty, I shall get the best seats in the house for her.

MME JOURDAIN: Madame Jourdain kisses your hands with gratitude.

DORANTE (*aside to* MONSIEUR JOURDAIN): As I told you in my note, our lovely Marquise will come here soon for the ballet and the refreshments. I have finally persuaded her to accept the party you want to give her.

M. JOURDAIN (*aside to* DORANTE): Let's move farther off, for good reason.

DORANTE: I haven't seen you for a week, and I haven't given you any news of the diamond ring you asked me to present to her in your name. But the fact is I had all sorts of trouble in overcoming her scruples, and it's only today she made up her mind to accept it.

M. JOURDAIN: How did she find it?

DORANTE: Marvelous! And unless I'm much mistaken, the beauty of the diamond will work wonders for you.

M. JOURDAIN: Would to God it were so!

MME JOURDAIN (*to* NICOLE): When he once gets with that Count, he can't leave him.

DORANTE (*to* MONSIEUR JOURDAIN): I played up to her properly the value of the present and the greatness of your love.

M. JOURDAIN: Your kindness overwhelms me, sir. I am embarrassed beyond words to see a person of your rank lower himself to do what you are doing for me.

DORANTE: Are you joking? Between friends, does one worry about scruples of that sort? Wouldn't you do the same thing for me, if the occasion should arise?

M. JOURDAIN: Oh, assuredly; with the utmost willingness.

MME JOURDAIN (*to* NICOLE): I can't abide seeing that fellow around.

DORANTE: Personally, I stick at nothing when it's a question of serving a friend. And when you confided to me your passion for my friend, the charming Marquise, you saw that I immediately offered to aid your love.

M. JOURDAIN: That's true. I am confounded by your kindnesses.

MME JOURDAIN (*to* NICOLE): Won't he ever go away?

NICOLE: They just like each other's company.

DORANTE: You have taken the right course to touch her heart. Women love above all things to have people spend money on them; and your frequent serenades, and the continual offerings of flowers, and the superb fireworks on the lake, and the diamond ring she received in your name, and the party you are preparing for her—that sort of thing speaks far better in favor of your love than all the words you might utter to her in person.

M. JOURDAIN: There are no expenditures I wouldn't make, if they would help me find the way to touch her heart. A lady of quality has ravishing charms for me; I would pay any price for the honor of her love.

MME JOURDAIN (*to* NICOLE): What can they be argufying so

much about? Sneak over and see if you can't pick up something.

DORANTE: Very soon you will enjoy at your ease the pleasure of seeing her; and your eyes will have plenty of time to satisfy their longing.

M. JOURDAIN: To get free, I have arranged that my wife shall go and dine with her sister, and she'll spend the whole afternoon there.

DORANTE: That's very prudent. Your wife might have made trouble. I have given all the directions to the caterer, in your name; and I've done everything necessary for the ballet. I worked out the scheme for it myself; if the execution comes up to my idea, I am sure it will be found—

M. JOURDAIN (*perceiving that* NICOLE *is listening, gives her a box on the ear*): What's this, saucebox! (*To* DORANTE) Please, let's get out of here.

(*Exit* MONSIEUR JOURDAIN *and* DORANTE.)

NICOLE: My stars, madame, curiosity cost me something. But I think there's more here than meets the eye. They're talking about some affair they don't want you to know about.

MME JOURDAIN: Well, Nicole, this isn't the first time I've had some suspicions about my husband. Unless I am very much mistaken, he's setting his cap at someone, and I'm trying to find out who it is. But let's think about my daughter a moment. You know how Cléonte loves her. He's a man I like, and I want to help his suit, and give Lucile to him, if I can.

NICOLE: Really, madame, I am just delighted to know you feel that way; for if you like the master, I like the manservant just as much, and it would make me very happy if our marriage could take place in the shadow of theirs.

MME JOURDAIN: Go and give him a message from me. Tell him to come and see me soon, and we'll go together to my husband and ask my daughter's hand.

NICOLE: I'll do so right away, madame, and very gladly. I couldn't do a pleasanter errand. (*Exit* MADAME JOURDAIN) I think I'm going to make some people very happy. (*Enter*

CLÉONTE *and* COVIELLE) Ah, here you are, by a lucky chance! I bring you good news. I've come—

CLÉONTE: Withdraw, perfidious creature! Don't try to distract me with your treacherous words!

NICOLE: So that's the way you take—

CLÉONTE: Withdraw, I tell you! And go straightway and tell your faithless mistress that she will never befool the too confiding Cléonte!

NICOLE: What kind of a fit is this? My dear Covielle, do tell me what this means.

COVIELLE: Your dear Covielle! You scoundrel! Quick, out of my sight, villain! Leave me in peace!

NICOLE: What! You too—

COVIELLE: Out of my sight, I tell you! Never speak to me again!

NICOLE (*aside*): Ouch! What's biting them both? I'd better go right away and tell my mistress of this fine to-do.

(*Exit* NICOLE.)

CLÉONTE: What! To treat in such a way a lover, the most faithful and ardent of all lovers!

COVIELLE: It's appalling, how they treat us both.

CLÉONTE: I display for a certain person all the ardor and affection conceivable. I love only her in all the world; I have her alone in my thought; she has all my devotion, all my desires, all my joy; I speak only of her, I think only of her, I dream only of her, I breathe only for her, my heart exists only for her; and here is the fit reward for so much love! I pass two days without seeing her, which are to me two frightful centuries; I meet her by chance; and at the sight my heart is utterly transported, my joy manifests itself upon my countenance. Ravished with delight, I fly to her; and the faithless one turns her face from me, and passes grimly by, as if she had never seen me in her life!

COVIELLE: I say—exactly the same thing.

CLÉONTE: Has anything, Covielle, ever matched the perfidy of the ingrate Lucile?

COVIELLE: Or that, sir, of the hussy Nicole?

CLÉONTE: After so many devout sacrifices, sighs, and vows that I have offered to her charms!

COVIELLE: After so many attentions, services, and helping hands I have extended to her in her kitchen!

CLÉONTE: So many tears I have shed at her knees!

COVIELLE: So many buckets of water I have pulled up out of the well for her!

CLÉONTE: So much ardor I have evidenced, in cherishing her more than my own self!

COVIELLE: So much heat I have endured in turning the spit for her!

CLÉONTE: She flees me with contempt!

COVIELLE: She turns her back on me with an uppity air!

CLÉONTE: It is perfidy deserving the utmost chastisement.

COVIELLE: It is treason deserving a thousand slaps in the face.

CLÉONTE: Never, I beg you, take it into your head to speak in her defense.

COVIELLE: I, sir? Heaven forbid!

CLÉONTE: Don't try to excuse the action of the faithless one.

COVIELLE: Don't be afraid, I won't.

CLÉONTE: No. For you see, all your efforts to defend her will avail nothing.

COVIELLE: Defend her? Who could have that idea?

CLÉONTE: I want to keep my resentment fresh, and break off all relations with her.

COVIELLE: I give my consent.

CLÉONTE: That Monsieur le Comte who goes to her house dazzles her perhaps; and I can see that she may let herself be allured by rank and quality. But, for my own honor, I must forestall the public revelation of her inconstancy. I can see her moving in the direction of a change of heart, and I want to keep step with her, and not let her have all the credit for quitting me.

COVIELLE: That's very well said. I share in all your feelings.

CLÉONTE: Come to the aid of my rancor, and support my resolution against any lingering remains of love that might speak in her favor. Tell me, please, all the evil you can about her; paint me a portrait of her person which will make her despicable to me; and to complete my disillusionment, point out all the defects you can see in her.

COVIELLE: What, in her, sir? She's a fine poser, an affected show-off, for you to fall in love with! She seems very ordinary to me; you could find a hundred girls worthier of you. In the first place, her eyes are too small.

CLÉONTE: That's true; her eyes are small. But they are full of fire, very brilliant and sparkling, and unusually touching.

COVIELLE: She has a big mouth.

CLÉONTE: Perhaps. But one sees in it graces that are not in ordinary mouths. That mouth, when one looks at it, inspires desires. It is the most attractive and amorous mouth on earth.

COVIELLE: For her figure, it isn't a tall one.

CLÉONTE: No; but it's dainty and flexible.

COVIELLE: She affects a kind of carefree speech and behavior.

CLÉONTE: True; but she does so gracefully, and her manners are engaging; she has a certain charm which insinuates itself into the heart.

COVIELLE: As for wit—

CLÉONTE: Ah, that she has, Covielle, the keenest and most delicate.

COVIELLE: Her conversation—

CLÉONTE: Her conversation is delightful.

COVIELLE: She is always serious.

CLÉONTE: Well, do you want broad gaiety, everlasting outbursts of glee? Is there anything more tiresome than those women who are always laughing at everything?

COVIELLE: But finally, she's as capricious as anybody alive.

CLÉONTE: Yes, she's capricious, I agree. But that suits a beauty. We can bear anything from a beauty.

COVIELLE: Since that's the way of it, I can see that you want to love her forever.

CLÉONTE: I? I'd rather die. I am going to hate her as much as I have loved her.

COVIELLE: And how will you do that, if you find her so perfect?

CLÉONTE: That is exactly how my revenge is going to be so sensational, and how I'm going to show so clearly the resolution of my heart, in hating and leaving her, beautiful, attractive, and lovable as she is . . . But here she is.

(*Enter* LUCILE *and* NICOLE.)

NICOLE (*to* LUCILE): As for me, I was quite scandalized.

LUCILE: The only explanation, Nicole, is what I was telling you . . . But there he is.

CLÉONTE (*to* COVIELLE): I won't even speak to her.

COVIELLE: I'll do just like you.

LUCILE: What is it, Cléonte? What is the matter?

NICOLE: What's got into you, Covielle?

LUCILE: Why this distress of mind?

NICOLE: Why are you so sulky?

LUCILE: Are you dumb, Cléonte?

NICOLE: Has the cat got your tongue, Covielle?

CLÉONTE (*to* COVIELLE): What an outrageous way to act!

COVIELLE: Just a couple of Judases!

LUCILE (*to* CLÉONTE): I see that our recent encounte has troubled you.

CLÉONTE (*to* COVIELLE): Aha! She realizes what she has done.

NICOLE (*to* COVIELLE): Our greeting this morning has got your goat.

COVIELLE (*to* CLÉONTE): They've guessed where the shoe pinches.

LUCILE: Isn't it true, Cléonte, that that is the cause of your ill humor?

CLÉONTE: Yes, perfidious one, it is, since I must speak. And I have this information for you: that you won't laugh off your infidelity as you expect, that I intend to be the first to break with you, and that you won't have the satisfaction of dismissing me. No doubt I shall have trouble in conquering my love for you. That will cause me some pain; I shall suffer for a time. But I shall overmaster it, and I'll sooner pierce my own heart than be so weak as to return to you.

COVIELLE: With me, ditto.

LUCILE: That's a lot of fuss about nothing, Cléonte. I want to tell you why I avoided your greeting this morning.

CLÉONTE (*turning his back*): No, I don't want to hear a word.

NICOLE (*to* COVIELLE, *who turns his back*): I want to tell you the reason we went by so quick.

COVIELLE: I won't listen.

LUCILE: Know, then, that this morning—

CLÉONTE: No, I tell you.

NICOLE: Here are the facts—

COVIELLE: No, traitor.

LUCILE: Listen—

CLÉONTE: There's no use talking.

NICOLE: Let me tell you—

COVIELLE: I'm deaf.

LUCILE: Cléonte!

CLÉONTE: No.

LUCILE: Covielle!

COVIELLE: I won't!

LUCILE: But stop—

CLÉONTE: Rubbish!

NICOLE: Listen to me!

COVIELLE: Fiddlededee!

LUCILE: Just a moment!

CLÉONTE: Not at all!

NICOLE: Be patient.

COVIELLE: Applesauce!

LUCILE: Just two words—

CLÉONTE: No, it's all over.

NICOLE: Just one word—

COVIELLE: I'll have no truck with you.

LUCILE: Well, since you won't listen to me, think what you please, and do what you please.

(LUCILE *and* NICOLE, *who have been following* CLÉONTE *and* COVIELLE *about the stage, cease their pursuit. The business is reversed, the men interceding with the girls.*)

NICOLE: Since that's the way you behave, take it any way you like.

CLÉONTE (*to* LUCILE): You might as well tell me why you greeted me so coldly.

LUCILE: I don't feel like telling you now.

COVIELLE: Go on, tell us the story.

NICOLE: I don't want to any more.

CLÉONTE: Tell me—

LUCILE: No, I won't say a thing.

COVIELLE: Go ahead; speak up.

NICOLE: Not a word.

CLÉONTE: Please!

LUCILE: No, I tell you.

COVIELLE: Oh, be nice—

NICOLE: Nothing doing.

CLÉONTE: I beg you—

LUCILE: Let me alone.

COVIELLE: I beseech you—

NICOLE: Get out!

CLÉONTE: Lucile!

LUCILE: No.

COVIELLE: Nicole!

NICOLE: Not on your life.

CLÉONTE: In heaven's name!

LUCILE: I don't want to.

COVIELLE: Speak to me!

NICOLE: I won't.

CLÉONTE: Explain my doubts away!

LUCILE: I'll do nothing of the sort.

COVIELLE: Cure my ailing mind!

NICOLE: I don't feel like it.

CLÉONTE: Well, since you care so little about relieving my suffering and justifying yourself for the unworthy way you have treated my devotion, you see me, ingrate, for the last time. I am going far away to die of grief and love.

COVIELLE: And I'll be right behind you.

(COVIELLE *and* CLÉONTE *start for the exit.*)

LUCILE: Cléonte!

NICOLE: Covielle!

CLÉONTE: Eh?

COVIELLE: What is it?

LUCILE: Where are you going?

CLÉONTE: Where I told you.

COVIELLE: We're going to die!

LUCILE: You are going to die, Cléonte?

CLÉONTE: Yes, cruel beauty, since that is what you wish.

LUCILE: You mean I wish you to die?

CLÉONTE: Yes, you wish it.

LUCILE: Who told you so?

CLÉONTE: Don't you wish my death, if you refuse to clear up my suspicions?

LUCILE: Is that my fault? If you had been willing to listen to me, wouldn't I have told you that the occurrence this morning, which you're complaining about, was caused by the presence of my old aunt, who is convinced that the mere approach of a man dishonors a girl? She lectures us perpetually on this theme, and she pictures all men to us as devils we must flee from.

NICOLE: That's the secret of the whole business.

CLÉONTE: You aren't deceiving me, Lucile?

COVIELLE: You aren't trying to bamboozle me?

LUCILE: It's absolutely true.

NICOLE: That's just the way things happened.

COVIELLE (*to* CLÉONTE): Do we surrender to that?

CLÉONTE: Ah, Lucile, how a word from your lips can appease my heart's tumult! How readily one lets oneself be convinced by a loved one!

COVIELLE: How easily a man is hooked by those confounded creatures!

(*Enter* MADAME JOURDAIN.)

MME JOURDAIN: I am very glad to see you, Cléonte; you are here at just the right moment. My husband is coming; so take this chance to ask him for Lucile's hand.

CLÉONTE: Ah, madame, how sweet are these words! How they

flatter my desires! Could I receive a more delightful order? A more precious favor? (*Enter* MONSIEUR JOURDAIN) Sir, I did not wish to get any intermediary to make to you a request I have been long meditating. This request touches me so closely that I have chosen to undertake it myself. Without further preamble, I shall tell you that the honor of being your son-in-law would be a glorious favor which I beg you to bestow upon me.

M. JOURDAIN: Before giving you an answer, sir, I ask you to tell me if you are a gentleman.

CLÉONTE: Sir, most people do not hesitate long at such a question. The word is easily spoken. People assume the appellation without scruple, and common usage today seems to authorize its theft. But as for me, I freely grant, I have somewhat more delicate feelings on the subject. I think that any imposture is unworthy of a decent man, and I think it is mean and base to conceal the state to which it has pleased God to call us, and to adorn oneself in the world's eye with a stolen title, and to try to pass oneself off for what one is not. Certainly, I am the son of a line which has held honorable offices. In the army I acquired the merit of six years of service; and I am possessed of sufficient wealth to sustain a very respectable position in society. But with all that, I am unwilling to give myself a name which others, in my place, would feel justified in assuming; and I will tell you frankly that I am not a gentleman.

M. JOURDAIN: Shake hands, sir; my daughter is not for you.

CLÉONTE: What?

M. JOURDAIN: You are not a gentleman; you won't have my daughter.

MME JOURDAIN (*to* MONSIEUR JOURDAIN): What do you mean, with this gentleman business? Are we descended from the rib of Saint Louis?

M. JOURDAIN: Shut up, wife. I see what you're driving at.

MME JOURDAIN: Were our ancestors anything but good bourgeois?

M. JOURDAIN: Slander!

MME JOURDAIN: And wasn't your father a merchant, just like mine?

M. JOURDAIN: Drat the woman! She never misses a chance! If your father was a merchant, so much the worse for him; but as for my father, it's only the ignorant who say so. All I have to tell you is that I want a son-in-law who's a gentleman.

MME JOURDAIN: What your daughter needs is a husband who suits her, and she'd much better have an honorable man who is rich and handsome than some ugly gentleman without a penny.

NICOLE: That's right. There's the son of the gentleman in our village, he's the biggest booby and ninny ever seen.

M. JOURDAIN: Shut up, saucebox. You're always sticking your oar in the conversation. I have enough property for my daughter; all I need is honor; and I want to make her a marquise.

MME JOURDAIN: Marquise?

M. JOURDAIN: Yes, marquise.

MME JOURDAIN: Alas, God forbid!

M. JOURDAIN: It's something I've made up my mind to.

MME JOURDAIN: As for me, it's something I'll never consent to. Alliances with people above our own rank are always likely to have very unpleasant results. I don't want to have my son-in-law able to reproach my daughter for her parents, and I don't want her children to be ashamed to call me their grandma. If she should happen to come and visit me in her grand lady's carriage, and if by mistake she should fail to salute some one of the neighbors, you can imagine how they'd talk. "Take a look at that fine Madame la Marquise showing off," they'd say. "She's the daughter of Monsieur Jourdain, and when she was little, she was only too glad to play at being a fine lady. She wasn't always so high and mighty as she is now, and both her grandfathers sold dry goods besides the Porte Saint Innocent. They both piled up money for their children, and now perhaps they're paying dear for it in the next world; you don't get so rich by being honest." Well, I don't want that kind of talk to go on; and in short, I want a man who will feel under obligation to my daughter, and I want to be able to say to him: "Sit down there, my boy, and eat dinner with us."

M. JOURDAIN: Those views reveal a mean and petty mind, that wants to remain forever in its base condition. Don't answer back to me again. My daughter will be a marquise in spite of everyone; and if you get me angry, I'll make her a duchess. (*Exit* MONSIEUR JOURDAIN.)

MME JOURDAIN: Cléonte, don't lose courage yet. Lucile, come with me; and tell your father straight out that if you can't have him, you won't marry anybody.

(*Exit* MADAME JOURDAIN, LUCILE, *and* NICOLE.)

COVIELLE: You've got yourself into a nice mess with your high principles.

CLÉONTE: Well, what can I do? I have serious scruples on that point, that can't be overcome by the example others set us.

COVIELLE: It's foolish to take your scruples seriously with a man like that. Don't you see he's crazy? Would it have cost you anything to fall in with his fancies?

CLÉONTE: No doubt you're right. But I didn't think one had to give proofs of nobility to be the son-in-law of Monsieur Jourdain.

COVIELLE: Ha, ha, ha!

CLÉONTE: What are you laughing at?

COVIELLE: At an idea I had to take the fellow in, and get you what you want.

CLÉONTE: How's that?

COVIELLE: It's rather funny.

CLÉONTE: What is it, then?

COVIELLE: There's been a comic performance recently which would fit in perfectly here. I could work the troupe into a practical joke we could play on our joker. It would be rather on the burlesque side, perhaps; but with him you can go to any lengths; you don't have to be too fussy. He could act his own part in it perfectly; he'd play up to all the farce. I can get the actors, and they have the costumes all ready. Just let me manage it.

CLÉONTE: But tell me—

COVIELLE: I'll tell you everything. But's he's coming back; let's get out.

(*Exit* COVIELLE *and* CLÉONTE. *Enter* MONSIEUR JOURDAIN.)

M. JOURDAIN: What the devil! The only thing they have to reproach me for is my noble friends; and as for me, I think there's nothing so splendid as to associate with noble lords. They have the monopoly of honor and civility. I'd gladly give two fingers off my hand, to have been born a count or a marquis.

(*Enter a* LACKEY.)

LACKEY: Monsieur, here is Monsieur le Comte, and a lady on his arm.

M. JOURDAIN: Oh, good God! I have some orders to give. Tell them I'll be here right away.

(*Exit* MONSIEUR JOURDAIN. *Enter* DORANTE *and* DORIMÈNE.)

LACKEY: The master has just gone and said he'd be here right away.

DORANTE: Very well. (*Exit* LACKEY.)

DORIMÈNE: I don't know, Dorante; it seems to me rather peculiar, to let you bring me into a house where I don't know anyone.

DORANTE: Well, my dear lady, what place can my love find to entertain you properly, since, to avoid gossip, you won't let me use either your house or mine?

DORIMÈNE: Yes, but you don't say that I am becoming involved every day, by accepting such excessive evidences of your devotion. I do my best to refuse, but you wear down my resistance; and you show a polite obstinacy which makes me yield gently to anything you like. The frequent visits began it; and then the impassioned declarations; and they brought along the serenades and the parties; and then came the presents. I made opposition to everything; but you don't let yourself be discouraged, and step by step you are breaking down my resolutions. Really, I can no longer be quite sure of myself; and I think that in the end you will drag me into marriage, in spite of my reluctance.

DORANTE: My word, madame, you ought to be already in that happy state. You are a widow; you have no obligations to anyone but yourself. I am independent; and I love you more than my life. What obstacle is there to your making me immediately the happiest of men?

DORIMÈNE: Good heavens, Dorante, for a happy married life many qualities are necessary in both parties; and the most reasonable pair of people alive often have much trouble in forming a quite satisfactory union.

DORANTE: You are absurd, my dear, in imagining so many difficulties. From one unfortunate experience you should not draw conclusions about all the others.

DORIMÈNE: Anyway, I keep coming back to the same point. I am disturbed by the expenditures I see you making for me, and for two reasons: one, that they obligate me more than I like; and two, that I am sure—if you will forgive me—that you aren't making them without embarrassment; and I don't want that.

DORANTE: Ah, madame, they are mere trifles! It is not by such means—

DORIMÈNE: I know what I am saying. Among other things, the diamond you forced me to accept is of such value—

DORANTE: Oh, madame, please! Don't rate so highly something my love regards as all unworthy of you! And permit— But here comes the master of the house.

(*Enter* MONSIEUR JOURDAIN. *He makes two sweeping bows, stepping forward. He finds himself close to* DORIMÈNE.)

M. JOURDAIN: Stand back a little, madame.

DORIMÈNE: What?

M. JOURDAIN: One step back, please.

DORIMÈNE: What for?

M. JOURDAIN: Back up a little, for the third.

DORANTE: Madame, Monsieur Jourdain knows his etiquette.

M. JOURDAIN: Madame, it is a very great distinction to me to find myself so fortunate as to be so happy as to have the happiness that you have had the kindness to grant me the grace of doing me the honor of honoring me with the favor of your presence; and if I had also the merit of meriting a merit like yours, and if heaven . . . envious of my bliss . . . had granted me . . . the privilege of finding myself worthy . . . of the . . .

DORANTE: Monsieur Jourdain, that is enough. Madame does not care for high compliments, and she knows that you are an intelligent man. (*Aside to* DORIMÈNE) He is a good bourgeois, and rather ridiculous in his behavior, as you see.

DORIMÈNE (*aside to* DORANTE): That's not hard to recognize.

DORANTE: Madame, this is the best of my friends.

M. JOURDAIN: You do me too much honor.

DORANTE: A man of the world, absolutely.

DORIMÈNE: I have much esteem for him.

M. JOURDAIN: I have done nothing as yet, madame, to deserve such kindness.

DORANTE (*aside to* MONSIEUR JOURDAIN): Be sure, anyway, you don't mention the diamond ring you've given her.

M. JOURDAIN (*aside to* DORANTE): Couldn't I even ask her how she likes it?

DORANTE (*aside to* MONSIEUR JOURDAIN): Not by any means. That would be horribly vulgar. As a man of the world, you must act as if you hadn't made the present at all. (*To* DORIMÈNE) Madame, Monsieur Jourdain says he is overjoyed to see you in his house.

DORIMÈNE: He honors me deeply.

M. JOURDAIN (*aside to* DORANTE): How much obliged I am to you for speaking to her in such a way!

DORANTE (*aside to* MONSIEUR JOURDAIN): I had a dreadful time getting her to come here.

M. JOURDAIN (*aside to* DORANTE): I don't know how to thank you.

DORANTE: He says, madame, that he thinks you are the most beautiful person on earth.

DORIMÈNE: It is very kind of him.

M. JOURDAIN: Madame, the kindness is all on your side, and . . .

(*Enter a* LACKEY.)

DORANTE: Let's think about dinner.

LACKEY: Everything is ready, sir.

DORANTE: Then let's sit down; and send in the musicians.

(*Six* COOKS *enter dancing. They bring in a table covered with various dishes. This makes the third* Interlude.)

Act IV

After the Interlude, DORIMÈNE, DORANTE, MONSIEUR JOURDAIN, *two* MALE SINGERS, *a* WOMAN SINGER, *and several* LACKEYS *remain on the stage.*

DORIMÈNE: Why, Dorante! What a magnificent repast!

M. JOURDAIN: You are joking, madame. I wish it were more worthy of being offered to you.

(DORIMÈNE, DORANTE, MONSIEUR JOURDAIN *and the* SINGERS *sit at table.*)

DORANTE: Monsieur Jourdain is quite right, madame, in speaking in that way, and he puts me under a deep obligation by doing so well the honors of his house. I agree with him that the repast is unworthy of you. As it was I who ordered it, and as I have not the finesse of some of our friends on this subject, you will not find here a culinary symphony, and you will perhaps notice some gastronomic incongruities, some solecisms of good taste. If Damis had had a hand in it, the rules would be strictly observed; you would recognize a mingling of elegance and erudition. He would not fail to call your attention to the dishes he would serve; he would make you applaud his high capacity in the science of cookery. He would mention the rolls, cooked golden-brown on the hearth's edge with a uniform crust, crumbling delicately under the tooth; the wine with a velvet bouquet, somewhat young and saucy, but not to the point of impudence; a breast of lamb pinked with parsley; a loin of riverside veal from Normandy, no longer than that, white, dainty, like almond paste on the tongue; partridges prepared with a special spice and mushroom sauce; and for his crowning triumph, a young fat turkey flanked by squabs, crested with white onions blended with chicory, swimming in a pearl bouillon. But for my part, I must admit my ignorance; and as Monsieur Jourdain has very well said, I could wish that the repast was more worthy of being offered you.

DORIMÈNE: I reply to this compliment by devouring the dinner as I do.

M. JOURDAIN: Oh, what beautiful hands!

DORIMÈNE: The hands are ordinary hands, Monsieur Jourdain; but you notice the diamond, which is indeed beautiful.

M. JOURDAIN: I, Madame? God forbid that I should mention it. That would not be the action of a man of the world. The diamond is nothing much.

DORIMÈNE: You are hard to please.

M. JOURDAIN: You are too kind—

DORANTE (*with a cautionary gesture to* MONSIEUR JOURDAIN): Come, some wine for Monsieur Jourdain, and for our musical guests, who will give us the pleasure of singing us a drinking song.

DORIMÈNE: There's no better seasoning for good cheer than to combine it with music. I am being magnificently regaled here.

M. JOURDAIN: Madame, it is not—

DORANTE: Monsieur Jourdain, let us lend an ear to the musicians; their songs will express our feelings better than we could in words.

(*The* SINGERS *take glasses in hand, and sing two drinking songs, accompanied by the orchestra.*)

DUET

Phyllis, a drop of wine, to make the moment pass!
How daintily your hand holds the delightful glass!
Ah, Phyllis, you and wine, you lend each other arms,
For wine and love together increase each other's charms.
So you and wine and I, come let us vow to be
  A constant trinity.
The wine that wets your lip itself doth beautify;
And yet your lovely lip is lovelier thereby.
The lips, they bid me drink; the wine, it bids me kiss!
Ah, what intoxication can ever equal this!
So you and wine and I, come let us vow to be
  A constant trinity.

DUET

Drink, my comrades, drink;
  The hour's propitious.
Let your glasses clink;
  The wine's delicious.
Too swift our steps we bend
  To the dark shore,
Where love is at an end,
  And we drink no more.
The scholars can't agree
  Where lives the soul;
By our philosophy
  It's in the bowl.
Not glory, wealth, nor wit
  Chase care away;
But wine doth still permit
  Man to be gay.

CHORUS

Come, wine for all, my lads; and never cease to pour,
And pour and pour again, while men can ask for more!

DORIMÈNE: That couldn't be better sung; it's really lovely.

M. JOURDAIN: I can see something even lovelier around here.

DORIMÈNE: Oho! Monsieur Jourdain is more gallant than I thought.

DORANTE: Why, madame, what do you take Monsieur Jourdain for?

M. JOURDAIN: I wish she would take me for something I could suggest.

DORIMÈNE: You're still at it?

DORANTE (*to* DORIMÈNE): You don't know him.

M. JOURDAIN: She can know me better whenever she likes.

DORIMÈNE: Oh, I give up!

DORANTE: He always has an answer ready. But you haven't noticed, madame, that Monsieur Jourdain eats all the bits that your spoon has touched in the serving dish.

DORIMÈNE: Monsieur Jourdain is a man who ravishes me.

M. JOURDAIN: If I could ravish your heart, I would be—

(*Enter* MADAME JOURDAIN.)

MME JOURDAIN: Aha! I find some fine company here, and I can see that I wasn't expected. So, it's for this pretty business, my good husband, that you were so anxious to send me off to dine with my sister? I've just seen a kind of a theatre downstairs; and here I see a kind of a wedding feast. So that's how you spend your money? And that's the way you put on a big party for ladies in my absence, and you give them music and a play, while you send me to Jericho?

DORANTE: What do you mean, Madame Jourdain? You must have hallucinations, to get it into your head that your husband is spending his own money, and that he's the one who is giving the party for Madame. Let me inform you that I'm footing the bill. He is merely lending me his house; you ought to be more careful about what you say.

M. JOURDAIN: Yes, insolence! It's Monsieur le Comte who is giving all this to Madame, who is a lady of quality. He does me the honor to borrow my house, and to ask me to join him.

MME JOURDAIN: Stuff and nonsense! I know what I know.

DORANTE: Madame Jourdain, you need some new spectacles.

MME JOURDAIN: I don't need any spectacles at all, monsieur; I can see all right without them. I've known what's up for quite some time now; I'm not such a fool. It's a very cheap business for you, a great lord, to encourage my husband's follies the way you're doing. And you, madame, for a great lady, it's neither pretty nor decent for you to bring trouble into a family, and to allow my husband to be in love with you.

DORIMÈNE: What is the meaning of all this? Dorante, you're unpardonable, to expose me to the delusions of this fantastic creature. (*She starts to leave.*)

DORANTE (*following* DORIMÈNE): Madame, look here! Madame, where are you running off to? (*Exit* DORIMÈNE.)

M. JOURDAIN: Madame! . . . Monsieur le Comte, make my apologies to her, and try to bring her back. (*Exit* DORANTE. *To* MADAME JOURDAIN) Impudence! These are nice tricks of yours! You come and insult me before everybody, and you drive people of quality out of the house!

MME JOURDAIN: I don't care a straw for their quality.

M. JOURDAIN: You cursèd troublemaker, I don't know why I don't crack your skull with the leftovers of the dinner you ruined!

(*The* LACKEYS *carry out the table and dishes.*)

MME JOURDAIN: I don't care a pin. I'm defending my rights; and every woman will be on my side. (*She starts for the door.*)

M. JOURDAIN: You do well to escape my anger. (*Exit* MADAME JOURDAIN) What a time she picked to interrupt! I was just in the mood to say some very neat things. I never felt myself so bubbling over with inspiration . . . But what's all this?

(*Enter* COVIELLE, *wearing an Oriental costume and a long beard.*)

COVIELLE: Monsieur, I don't know if I have the honor of being known to you.

M. JOURDAIN: No, sir.

COVIELLE: I last saw you when you weren't any bigger than that. (*Holds his hand a foot from the floor.*)

M. JOURDAIN: Me?

COVIELLE: Yes, you were the prettiest child ever seen, and all the ladies would take you in their arms to kiss you.

M. JOURDAIN: To kiss me!

COVIELLE: Yes. I was a great friend of your late honorable father.

M. JOURDAIN: My late honorable father?

COVIELLE: Yes. He was a very worthy gentleman.

M. JOURDAIN: What did you say?

COVIELLE: I said he was a very worthy gentleman.

M. JOURDAIN: My father?

COVIELLE: Yes.

M. JOURDAIN: You knew him well?

COVIELLE: Certainly.

M. JOURDAIN: And you knew him to be a gentleman?

COVIELLE: Of course.

M. JOURDAIN: The world is certainly a funny place!

COVIELLE: How is that?

M. JOURDAIN: There are some stupid people who try to tell me he was a merchant.

COVIELLE: He, a merchant? It's pure slander; he never was anything of the sort. The fact is, he was very obliging, very helpful by nature. And as he was a remarkable judge of woolens, he used to go here and there and pick them out, and have them brought to his house; and then he would give them to his friends—for money.

M. JOURDAIN: I am delighted to know you, and to have your testimony that my father was a gentleman.

COVIELLE: I will testify to the fact before everyone.

M. JOURDAIN: That's very kind. And what brings you here?

COVIELLE: Since the time when I knew your late honorable father, that worthy gentleman, I have been roving the wide world.

M. JOURDAIN: The wide world!

COVIELLE: Yes.

M. JOURDAIN: That must be quite a trip.

COVIELLE: It is, certainly. I returned from my far journeys only four days ago; and because of my interest in everything that concerns you, I have come to announce to you some excellent news.

M. JOURDAIN: What's that?

COVIELLE: You know that the son of the Grand Turk is here?

M. JOURDAIN: Me? No.

COVIELLE: Really! He has come with a magnificent retinue. Everyone goes to see him; and he was received in this country as a noble lord of great importance.

M. JOURDAIN: Bless me! I didn't know that.

COVIELLE: And what concerns you, to your great advantage, is that he has fallen in love with your daughter.

M. JOURDAIN: The son of the Grand Turk?

COVIELLE: Yes. And he wants to be your son-in-law.

M. JOURDAIN: My son-in-law? The son of the Grand Turk?

COVIELLE: The son of the Grand Turk wants to be your son-in-law. I went to call on him; and as I understand his language perfectly, he said to me, after discussing various matters: "Acciam croc soler ouch alla moustaph gidelum amanahem varahini oussere carbulath?" [4] That is, "Have you by chance seen a beautiful girl, the daughter of Monsieur Jourdain, a Parisian gentleman?"

M. JOURDAIN: The son of the Grand Turk said that about me?

COVIELLE: Yes. When I replied that I had a particular

[4] [Molière's Turkish is a mingling of genuine Turkish, Arabic, and Hebrew with mere gibberish.—Trans.]

acquaintance with you, and that I had chanced to see your daughter, he said: "Ah! marababa sahem!" That means: "Oh, how much I love her!"

M. JOURDAIN: "Marababa sahem" means "Oh, how much I love her"?

COVIELLE: Yes.

M. JOURDAIN: Bless my soul, I'm glad you told me, for personally I would never have imagined that "marababa sahem" could mean "Oh, how much I love her." Turkish is certainly a wonderful language.

COVIELLE: More wonderful than you would think. Do you know what "cacaracamouchen" means?

M. JOURDAIN: "Cacaracamouchen"? No.

COVIELLE: That means "my darling."

M. JOURDAIN: "Cacaracamouchen" means "my darling"?

COVIELLE: Yes.

M. JOURDAIN: That's really marvelous. "Cacaracamouchen; my darling." Can you imagine? You amaze me.

COVIELLE: In short, to fulfill the purpose of my embassy, he wants to ask the hand of your daughter in marriage. And to have a father-in-law of a rank suitable for him, he wants to make you a mamamouchi, which is a certain high dignity of his own country.

M. JOURDAIN: A mamamouchi?

COVIELLE: Yes, a mamamouchi. That is to say, in our language, a paladin. The paladins, they were those old-time—well, in short, paladins. There is nothing nobler than that anywhere. You will be the equal of the greatest lords on earth.

M. JOURDAIN: The son of the Grand Turk honors me very profoundly. I beg you to take me to his presence so that I can express my thanks.

COVIELLE: It's unnecessary. He is coming here.

M. JOURDAIN: He's coming here?

COVIELLE: Yes. And he's bringing everything needful for the ceremony of your ennoblement.

M. JOURDAIN: He certainly works fast.

COVIELLE: His love is such that he can bear no delay.

M. JOURDAIN: There's just one awkward thing. My daughter is very stubborn, and she's gone and set her mind on a certain Cléonte, and she swears she won't marry anyone else but him.

COVIELLE: She will change her views when she sees the son of the Grand Turk. And also—a very remarkable fact—the son of the Grand Turk has a striking resemblance to Cléonte. I've just seen this Cléonte; I had him pointed out to me. Her love for the one may easily shift to the other; and . . . But I think I hear him coming. Indeed, here he is.

(*Enter* CLÉONTE *in Turkish costume, with three* PAGES *carrying his train.*)

CLÉONTE: Ambousahim oqui boraf, Jordina salamalequi!

COVIELLE (*to* MONSIEUR JOURDAIN): That is, "Monsieur Jourdain, may your heart be all year long like a rosebush in bloom!" That is a courteous expression in those countries.

M. JOURDAIN: I am the very humble servant of his Turkish Highness.

COVIELLE: Carigar camboto oustin moraf.

CLÉONTE: Oustin yoc catamalequi basum base alla moran!

COVIELLE: He says: "May Heaven give you the strength of lions and the prudence of serpents!"

M. JOURDAIN: His Turkish Highness does me too much honor, and I wish him every kind of prosperity.

COVIELLE: Ossa binamen sadoc baballý oracaf ouram.

CLÉONTE: Bel-men.

COVIELLE: He says you must go with him right away to make preparations for the ceremony, and afterwards you'll see your daughter and conclude the marriage.

M. JOURDAIN: All that in two words?

COVIELLE: Yes, the Turkish language is like that. It says a great deal in very few words. You go where he wants you to, quickly.

(*Exit* MONSIEUR JOURDAIN, CLÉONTE, *and* PAGES.)

COVIELLE: Ha, ha, ha! That was a good one! What a dupe he is! He couldn't play his part better if he'd learned it by heart! Ha, ha, ha! (*Enter* DORANTE) I beg you, sir, to help us out in a little performance we're staging.

DORANTE: Ha, ha! Covielle, I would never have recognized you! What kind of getup is this?

COVIELLE: Well, take a look. Ha, ha!

DORANTE: What are you laughing at?

COVIELLE: At something, sir, which deserves a laugh.

DORANTE: How's that?

COVIELLE: You'd never guess, sir, the trick we're playing on Monsieur Jourdain, to induce him to give his daughter to my master.

DORANTE: I can't guess the trick, but I can guess that it is pretty sure to work, since you are organizing it.

COVIELLE: Evidently, sir, you are a judge of character.

DORANTE: Tell me the story.

COVIELLE: Be so kind as to come to one side, and give room to what I see coming in. You will see a part of the story, and I will tell you the rest.

(*The Turkish ceremony of the ennobling of* MONSIEUR JOURDAIN, *performed with music and dance, forms the fourth* Interlude.

Six DANCING TURKS *enter gravely, two by two, to the full orchestra. They carry three long carpets, with which they make various evolutions, and finally raise them high. The* TURKISH MUSICIANS *and other instrumentalists pass beneath. Four* DERVISHES, *accompanying the* MUFTI, *or legal-religious dignitary, close the procession.*

The TURKS *spread the carpets on the ground and kneel upon them. The* MUFTI, *standing in the middle, makes an invocation with contortions and grimaces, turning up his face, and wiggling his hands outward from his head, like wings. The* TURKS *bow forward, touching their foreheads to the floor, singing "Ali"; they resume the kneeling position, singing "Allah." They continue thus to the end of the invocation; then they all stand, singing "Allah akbar."*

Then the DERVISHES *bring before the* MUFTI MONSIEUR JOURDAIN, *dressed in Turkish costume, clean-shaven, without turban or sword. The* MUFTI *sings in solemn tones.*)

MUFTI:

Se ti sabir,
Ti respondir;
Se non sabir,
Tazir, tazir.

Mi star muphty;
Ti qui star ti?
Non intendir:
Tazir, tazir.[5]

(*Two* DERVISHES *lead out* MONSIEUR JOURDAIN. The MUFTI *questions the* TURKS *as to the candidate's religion.*)

MUFTI:

Dice, Turque, qui star quista?
Anabatista, anabatista? [6]

TURKS:

Ioc.[7]

MUFTI:

Zwinglista? [8]

TURKS:

Ioc.

MUFTI:

Coffita? [9]

[5] ["If you know, answer; if you don't know, keep still, keep still. I am a mufti; you, who are you? You don't understand; keep still, keep still." Most of the language of the Turkish ceremony is *lingua franca,* once used for commercial and diplomatic purposes around the Mediterranean, still known to sailors and harbor men. It is a blend mostly of French, Spanish, Italian, and Arabic. All grammatical forms are simplified; verbs have only the infinitive form. (A sort of Basic Romance.) Any Frenchman, or Spaniard or Italian, could understand the Mufti well enough.—Trans.]

[6] ["Tell me, Turks, what is this man? An Anabaptist?"—Trans.]

[7] ["No." An authentic Turkish word.—Trans.]

[8] [Follower of Zwingli, Protestant reformer.—Trans.]

[9] [Member of the Coptic Church.—Trans.]

TURKS:

Ioc.

MUFTI:

Hussita? Morista? Fronista? [10]

TURKS:

Ioc. Ioc. Ioc.

MUFTI:

Ioc, Ioc, Ioc!
Star pagana?

TURKS:

Ioc.

MUFTI:

Luterana?

TURKS:

Ioc.

MUFTI:

Puritana?

TURKS:

Ioc.

MUFTI:

Bramina? Moffina? Zurina? [11]

TURKS:

Ioc. Ioc. Ioc.

MUFTI:

Ioc. Ioc. Ioc.
Mahametana? Mahametana?

TURKS:

Hey valla! Hey valla! [12]

MUFTI:

Como chamara? Como chamara? [13]

TURKS:

Giourdina, Giourdina.

[10] [A Hussite, follower of Bohemian reformer John Huss. The meaning of the other two words is obscure.—Trans.]

[11] [Brahmin; "Moffina" and "Zurina" are apparently invented words.—Trans.]

[12] ["Yes, by Allah!" (Arabic.)—Trans.]

[13] ["What is his name?"—Trans.]

MUFTI:

Giourdina! (*He leaps high, and peers in all directions*)
Giourdina? Giourdina? Giourdina?

TURKS:

Giourdina! Giourdina! Giourdina!

MUFTI:

Mahameta per Giourdina
Mi pregar sera e matina;
Voler far un paladina
De Giourdina, de Giourdina.
Dar turbanta e dar scarcina
Con galera e brigantina
Per deffender Palestina.
Mahameta per Giourdina
Mi pregar sera e mattina.[14]
(*Questioning the* TURKS)
Star bon Turca Giourdina?
Star bon Turca Giourdina?

TURKS:

Hey valla, hey valla!
Hey valla, hey valla!

MUFTI (*dancing*):

Hu la ba ba la chou ba la ba ba la da!

(*The* MUFTI *exits; the* TURKS *dance and sing.*)

TURKS:

Hu la ba ba la chou ba la ba ba la da!

(*The* MUFTI *returns, wearing an enormous ceremonial turban, adorned with four or five rows of blazing candles. Two* DERVISHES *accompany him, wearing pointed hats, also adorned with lighted candles. They solemnly bear the Koran. The two other* DERVISHES *conduct* MONSIEUR JOURDAIN, *who is terrified by the ceremony. They make him kneel down with his back to the* MUFTI: *then they*

[14] ["I pray to Mahomet for Jourdain night and morning. I want to make a paladin of Jourdain, of Jourdain. Give a turban and a scimitar, with a galley and a brigantine, to defend Palestine. I pray to Mahomet for Jourdain night and morning."—Trans.]

make him bend forward till his hands rest on the floor. They put the Koran on his back, which serves as a reading desk for the MUFTI. *The* MUFTI *makes a burlesque invocation, scowling and opening and shutting his mouth without uttering a word. Then he speaks vehemently, now muttering, now shouting with terrifying passion, slapping his sides as if to force out his words, occasionally striking the Koran, turning its leaves briskly. He finally raises his hands and exclaims loudly: "Hou!"* [15] *During this invocation, the* TURKS *sing, "Hou, hou, hou!" bending forward three times, then straightening up, singing, "Hou, hou, hou!" They continue doing so throughout the* MUFTI*'s invocation. After the invocation, the* DERVISHES *remove the Koran from* MONSIEUR JOURDAIN*'s back. He exclaims, "Ouf!" with relief. The* DERVISHES *raise him to his feet.)*

MUFTI (*to* MONSIEUR JOURDAIN):

Ti non star furba? [16]

TURKS:

No, no, no.

MUFTI:

Non star forfanta? [17]

TURKS:

No, no, no.

MUFTI (*to the* TURKS):

Donar turbanta, donar turbanta.[18]

(*Exit the* MUFTI. *The* TURKS *repeat the* MUFTI*'s words, and with song and dance present the turban to* MONSIEUR JOURDAIN. *The* MUFTI *re-enters with a scimitar, which he presents to* MONSIEUR JOURDAIN.)

MUFTI:

Ti star nobile, non star fabola.
Pigliar schiabola.[19]

[15] [He, or God, in Arabic.—Trans.]
[16] ["You aren't an evildoer?"—Trans.]
[17] ["You aren't a rascal?"—Trans.]
[18] ["Give the turban."—Trans.]
[19] ["You're a noble, it's no lie. Take this sword."—Trans.]

(*Exit the* MUFTI. *The* TURKS *draw their scimitars and repeat the* MUFTI*'s words. Six of them dance around* MONSIEUR JOURDAIN, *feigning to strike him with their weapons. The* MUFTI *returns.*)

MUFTI:

Dara, dara bastonara, bastonara, bastonara.[20]

(*Exit the* MUFTI. *The* TURKS *repeat his words, beating* MONSIEUR JOURDAIN *to music. Re-enter the* MUFTI.)

MUFTI:

Non tener honta;
Questa star l'ultima affronta.[21]

(*The* TURKS *repeat the* MUFTI*'s words. The* MUFTI, *leaning on the* DERVISHES, *makes another invocation, to the full orchestra. Evidently fatigued by the ceremony, he is respectfully supported by the* DERVISHES. *The* TURKS, *leaping, dancing, and singing around the* MUFTI, *conduct him offstage to the sound of Turkish musical instruments.*)

Act V

After the Interlude, *all retire except* MONSIEUR JOURDAIN. *Enter* MADAME JOURDAIN.

MME JOURDAIN: Lord have mercy on us! What's all this? What a figure of fun! You're dressing up for Hallowe'en at this time of year? Tell me, what's going on? Who rigged you up that way?

M. JOURDAIN: Insolent creature, to talk that way to a mamamouchi!

MME JOURDAIN: How's that?

M. JOURDAIN: Yes, now you've got to show me some respect. I've just been made a mamamouchi.

MME JOURDAIN: What do you mean with your mamamouchi?

[20] ["Give him a beating."—Trans.]
[21] ["Feel no shame; this is the last affront."—Trans.]

M. JOURDAIN: Mamamouchi, I tell you! I'm a mamamouchi!

MME JOURDAIN: What kind of a creature is that?

M. JOURDAIN: Mamamouchi! That is, in our language, a paladin.

MME JOURDAIN: Aballadin'! You're going to go around aballadin', at your age?

M. JOURDAIN: Such ignorance! I said a paladin. That's a dignity that just has been conferred upon me, with due ceremony.

MME JOURDAIN: What kind of ceremony?

M. JOURDAIN: Mahameta per Giourdina!

MME JOURDAIN: What does that mean?

M. JOURDAIN: Giourdina, that is, Jourdain.

MME JOURDAIN: Well, what of it, Jourdain?

M. JOURDAIN: Voler far un paladina de Giourdina.

MME JOURDAIN: What?

M. JOURDAIN: Dar turbanta con galera.

MME JOURDAIN: What sense is there in that?

M. JOURDAIN: Per deffender palestina.

MME JOURDAIN: What are you trying to say?

M. JOURDAIN: Dara dara bastonara.

MME JOURDAIN: What's all that gibberish?

M. JOURDAIN: Non tener honta; questa star l'ultima affronta.

MME JOURDAIN: What's the idea, anyway?

M. JOURDAIN (*singing and dancing*): Hou la ba ba la chou ba la ba ba la da.

MME JOURDAIN: Alas, dear God! My husband has gone crazy!

M. JOURDAIN: Silence, insolent woman! Show proper respect to a noble mamamouchi. (*Exit* MONSIEUR JOURDAIN.)

MME JOURDAIN: How has he gone and lost his wits? I must keep him from going out. Oh, dear, oh, dear, this is the last straw! There's nothing but trouble everywhere!

(*Exit* MADAME JOURDAIN. *After a moment, enter* DORANTE *and* DORIMÈNE.)

DORANTE: Yes, madame, you will see a very amusing sight. I don't think you will ever find a crazier man than he is. And besides, madame, we must try to aid Cléonte's love affair, and fall in with his masquerade. He's a very decent fellow, who deserves our interest and help.

DORIMÈNE: I think very highly of him; he merits good fortune in his enterprise.

DORANTE: Besides, we have a ballet due us. We shouldn't let it be wasted. And I want to see if my scheme for the performance works out well.

DORIMÈNE: I've just seen some of the preparations; they are magnificent. And I must tell you, Dorante, that I simply cannot allow this sort of thing. I must put a stop to your lavishness; and to check your mad spending of money on me, I have decided to marry you very soon. That's the best solution; with marriage, all the extravagances stop.

DORANTE: Ah, madame, is it possible that you have made so welcome a resolution in my favor?

DORIMÈNE: It's only to prevent you from ruining yourself. Otherwise, I can see that soon you wouldn't have a penny.

DORANTE: What an obligation I have, my dear, to your concern for preserving my property! It is all yours, and my heart is too; you can do with them what you will.

DORIMÈNE: I shall take proper care of both of them . . . But here is our good man; he certainly looks extraordinary.

(*Enter* MONSIEUR JOURDAIN.)

DORANTE: Sir, madame and I have come to render homage to your new dignity, and to felicitate you on the proposed marriage of your daughter to the son of the Grand Turk.

M. JOURDAIN (*after making obeisances in the Turkish style*): Sir, I wish you the strength of serpents and the wisdom of lions.

DORIMÈNE: I am happy to be one of the first, Monsieur, to congratulate you upon the high degree of glory you have attained.

M. JOURDAIN: Madame, I wish your rosebush may be in bloom all year long. I am infinitely obliged to you for your sympathetic interest in the honors which have come to me, and I take great joy in seeing you here again, so that I may make my very humble apologies for my wife's excesses.

DORIMÈNE: It was nothing at all; I can readily excuse her impulse. Your heart is no doubt precious to her; it is not strange that the possession of a man like you may expose her to some alarms.

M. JOURDAIN: The possession of my heart is entirely yours to dispose of.

DORANTE: You see, madame, that Monsieur Jourdain is not one of those people who are dazzled by prosperity. Even in his glory, he does not forget his old friends.

DORIMÈNE: That is the character of a really noble soul.

DORANTE: But where is His Turkish Highness? As your friends, we should like to pay him our respects.

M. JOURDAIN: There he is, coming now. I have sent for my daughter, in order to give him her hand.

(*Enter* CLÉONTE, *in Turkish costume.*)

DORANTE (*to* CLÉONTE): Sir, as friends of your honorable father-in-law, we have come to make obeisance to Your Highness, and to respectfully assure Your Highness of our humble service.

M. JOURDAIN: Where is the interpreter, to tell him who you are, and make him understand what you are saying? You'll see that he'll answer you; he speaks Turkish wonderfully. Hello, hello! Where the deuce did he go to? (*To* CLÉONTE) Strouf, strif, strof, straf. This gentleman is a *grande segnore, grande segnore, grande segnore;* and Madame is a *granda dama, granda dama.* (*Recognizing that he fails to make himself understood*) Oh, dear! Sir, him French mamamouchi; Madame here, French female mamamouchi. I can't make it any clearer . . . Good! Here's the interpreter! (*Enter* COVIELLE) Where did you get off to? We can't say a thing without you. Just tell him that the gentleman and lady are persons of high rank, who have come to salute him, as my friends, and to assure him of their regards. (*To* DORIMÈNE *and* DORANTE) You'll see how he'll answer you.

COVIELLE: Alabala crociam acci boram alabamen.

CLÉONTE: Catalequi tubal ourin soter amalouchan.

M. JOURDAIN: You see?

COVIELLE: He says: "May the rain of prosperity forever sprinkle the garden of your family."

M. JOURDAIN: Didn't I tell you he spoke Turkish?

DORANTE: It's certainly amazing.

(*Enter* LUCILE.)

M. JOURDAIN: Come here, daughter, come here. Come and give your hand to the gentleman, who does you the honor of asking to marry you.

LUCILE: Father! How you're gotten up! Are you acting in a play?

M. JOURDAIN: No, no; it isn't a play. It's a very serious matter, and one that does you the greatest honor you could conceive. Here is the husband I'm giving you.

LUCILE: Husband—to me, Father?

M. JOURDAIN: Yes, to you. Go on, shake hands with him, and thank heaven for your good fortune.

LUCILE: I don't want to get married.

M. JOURDAIN: Well, I want you to, and I'm your father.

LUCILE: Well, I won't.

M. JOURDAIN: Oh, talk, talk! Come on, I tell you. Here, give me your hand.

LUCILE: No, Father, I have told you, no power on earth can force me to take any other husband than Cléonte; and I'll go to any lengths, rather than— (*She recognizes* CLÉONTE) It is true that you are my father, and I owe you entire obedience, and it is your right to dispose of me according to your decision.

M. JOURDAIN: Ah, I'm delighted to see you recognize your duty so quickly. It's always a pleasure to have an obedient daughter.

(*Enter* MADAME JOURDAIN.)

MME JOURDAIN: What's this? What in the world is up? They say you're trying to marry your daughter to a circus clown!

M. JOURDAIN: Will you shut up, impertinence? You always come sticking your oar into everything, and there's no way to teach you to be reasonable.

MME JOURDAIN: You're the one there's no getting any sense into; you go from one crazy fool trick to another. What's your idea? And what are you trying to do with this tomfool marriage?

M. JOURDAIN: I want to marry our daughter to the son of the Grand Turk.

MME JOURDAIN: The son of the Grand Turk!

M. JOURDAIN: Yes. You can have the interpreter there pay him your compliments for you.

MME JOURDAIN: I don't care a hoot for any interpreter, and I'll tell him myself to his face that he won't have my daughter.

M. JOURDAIN: Once more, will you shut up?

DORANTE: What, Madame Jourdain, you are opposing such a happy opportunity as this? You refuse His Turkish Highness for a son-in-law?

MME JOURDAIN: My good sir, mind your own business.

DORIMÈNE: It's a glorious honor, hardly to be turned down.

MME JOURDAIN: Madame, I shall beg you also not to interfere in matters with which you have no concern.

DORANTE: It is our friendly feeling for you which makes us take an interest in your welfare.

MME JOURDAIN: I don't need any of your friendly feelings.

DORANTE: But your daughter has yielded to her father's wishes.

MME JOURDAIN: My daughter consents to marry a Turk?

DORANTE: Certainly.

MME JOURDAIN: She can forget Cléonte?

DORANTE: Ah, well, what won't a girl do to be a great lady?

MME JOURDAIN: I would strangle her with my own hands, if she ever did a trick like that.

M. JOURDAIN: Talk, talk, talk! I tell you that this marriage will take place.

MME JOURDAIN: And I tell you it won't.

M. JOURDAIN: Gabble, gabble, gabble!

LUCILE: Mother!

MME JOURDAIN: You're a nasty girl!

M. JOURDAIN (*to* MADAME JOURDAIN): You're scolding her because she obeys me?

MME JOURDAIN: Yes; she belongs to me as well as to you.

COVIELLE (*to* MADAME JOURDAIN): Madame!

MME JOURDAIN: What are you trying to tell me, you?

COVIELLE: Just a word—

MME JOURDAIN: I don't want to hear any "just a word" out of you.

COVIELLE (*to* MONSIEUR JOURDAIN): Sir, if she will listen to me a moment in private, I promise you I'll make her consent to your desires.

MME JOURDAIN: I won't consent.

COVIELLE: But just listen to me!

MME JOURDAIN: I won't.

M. JOURDAIN: Listen to him!

MME JOURDAIN: I don't want to listen to him.

M. JOURDAIN: He will tell you—

MME JOURDAIN: I don't want him to tell me anything.

M. JOURDAIN: How obstinate women are! Will it do you any harm to hear what he says?

COVIELLE (*to* MADAME JOURDAIN): Just listen to me; and afterwards you can do whatever you please.

MME JOURDAIN: Well, all right. What?

COVIELLE (*to* MADAME JOURDAIN): We've been trying to signal to you for the last half-hour. Don't you see that we're doing all this just to fall in with your husband's mania, and we're fooling him under this disguise, and it's Cléonte himself who is the son of the Grand Turk?

MME JOURDAIN: Aha!

COVIELLE: And I'm Covielle!

MME JOURDAIN (*aside to* COVIELLE): Oh, well, in that case, I surrender.

COVIELLE: Don't give anything away.

MME JOURDAIN (*to* MONSIEUR JOURDAIN): Well, all right. I consent to the marriage.

M. JOURDAIN: Ah, now everybody's reasonable at last. You wouldn't listen to me. But I knew very well he would explain to you what it means to be the son of the Grand Turk.

MME JOURDAIN: He's explained it to me very nicely, and I'm satisfied. Let's send out for a notary.

DORANTE: That's very well said. And Madame Jourdain, in order that you may have your mind entirely at ease, and dismiss any suspicion you may have conceived about your husband, Madame Dorimène and I shall make use of the same notary for our own marriage contract.

MME JOURDAIN: I consent to that too.

M. JOURDAIN (*aside to* DORANTE): That's just to throw dust in her eyes, I suppose?

DORANTE (*aside to* MONSIEUR JOURDAIN): It's a good thing to play her along with this pretense.

M. JOURDAIN (*aside*): Good, good. (*Aloud*) Have the notary sent for, right away.

DORANTE: While we're waiting for him to come and draft the contracts, let's have a look at our ballet. It will be a nice entertainment for His Turkish Highness.

M. JOURDAIN: A very good idea. Let's take our seats.

MME JOURDAIN: How about Nicole?

M. JOURDAIN: I'll give her to the interpreter; and my wife to anyone that wants her.

COVIELLE: Sir, I thank you. (*Aside*) If anyone can find a madder madman, I'll go to Rome and tell it to the world. (*The play concludes with the Ballet of the Nations. As this has nothing to do with the previous action and characters, it is here omitted.*)

Phaedra

by RACINE

TRANSLATED BY *Kenneth Muir*

PREFACE

Here is another tragedy of which the subject is taken from Euripides. Although I have followed a slightly different road from that author's for the conduct of the action, I have not scrupled to enrich my play with all that seemed to me most striking in his. While I owe only the single idea of the character of Phaedra to him, I could say that I owe to him that which I could reasonably show on the stage. I am not surprised that this character had so great a success in the time of Euripides, and that it has also succeeded so well in our century, since it has all the qualities which Aristotle demanded in the heroes of a tragedy, and which are proper to excite pity and terror. Indeed, Phaedra is neither entirely guilty, nor entirely innocent; she is involved, by her fate and the wrath of the gods, in an unlawful passion, of which she is the first to feel horror; she makes every effort to overcome it; she prefers to let herself die rather than to confess it to anyone; and when she is forced to discover it, she speaks of it with a confusion that makes plain that her crime is rather a punishment of the gods than a movement of her will.

I have even taken care to render her a little less odious than she is in the tragedies of the ancients, where she resolves of herself to accuse Hippolytus. I thought that the calumny was too base and evil to put into the mouth of a princess who elsewhere displays such noble and virtuous sentiments. This baseness appeared to me more suitable to a nurse, who could have more servile inclinations, and who nevertheless undertakes this false accusation only to save the life and honor of her mistress. Phaedra consents to it only because she is in such agitation that she is beside herself; and she comes a moment after in the action to justify innocence and declare the truth.

Hippolytus is accused, in Euripides and Seneca, of having actually violated his stepmother: *vim corpus tulit.* But he is here accused of only having had the intention. I wished to spare Theseus a confusion which would have rendered him less agreeable to the audience.

With regard to the character of Hippolytus, I have noticed among the ancients that Euripides is reproached for having represented him as a philosopher exempt of all imperfection: which made the death of the young prince cause much more indignation than pity. I thought I should give him some weakness which would make him a little guilty towards his father, without however taking away from him any of the greatness of soul with which he spares Phaedra's honor and lets himself be oppressed without accusing her. I call weakness the passion which he feels, against his will, for Aricia, who is the daughter and the sister of mortal enemies of his father.

This Aricia is not a character of my invention. Virgil says that Hippolytus married her, and had a son by her, after Æsculapius had brought him back to life. And I have also read in some authors that Hippolytus had wedded and brought to Italy a young Athenian of high birth, called Aricia, and who had given her name to a small Italian town.

I mention these authorities because I have very scrupulously set myself to follow the fable. I have even followed the story of Theseus as given in Plutarch.

It is in this historian that I have found that what gave occasion to believe that Theseus descended into the underworld to rescue Proserpine was a journey that the prince had made in Epirus towards the source of the Acheron, at the home of a king whose wife Peirithous wishes to bear off, and who took Theseus prisoner after slaying Peirithous. So I have tried to keep the verisimilitude of the story, without losing anything of the ornaments of the fable, which is an abundant storehouse of poetical imagery; and the rumor of Theseus' death, based on this fabulous voyage, gives an opportunity to Phaedra to make a declaration of love which becomes one of the principal causes of her misfortune, and which she would never have dared to make so long as she believed that her husband was alive.

For the rest, I dare not yet assert that this play is indeed the best of my tragedies. I leave it to readers and to time to decide its true value. What I can assert is that I have not made one where virtue is put in a more favorable light than in this one; the least faults are severely punished; the very thought of a crime is regarded with as much horror as the crime itself; the weaknesses of love are shown as true weaknesses; the passions are displayed only to show all the disorder of which they are the cause; and vice is everywhere depicted in colors which make the deformity recognized and hated. That is properly the end which every man who works for the public should propose to himself; and it is that which the first tragic poets kept in sight above everything. Their theatre was a school where virtue was not less well taught than in the schools of the philosophers. So Aristotle was willing to give rules for the dramatic poem; and Socrates, the wisest of philosophers, did not disdain to set his hand to the tragedies of Euripides. It could be wished that our works were as solid and as full of useful instructions as those of these poets. That would perhaps be a means of reconciling tragedy with numerous people, celebrated for their piety and for their doctrine, who have condemned it in recent times, and who would doubtless judge it more favorably if the authors thought as much about instructing their audiences as about diverting them, and if they followed in this respect the true function of tragedy.

Dramatis Personae

THESEUS, *King of Athens*
PHAEDRA, *his wife*
HIPPOLYTUS, *son of Theseus and Antiope*
ARICIA, *Princess of the blood royal of Athens*
THERAMENES, *tutor to Hippolytus*
ŒNONE, *nurse and confidante of Phaedra*
ISMENE, *confidante of Aricia*
PANOPE, *woman of Phaedra's suite*
GUARDS

Scene—Troezen.

Act I

HIPPOLYTUS *and* THERAMENES.

HIPPOLYTUS: It is decided, dear Theramenes.
I'm leaving now, and cutting short my stay
In pleasant Troezen. In my state of doubt
I blush at my own sloth. Six months and more
My father has been absent, yet I stay
Still ignorant of his fate, not even knowing
In what part of the world he hides his head.

THERAMENES: Where will you seek him then? I have already,
My lord, to satisfy your natural fears,
Crossed the Corinthian sea, and asked for Theseus
Upon those distant shores where Acheron
Is lost among the dead. I went to Elidos
And sailed from Tenaros upon the sea
Where Icarus once fell. By what new hope,
Or in what lucky region will you find
His footprints now? Who knows, indeed, who knows
Whether it is the King your father's will,
That we should try to probe the mystery
Of his long absence? While we are afraid,
Even for his life, that hero, unperturbed,
Screening from us his latest love exploit,
May just be waiting till a woman . . .

HIPPOLYTUS: Stop,
Dear Theramenes; respect the King
Who has outgrown the headstrong faults of youth.
No such unworthy obstacle detains him.
Phaedra has conquered his inconstancy,
And fears no rival now. In seeking him,
I do my duty, and thereby escape
A place I dare not stay in.

THERAMENES: Since when, my lord,
Have you been frightened of the peaceful place
You used to love in childhood? You once preferred it
To the noisy pomp of Athens and the court.

What danger, or rather, should I say, what grief
Drives you away?

HIPPOLYTUS: Alas, that happy time
Is now no more. For everything has changed
Since to these shores the gods despatched the Queen,
The daughter of Minos and of Pasiphaë.

THERAMENES: I know the cause indeed; for Phaedra here
Vexes and wounds your sight—a dangerous
Stepmother, who had scarce set eyes on you
Ere she procured your exile. But her hatred
Is either vanished, or at least relaxed.
Besides, what perils can you undergo
From a dying woman, one who seeks to die?
Phaedra, who will not speak about her illness,
Tired of herself and even of the sunshine,
Is scarcely hatching plots against you.

HIPPOLYTUS: No:
Her vain hostility is not my fear.
In leaving her, I flee another foe:
I flee—I will admit it—young Aricia,
Last of a fatal race that has conspired
Against us.

THERAMENES: What? Do you yourself, my lord,
Persecute her? The Pallantids' lovely sister
Was not involved in her treacherous brothers' plots.
And should you hate her innocent charms?

HIPPOLYTUS: If I
Did hate her, I would not be fleeing.

THERAMENES: My lord,
May I explain your flight? Is it that you
No longer are that proud Hippolytus,
Relentless enemy of the laws of love,
And of a yoke to which your father bowed
So many times? Does Venus whom your pride
So long has slighted wish to justify
The amorous Theseus? While, like the rest of mortals,
You're forced to cense her altars? Are you in love,

My lord?
HIPPOLYTUS: What do you dare to ask, my friend?
You have known my heart since it began to beat,
And can you ask me to repudiate
My former proud, disdainful sentiments?
I sucked the pride which so amazes you
From an Amazonian mother; and when I reached
A riper age, and knew myself, I gloried
In what I was. Then in your friendly zeal
You told me all my father's history.
My soul, attentive to your voice, was thrilled
To hear the tale of his heroic deeds—
Consoling mortals for Alcides' absence,
By slaying monsters, putting brigands down,
Procrustes, Cercyon, Sciron, and Sinis,
The scattered bones of the giant of Epidaurus,
Crete reeking with the Minotaur's foul blood.
But when you told of deeds less glorious,
The way his faith was pledged a hundred times—
Helen of Sparta stolen from her kin,
Salamis witness of Periboea's tears,
And many more, whose names he has forgotten,
Of credulous women by his love deceived:
Ariadne on her rocky isle
Telling her wrongs; and Phaedra at the last,
Kidnapped, but under better auspices;
You know how listening to the sorry tale
I begged you cut it short, and would have been
Happy to blot out from my memory
The worser half of the tale. And shall I now
Be bound so ignominiously by the gods?
My base affections, unlike those of Theseus,
Can claim no heap of honors as excuse,
And so deserve more scorn. As I have slain
No monster yet, I have not earned the right
So to transgress; and if my pride must melt,
Should I have chosen for my conqueror

Aricia? Surely my wandering senses
Should have recalled that we are kept apart
By an eternal obstacle. My father
Holds her in reprobation, and forbids her
Ever to marry: of a guilty stem
He fears a shoot, and wishes to entomb
With her the memory of her brothers' name.
Under his tutelage until she dies,
Never for her shall Hymen's fires be lit.
Should I support her rights against a father
Incensed against her, give example to
Temerity, and let my youth embark
Upon a wild sea? . . .

THERAMENES: If your hour is come,
My lord, heaven cares not for our reasons. Theseus,
Wishing to shut your eyes, has opened them.
His hatred, rousing a rebellious flame,
Lends a new luster to his enemy.
But, after all, why fear an honest love?
If it is sweet, why should you not dare taste it?
Why will you trust a shy or sullen scruple?
Or fear to walk where Hercules once trod?
What spirits has not Venus tamed? And where
Would you be, you who fight against her, if
Antiope, always to her laws opposed,
Had not with modest ardor burned for Theseus?
But why do you affect a haughty speech?
Confess that all is changed: and for some days
You're seen less often, proud and solitary,
Racing the chariot on the shore, or skilled
In the art of Neptune, making the wild steeds
Obedient to the bit. The forest echoes
Less often to our shouts. Your eyes are heavy,
Charged with a secret passion. There is no doubt:
You love, you burn; you perish from an illness
Which you conceal. And are you now in love
With charming Aricia?

HIPPOLYTUS: Theramenes,
I'm setting off in quest of my lost father.
THERAMENES: Won't you see Phaedra, my lord, before you go?
HIPPOLYTUS: So I intend; and you may tell her so.
I'll see her—since my duty thus ordains.
But what's the new misfortune which disturbs
Her dear Œnone?

(*Enter* ŒNONE.) (I.2)

ŒNONE: Alas! my lord, what trouble
Can equal mine? The Queen has nearly reached
Her fatal term. In vain both night and day
I've watched beside her. She's dying of a sickness
She hides from me; and in her spirit reigns
Continual disorder. Restless affliction
Now drags her from her bed to see once more
The light of day; and her deep grief demands
That all should keep away. She's coming now.
HIPPOLYTUS: It is enough. I'll leave this place to her,
And not offend her with my hated face.
[*Exeunt* HIPPOLYTUS *and* THERAMENES.]

(*Enter* PHAEDRA.) (I.3)

PHAEDRA: Let's go no further, dear Œnone, stay.
I've reached the limit of my strength; my eyes
Are blinded by the daylight, and my knees
Give way beneath me.
[*She sits.*]
ŒNONE: O all-powerful Gods,
May all our tears appease you!
PHAEDRA: How these vain
Adornments, how these veils, now weigh me down.
What busy hand, in tying all these knots,
Has taken care to gather on my brow
This heavy load of hair? Now all afflicts me,
Hurts me, and conspires to hurt me.
ŒNONE: How

Her wishes seem now to destroy each other!
Madam, it was yourself, with your own hands,
Who dressed and decked your hair, wishing to show
Yourself, and see once more the light of day.
But now you see it, ready to hide yourself,
You hate the day you sought.

PHAEDRA: O shining Sun,
Author of my sad race, thou of whom my mother
Boasted herself the daughter, who blush perhaps
At these my sufferings, I see you now
For the last time.

ŒNONE: What! have you not lost
That cruel desire? And shall I see you still
Renouncing life and making of your death
The dreadful preparations?

PHAEDRA: O that I were seated
In the forest shade, where through a cloud of dust
I could behold a chariot racing by!

ŒNONE: What, madam?

PHAEDRA: Fool! Where am I? What have I said?
Where have my wits been wandering? I have lost them.
The gods have robbed me of them. I blush, Œnone.
I let you see too much my shameful sorrows,
And, spite of me, my eyes are filled with tears.

ŒNONE: If you must blush, blush rather at your silence
Which but augments your griefs. Deaf to our pleading,
Rebellious to our care, and without pity,
Do you wish to end your days? What madness now
Stops them in mid-career? What spell or poison
Has drained their source? Three nights have come and gone
Since sleep last entered in your eyes; three days
Have chased the darkness since you took some food.
What frightful scheme are you attempting now?
For you insult the gods who gave you life,
Betray the husband to whom your faith is given,
Betray your hapless children whom you throw

Under a rigorous yoke. Think that one day
Will snatch their mother from them, and give up
Their hopes to the stranger's son, to that proud foe
Of you, and of your blood, the Amazon's son,
Hippolytus.

PHAEDRA: Ah Gods!

ŒNONE: Does this reproach—?

PHAEDRA: Wretch! What name has issued from your mouth?

ŒNONE: You are right to be angry: I like to see you tremble
At that ill-omened name. Then live! Both love and duty
Reanimate you. Live. Do not let the son
Of the Scythian, crushing your children with his rule,
Command the noblest blood of Greece and heaven.
But don't delay: each moment threatens life.
Repair your weakened strength, while yet life's torch
Can be rekindled.

PHAEDRA: I have too much prolonged
Its guilty span.

ŒNONE: What! are you torn apart
By some remorse? What crime could have produced
Such agony? Your hands were never stained
With innocent blood.

PHAEDRA: Thanks to the gods, my hands
Are guiltless still. But would to heaven my heart
Were innocent as they!

ŒNONE: What frightful scheme
Have you conceived to terrify your heart?

PHAEDRA: I have said enough. Spare me the rest. I die
Because I cannot such confession make.

ŒNONE: Die then; and keep inhuman silence still.
But seek another hand to close your eyes.
Although there but remains a feeble flame
In you, my soul will journey to the dead
Before you, since there are a thousand ways
By which we can go thither—mine the shortest.
Cruel! When have I betrayed your confidence?
Think, that my arms received you at your birth,

For you I've left my country and my children.
Is this the price of my fidelity?

PHAEDRA: What fruit can come from so much violence?
You would be horror-struck if I should tell you.

ŒNONE: What will you say to me more horrible
Than seeing you expire before my eyes?

PHAEDRA: But when you know my crime and the dread fate
That crushes me, I shall die just the same,
And die more guilty.

ŒNONE: Madam, by all the tears
That I have shed for you, by your weak knees
That I embrace now, free my mind from doubt.

PHAEDRA: You wish it: rise.

ŒNONE: Speak: I am listening.

PHAEDRA: What shall I say? And where shall I begin?

ŒNONE: Cease to insult me by these needless fears.

PHAEDRA: O hate of Venus and her fatal wrath!
Love led my mother into desperate ways.

ŒNONE: Forget them, madam. Let an eternal silence
Hide their remembrance.

PHAEDRA: My sister, Ariadne,
Stricken with love, upon a desolate coast
Despairing died.

ŒNONE: What are you doing, madam?
What mortal spite enkindles you today
Against your nearest . . . ?

PHAEDRA: Since Venus so ordains,
Last and most wretched of my tragic race,
I too shall perish.

ŒNONE: Are you then in love?

PHAEDRA: All of love's frenzies I endure.

ŒNONE: For whom?

PHAEDRA: You're going to hear the last extreme of horror.
I love . . . I shudder at the fatal name . . .
I love . . .

ŒNONE: Whom do you love?

PHAEDRA: You know the son

Of the Amazon—the prince I've harshly used.
ŒNONE: Hippolytus! Great Gods!
PHAEDRA: 'Tis you have named him.
Not I.
ŒNONE: O righteous heaven! The blood in my veins
Is turned to ice. O crime! O hapless race!
Disastrous voyage! O unlucky coast!
Why did we travel to your perilous shores?
PHAEDRA: My evil comes from a more distant place.
Scarce had I wedded Theseus and established
My happiness, it seemed, I saw in Athens
My haughty foe. I saw him—blushed and blanched
To see him—and my soul was all distraught.
My eyes were blinded, and I could not speak.
I felt my body freeze and burn; I knew
The terrible fires of Venus, the tortures fated
To one whom she pursues. I hoped to avert them
By my assiduous prayers. I built for her
A temple, and took pains to adorn its walls.
Myself surrounded by the sacrifices,
I sought for my lost reason in their entrails.
Weak remedies of love incurable!
In vain upon the altars I burnt incense;
My lips implored the goddess, but I worshipped
Only Hippolytus; and seeing him
Each day even at the altar's foot
I offered all to the god I dared not name.
I shunned him everywhere. O heavy weight
Of misery! My eyes beheld the son
In the father's countenance. At length I dared
To rebel against myself. I spurred my spirit
To persecute him, striving thus to banish
The enemy I worshipped by assuming
A stepmother's proverbial cruelty.
I clamored for his exile till my cries
Tore my dear enemy from his father's arms.
I breathed again, Œnone. In his absence

My calmer days flowed by in innocence,
Compliant to my husband, while my griefs
Lay hidden. I bore him children. But in vain
Were all precautions, for Fate intervened.
Brought by my husband to Troezen, once more
I saw the enemy I had sent away.
My keen wound bled again—it is no more
A passion hidden in my veins, but now
It's Venus fastened on her helpless prey.
I have a just abhorrence of my crime;
I hate my life, abominate my lust;
Longing by death to rescue my good name
And hide my black love from the light of day.
Your tears have conquered me. I have confessed
All my dark secret; and I won't regret it
If you respect now my approaching death,
And do not wound me with unjust reproofs,
Or with vain remedies keep alive within me
The last faint spark of life.

(*Enter* PANOPE.) (I.4)

PANOPE: I would prefer
To hide these tidings from you, madam, but
I must reveal them. Death has robbed you now
Of your unconquerable husband, and
It is known to all but you.

ŒNONE: What do you say?

PANOPE: That the mistaken Queen in vain demands
Theseus' return from heaven; and that from ships
Arrived in port, Hippolytus, his son,
Has just heard of his death.

PHAEDRA: Heaven!

PANOPE: For the choice
Of ruler, Athens is divided. Some
Vote for the Prince, your son, and others, madam,
Forgetting the laws of the State, dare give their voices
To the son of the stranger. It is even said

An insolent faction has designed to place
Aricia on the throne. I thought you should
Be warned about this danger. Hippolytus
Is ready to depart, and it is feared,
If he becomes involved in this new storm,
Lest he draw to him all the fickle mob.

ŒNONE: No more, Panope. The Queen has heard you,
And won't neglect your warning. [*Exit* PANOPE.]

(I.5)

ŒNONE: I had ceased,
Madam, to urge that you should live. Indeed,
I thought that I should follow you to the grave;
I had no further voice to change your mind.
But this new blow imposes other laws.
Your fortune shows a different face; the King
Is now no more, and his place must be filled.
His death has left you with a son to whom
You have a duty; slave if he loses you,
A king if you live. On whom in his misfortune
Do you wish that he should lean? His tears will have
No hand but yours to wipe them; and his cries,
Borne even to the gods, would then incense
His ancestors against his mother. Live.
You have no longer reason to reproach
Yourself; your love becomes a usual love;
Theseus in dying cuts the sacred knots
Which made the crime and horror of your passion.
Hippolytus becomes less terrible to you,
And you can see him without guiltiness.
Perhaps, convinced of your aversion, he
Is going to lead the rebels. Undeceive him,
Appease his spirit. King of these happy shores,
Troezen is his portion; but he knows
That the laws give your son the lofty ramparts
Minerva builded. Both of you, indeed,
Have a true enemy. Unite together
To combat Aricia.

PHAEDRA: To your advice
I let myself be drawn. Well, let me live,
If I can be restored to life; and if
My love for a son can in this grievous moment
Reanimate the rest of my weak spirits.

Act II

ARICIA *and* ISMENE.

ARICIA: Hippolytus asks to see me in this place?
Hippolytus seeks me here to say good-by?
Ismene, is it true? You're not mistaken?
ISMENE: It is the first result of Theseus' death.
Madam, prepare yourself to see the hearts
Scattered by Theseus fly from every side
Towards you. Aricia at last is mistress
Of her fate, and soon will see the whole of Greece
Submit to her.
ARICIA: It's not a false report?
Do I cease to be a slave, and have no foe?
ISMENE: No, madam, the gods are now no more against you,
And Theseus has rejoined your brothers' shades.
ARICIA: Is it known what caused his death?
ISMENE: They spread
An unbelievable tale of it. It is said
That stealing a new love this faithless husband
Was swallowed by the waves. It is even said—
A widespread rumor this—that he descended
To Hades with Peirithous, and saw
Cocytus and the gloomy banks, and living
Appeared to the infernal shades, but then
Could not emerge from those sad regions,
And cross the bourn from which there's no return.
ARICIA: Shall I believe a man before his hour
Can enter the dark dwelling of the dead?

What spell could draw him to those fearsome coasts?
ISMENE: Theseus is dead, madam, and you alone
Have doubts of it. Athens is mourning for it,
Troezen, informed of it, acknowledges
Hippolytus as King; and Phaedra, here
In this palace, trembling for her son, now seeks
The advice of anxious friends.
ARICIA: Do you believe
Hippolytus, less cruel than his father,
Will make my chains less heavy, sympathize
With my misfortunes?
ISMENE: Madam, I do believe it.
ARICIA: But do you really know that heartless man?
By what fond hope do you think he'll pity me?
In me alone respect a sex he scorns?
You've seen how he avoids me, seeks those places
Where I am not.
ISMENE: I know all that is said
About his coldness. But I've seen when near you
This proud Hippolytus; and in seeing him,
The rumor of his pride has doubly whetted
My curiosity. His actual presence
Seemed not to correspond. At your first glances
I've seen him get confused. His eyes, which wished
Vainly to shun you, could not leave your face.
The name of lover would offend his heart,
But yet he has a lover's tender eyes,
If not his words.
ARICIA: How my heart, dear Ismene,
Drinks in a speech which may have little basis.
Is it believable to you who know me
That the sad plaything of a pitiless fate,
Whose heart is fed on bitterness and tears,
Should be acquainted with the trivial griefs
Of love? The remnant of the blood of a king,
Erechtheus, the noble son of Earth,
Alone I have escaped war's ravages.

I've lost six brothers in the flower of youth—
Hope of a famous house!—all reaped by the sword.
The moistened earth regretfully drank the blood
Of the offspring of Erechtheus. You know
How since their death a cruel law was made,
Forbidding Greeks to breathe a lover's sighs
For me. It is feared the sister's reckless flames
May kindle once again her brothers' ashes.
But you know well with what disdainful eye
I looked upon a conqueror's suspicions;
And how, opposed to love, I often thanked
The unjust Theseus whose convenient harshness
Aided my scorn. But then my eyes had not
Beheld his son. Not that by eyes alone
Basely enchanted, I love his beauty and charm,
Gifts with which nature wishes to honor him,
And which he scorns, or seems unconscious of;
I love in him his nobler wealth, his father's virtues,
Without his faults. I love—I do confess it—
That generous pride that never yet has bowed
Beneath the amorous yoke. Phaedra took pride
In Theseus' practiced sighs. But as for me,
I am more proud, and shun the easy glory
Of gaining homage that a thousand others
Have had before me, and of penetrating
A heart completely open. But to bend
A heart inflexible, to make a soul
Insensible to love feel all its pain,
To enchain a captive by his bonds amazed,
In vain rebellion against the pleasing yoke,
That's what I wish; and that is what provokes me.
It's easier to disarm Hercules
Than Prince Hippolytus; and conquests soon
And often made will bring less glory to
The victor's eyes. But, dear Ismene, how
Unwise I am! for I shall be resisted
Only too much; and you perhaps will hear me

Lament the pride that I admire today.
If he would love! With what extreme delight
Would I make him . . .

ISMENE: You'll hear him now, himself.
He comes to you.

(*Enter* HIPPOLYTUS.) (II.2)

HIPPOLYTUS: Madam, before I leave,
I thought that I should tell you of your fate.
My father lives no more. My apprehension
Presaged the reasons of his too long absence;
And death alone, stopping his famous deeds,
Could hide him for so long within this world.
The gods have yielded to the Fates at last
The friend and the successor of Alcides.
I think your hatred, allowing him his virtues,
Will hear without regret what is his due.
One hope allays my deadly sorrow now.
From your strict tutelage I'll deliver you,
Revoke the laws whose rigor I've deplored.
Do what you will. Dispose of your own heart,
And in this Troezen, my heritage,
Which has forthwith accepted me as King,
I leave you as free, nay freer, than myself.

ARICIA: Temper your generosity, my lord,
For its excess embarrasses me. So
To honor my disgrace will put me—more
Than you think—under the harsh laws from which
You would exempt me.

HIPPOLYTUS: Athens, undecided
In the choice of a successor, speaks of you,
Names me and the Queen's son.

ARICIA: Me, my lord?

HIPPOLYTUS: I know, without self-flattery, that a law
Seems to reject me. Greece reproaches me
With an alien mother. But if my brother were
My only rival, over him I have

Some veritable claims that I would save
Out of the law's caprice. Another bridle,
More lawful, checks my boldness. I yield to you,
Or rather give you back what is your own,
A scepter which your ancestors received
From the most famous man that ever lived;
Adoption placed it in Ægeus' hands;
Athens protected and enlarged by Theseus
Joyfully recognized so good a king,
And left in oblivion your luckless brothers.
Now Athens calls you back within her walls;
With a long quarrel she has groaned enough;
Enough her fields have reeked with blood of thine.
Troezen obeys me; and the plains of Crete
Offer to Phaedra's son a rich domain.
Attica is yours, and I am going
On your behalf to reunite the suffrages
We share between us.

ARICIA: Astonished and confused
At all I hear, I am afraid . . . afraid
A dream abuses me. Am I awake?
Can I believe in such a plan? What god,
My lord, what god has put it in your breast?
How justly is your glory spread abroad
In every place! And how the truth surpasses
Your fame! You would betray yourself for me?
Would it not be enough for you to refrain
From hating me? And to prevent your soul
So long from this hostility . . .

HIPPOLYTUS: I hate you,
Madam? However they depict my pride,
Do you think it bore a monster? What settled hate,
What savage manners could, in seeing you,
Not become milder? Could I have resisted
The charm that . . .

ARICIA: What, my lord?

HIPPOLYTUS: I've gone too far.

I see that reason yields to violence.
Since I've begun to speak, I must continue.
I must inform you, madam, of a secret
My heart no longer can contain. You see
Before you a lamentable prince, a type
Of headstrong pride. I, rebel against love,
For long have scorned its captives. I deplored
The shipwreck of weak mortals, and proposed
To contemplate the tempests from the shore.
But now enslaved under the common law,
I see myself transported. In a moment
My mad audacity has been subdued.
My proud soul is at last enslaved. For nearly
Six months, ashamed and desperate, and wearing
The marks of torture, against you, against myself,
Vainly I strove. Present I fled from you,
Absent I sought you. In the midst of forests
Your image followed me; the light of day,
The shadows of the night, brought to my eyes
The charms I shunned, and everything conspired
To make the rebel Hippolytus your captive.
Now for all fruit of my superfluous cares,
I seek but do not find myself. My bow, my spears,
My chariot call to me in vain. No more
Do I remember Neptune's lessons; the woods
Now echo to my groans. My idle steeds
Have now forgot my voice. Perhaps the tale
Of love so wild will make you, as you listen,
Blush for your work. What an uncouth recital
Of a heart that's offered you. What a strange captive
For bonds so beautiful! But to your eyes
The offering should be the richer for it;
Remember that I speak an alien tongue,
And don't reject vows that are ill expressed,
Vows that without you I had never formed.

(*Enter* THERAMENES.) (II.3)

THERAMENES: My lord, the Queen is coming. I come before
To tell you that she seeks you.
HIPPOLYTUS: Me?
THERAMENES: I don't know why.
But she has sent to ask for you. She wishes
To speak with you before you go.
HIPPOLYTUS: Phaedra!
What shall I say to her? And what can she
Expect . . .
ARICIA: My lord, you can't refuse to hear her.
Though you are sure of her hostility,
You ought to have some pity for her tears.
HIPPOLYTUS: Yet you are going. And I depart, not knowing
Whether I have offended by my words
The charms that I adore. I do not know
Whether this heart I leave now in your hands . . .
ARICIA: Go, Prince, pursue your generous designs;
Put tributary Athens in my power.
And all those gifts that you have wished to make me,
I accept. But yet that Empire, great and glorious,
Is not to me the richest of your gifts.
[*Exeunt* ARICIA *and* ISMENE.]

(II.4)

HIPPOLYTUS: Friend, is all ready? But the Queen approaches.
Go, see that all's prepared for our departure.
Run, give the signal, and return at once
To free me from a vexing interview. [*Exit* THERAMENES.]

(*Enter* PHAEDRA *and* ŒNONE.) (II.5)

PHAEDRA: He's here: my blood retreats towards my heart,
And I forget what I had meant to say.
ŒNONE: Think of a son whose sole hope lies in you.
PHAEDRA: It is said that your immediate departure
Is sundering us, my lord. I come to wed
My tears unto your griefs; and to explain
My anxious fears to you. My son is now
Without a father; and the day is near

Which of my death will make him witness too.
His youth is threatened by a thousand foes,
And you alone can arm against them—but
Secret remorse is fretting in my soul.
I fear you're deaf to his cries, and that you'll wreak
On him your wrath against an odious mother.

HIPPOLYTUS: Madam, I do not harbor such base feelings.

PHAEDRA: Although you hate me, I shall not complain,
My lord: for you have seen me bent to harm you.
You could not read the tables of my heart.
I've taken care to invite your enmity,
And could not bear your presence where I dwelt.
In public, and in private, your known foe,
I've wished the seas to part us, and even forbidden
The mention of your name within my hearing.
But if one measures punishment by the offense,
If only hatred can attract your hate,
Never was woman who deserved more pity,
My lord, and less deserved your enmity.

HIPPOLYTUS: A mother jealous for her children's rights
Seldom forgives her stepson. I know it, madam.
Nagging suspicions are the commonest fruits
Of second marriage; and another wife
Would have disliked me just the same; and I
Might well have had to swallow greater wrongs.

PHAEDRA: Ah, my lord! Heaven—I dare avow it now—
Has made me an exception to that rule.
And what a different care perplexes me
And eats me up.

HIPPOLYTUS: Madam, it is not time
To grieve. Perhaps your husband is alive.
Heaven to our tears may grant his swift return.
Neptune, his tutelary god, protects him,
To whom my father never prayed in vain.

PHAEDRA: None has beheld the marches of the dead
A second time, my lord. Since he has seen
Those dismal shores, you hope in vain some god

Will send him back. The greedy Acheron
Never lets go its prey. What do I say?
He is not dead since he still lives in you.
Ever before my eyes I see my husband.
I see him, speak with him, and my heart still . . .
I'm wandering, my lord. My foolish feelings,
In spite of me, declare themselves.

HIPPOLYTUS: I see
Love's wonderful effects. Dead though he is,
Theseus is always present to your eyes:
Your soul is ever burning with your love.

PHAEDRA: Yes, Prince, I pine and burn for Theseus.
I love him, not as when he visited
The underworld, a fickle lover, bent
To stain great Pluto's bed, but faithful, proud,
Attractive, young, and even a little shy,
Charming all hearts, an image of the gods,
Or even as you are now. He had your bearing,
Your eyes, your speech; and such a modesty
Made flush his face when over the Cretan waves
He came and turned the hearts of Minos' daughters.
What were you doing then? Why without you
Did he assemble there the flower of Greece?
And why were you too young to sail with him
Unto our shores? For then you would have slain
The Minotaur, despite the devious ways
Of his vast lair: my sister, to redeem you
From your confusion, with the fateful thread
Would have armed your hand—but no, for I myself,
Inspired by love, would have forestalled her plan.
It would have been me, Prince; by timely aid,
I would have led you through the labyrinth.
How many cares that charming head of yours
Would then have cost me! I would not have trusted
To that weak thread alone, but walked before you,
Companion in the peril which you chose:
And going down into the labyrinth,

Phaedra would have returned with you, or else
Been lost with you.

HIPPOLYTUS: O Gods! What do I hear?
Do you forget that Theseus is my father,
And you his wife?

PHAEDRA: By what do you judge that I
Have done so, Prince? Would I forget my honor?

HIPPOLYTUS: Forgive me, madam. I admit, with blushing,
I misinterpreted an innocent speech.
I am ashamed to stay within your sight;
I'm going. . . .

PHAEDRA: Ah! cruel! You've understood too well.
I've said enough to save you from mistaking.
Know Phaedra, then, and all her madness. Yes,
I love; but do not think that I condone it,
Or think it innocent; nor that I ever
With base complaisance added to the poison
Of my mad passion. Hapless victim of
Celestial vengeance, I abhor myself
More than you can. The gods are witnesses—
Those gods who kindled in my breast the flame
Fatal to all my blood, whose cruel boast
Was to seduce a weak and mortal heart.
Recall what's past. I did not flee from you,
Hardhearted man, I drove you away. I wished
To seem to you both hateful and inhuman.
To resist you better I aroused your hatred.
But what have profited my useless pains?
You loathed me more: I did not love you less;
And your misfortunes lent you further charms.
I've languished, shriveled in the flames, in tears
Your eyes will tell you so—if for a moment
Your eyes could look at me. What am I saying?
Think you that this confession I have made
Was voluntary? I trembled for a son
I did not dare betray and came to beg you
No more to hate him—futile schemes devised

By a heart too full of what it loves. Alas!
I could only speak to you about yourself.
Avenge yourself; punish an odious love,
Son worthy of a noble father, free
The universe of a monster who offends you.
Theseus' widow dares to love Hippolytus!
Believe me, Prince,
This dreadful monster would not seek to flee.
There is my heart: there you should aim your blow.
I feel it now, eager to expiate
Its sin, advance towards your arm. Strike.
Or if you think it unworthy of your blows,
Your hatred envying me a death so sweet,
Or if you think your hand with blood too vile
Would be imbrued, lend me your sword instead.
Give it me.
[*She takes sword.*]

ŒNONE: What are you doing, madam?
O righteous Gods! But someone's coming. Leave
These hateful testimonies. Come inside,
And flee a certain shame. [*Exeunt* ŒNONE *and* PHAEDRA.]

(*Enter* THERAMENES.) (II.6)

THERAMENES: Is it Phaedra who flees,
Or rather is led away? O why, my lord,
These marks of sorrow? I see you without sword,
Speechless and pale.

HIPPOLYTUS: Theramenes, let's flee.
I am amazed, and cannot without horror
Behold myself. Phaedra . . . but no, great Gods!
In deep oblivion may this horrid secret
Remain entombed!

THERAMENES: If you would now depart,
The sails are ready. But Athens has decided.
Her chiefs have taken the votes of all the tribes.
Your brother wins, and Phaedra gets her way.

HIPPOLYTUS: Phaedra?

THERAMENES: A herald, bearing Athens' will,
Comes to remit the reins of government
Into her hands. Her son is King, my lord.
HIPPOLYTUS: O Gods, who know her heart, is it her virtue
That thus you recompense?
THERAMENES: There is, however,
A muffled rumor that the King's alive.
It is said that in Epirus he's appeared.
But I, who sought him there, I know too well . . .
HIPPOLYTUS: No matter. Let us listen to everything,
And neglect nothing. Examine this report
And trace it to its source. If it should prove
Unfounded, let's depart. Whatever the cost,
Let's put the scepter into worthy hands.

Act III

PHAEDRA *and* ŒNONE.

PHAEDRA: O! that the honors which are brought to me
Were paid elsewhere! Why do you urge me so?
Can you wish me to be seen? What do you come with
To flatter my desolation? Hide me rather.
Not only have I spoken; but my frenzy
Is noised abroad. I've said those things which ought
Never to be heard. O heavens! The way he listened!
By devious means he somehow failed to grasp
What I was saying—then he recoiled. His blush
Doubled my shame. Why did you turn aside
The death I sought? Did he turn pale with fear
When with his sword I sought my breast, or seek
To snatch it from me? Since my hands had touched it
But once, it was made horrible in his eyes,
And would profane his hands.
ŒNONE: Thus in your woes
Lamenting to yourself, you feed a flame

That ought to be put out. Would it not be better,
Worthy the blood of Minos, in nobler cares
To seek your peace. To spite a heartless man
Who had recourse to flight, assume the conduct
Of affairs, and reign.

PHAEDRA: I reign? To place the State
Under my law, when reason reigns no longer
Over myself; when I have abdicated
From the empire of my senses; when beneath
A yoke of shame I scarcely breathe; when I
Am dying.

ŒNONE: Fly.

PHAEDRA: I cannot leave him.

ŒNONE: You dared
To banish him, and dare not shun him now?

PHAEDRA: Too late. He knows of my mad passion.
I've crossed the bounds of rigid modesty,
Declared my shame before my conqueror's eyes,
And hope has slipped perforce into my heart.
It was you who rallied my declining strength,
When my departing soul was on my lips,
And by your flattering counsels knew the way
To bring me back to life. You made me glimpse
How I could love him.

ŒNONE: To save you from your ills,
Guilty or innocent, what would I not
Have done? But if an insult ever touched you,
Can you forget his haughty scorn? And how
With cruel eyes his obstinate rigor let you
Lie prostrate at his feet. How his fierce pride
Rendered him odious! If only Phaedra
Had seen him, at that moment, with my eyes!

PHAEDRA: Œnone, he may leave this native pride
Which wounds you. Nurtured in the pathless woods,
He has their roughness. Hardened by savage laws,
He hears love spoken of for the first time;
Perhaps it was surprise that caused his silence;

Perhaps my pleas had too much violence.
ŒNONE: Remember a barbarian gave him birth.
PHAEDRA: Although a Scythian and barbarian,
She yet has loved.
ŒNONE: He has for all our sex
A deadly hatred.
PHAEDRA: So I shall not see him
Prefer a rival. All your counsels now
Are out of season. Serve my passion, Œnone,
And not my reason. He opposes now
To love a heart impenetrable; let us
Discover some more vulnerable place.
The charms of ruling have appeared to touch him.
Athens attracts him; he has not been able
To hide it. His ships have turned their prows; their sails
Flap in the wind. Find this ambitious youth,
Œnone; make the royal crown to glitter
Before his eyes. Let him wear upon his brow
The sacred diadem. I only wish
The honor of his love, and yield to him
The power I cannot keep. He will instruct
My son in the art of ruling, who may perhaps
Regard him as a father. Both son and mother
I put under his power. Try every means
To bend him; he will listen to your speech
More readily than to mine. Urge, weep, and moan.
Paint Phaedra dying; do not blush to use
The tone of a suppliant. I will approve
Of all you do. You are my only hope.
I await your coming to decide my fate. [*Exit* ŒNONE.]

(III.2)

PHAEDRA: O thou who seest the shame to which I've come,
Venus implacable, am I confounded
Enough for thee? Thou canst not further urge
Thy cruelty; thy victory is complete.
O cruel! If thou wishest another triumph
Attack an enemy who is more rebellious.

Hippolytus flees thee; and, thy wrath defying,
Has never to thy altars bowed the knee.
Thy name appears to shock his haughty ears.
Goddess, avenge thyself. Thy cause is mine.
O let him love! Œnone is returned.
I am detested then. He would not hear you?

(*Enter* ŒNONE.) (III.3)

ŒNONE: Madam, you must repress the very thought
Of your vain passion, and recall again
Your former virtue. The King that we thought dead
Will soon appear before your eyes. Theseus
Is come. The people rush to see him. I went,
At your command, to seek Hippolytus,
When I heard a thousand shouts. . . .

PHAEDRA: My husband lives,
Œnone. It is enough. I have confessed
A love which foully wrongs him. Theseus lives.
I wish to know no more.

ŒNONE: What?

PHAEDRA: I foretold it,
But you would not believe it. Your tears prevailed
Over my shame. I would have died today
Worthy of tears. I followed your advice—
I die dishonored.

ŒNONE: Die?

PHAEDRA: O righteous heaven!
What have I done today? My husband's coming,
And his son with him. I shall see the witness
Of my adulterous passion watch how boldly
I greet his father—my heart still full of sighs
To which he would not listen, and my eyes
Still moist with tears he scorned. Do you suppose
That he, so sensitive to Theseus' honor,
Will hide the fires that burn me—and betray
His father and his king? Could he contain
The horror I inspire? He would keep silence

In vain. I know my perfidies, Œnone;
I am not one of those who in their crimes
Enjoy a tranquil peace, and know the art
To keep their countenance without a blush.
I know my madness: I recall it all.
I think already that these walls, these arches,
Are going to speak; they but await my husband
Before they utter forth my crimes. Die, then.
My death will free me from a crowd of horrors.
Is it a great mischance to cease to live?
Death has no terrors for the unfortunate.
I only fear the name I leave behind me.
A dreadful heritage for my poor children!
The blood of Jupiter should puff up their courage,
With a just pride; but yet a mother's crime
Will be a heavy burden. One day, I fear,
A speech—too true!—will cast it in their teeth
They had a guilty mother; and I fear
That crushed by such a hateful load, they'll never
Dare raise their eyes.

ŒNONE: It is true. I pity them.
Never was fear more justified than yours.
But why expose them to such insults? Why
Against yourself give evidence? All would be lost.
It will be said that guilty Phaedra fled
The terrible sight of husband she betrayed.
Hippolytus will rejoice that by your death
You corroborate his tale. What could I say
To your accuser? Face to face with him
I shall be easy to confound, and see him
Rejoicing in his triumph, while he tells
Your shame to all who listen. Rather let
Fire from heaven consume me! But tell me true
Is he still dear to you? And with what eyes
Do you behold this insolent prince?

PHAEDRA: I see him
Even as a monster hideous to my eyes.

ŒNONE: Why yield him then a total victory?
You fear him, madam. Dare to accuse him first
Of the crime that he will charge you with today.
Who will contradict you? Everything
Speaks against him—his sword by lucky chance
Left in your hands, your present sore distress,
Your former sorrow, his father long ago
Warned by your outcries, and his actual exile
Obtained by you yourself.

PHAEDRA: How should I dare
Oppress and slander innocence?

ŒNONE: My zeal
Only requires your silence. Like you I shrink
From such an action. You would find me readier
To face a thousand deaths; but since I'd lose you
Without this painful remedy, and your life
For me is of such value that all else
Must yield to it, I'll speak. And Theseus, angered
By what I tell him, will restrict his vengeance
To his son's exile. When he punishes,
A father is always father, satisfied
With a light penalty. But even if
His guiltless blood is spilt, your threatened honor
Is yet too valuable to be exposed.
Whatever it demands, you must submit,
Madam. And to save your threatened honor
All must be sacrificed, including virtue.
Someone is coming. I see Theseus.

PHAEDRA: Ah!
I see Hippolytus. In his haughty eyes
I see my ruin written. Do what you will,
I resign myself to you. In my disorder,
I can do nothing for myself.

(*Enter* THESEUS, HIPPOLYTUS, *and* THERAMENES.) (III.4)

THESEUS: Now Fortune,
Madam, no longer frowns, and in your arms . . .

PHAEDRA: Stay, Theseus. Do not profane the love you feel.
I am not worthy of your sweet caresses.
You are insulted. Fortune has not spared
Your wife during your absence. I am unworthy
To please you, or approach you; and henceforward
I ought to think only of where to hide.

[*Exeunt* PHAEDRA *and* ŒNONE.]

(III.5)

THESEUS: What is the reason for this strange reception?

HIPPOLYTUS: Phaedra alone the mystery can explain.
But if my ardent prayers can move your heart,
Permit me not to see her any more.
And let Hippolytus disappear forever
From places where she dwells.

THESEUS: Leave me, my son?

HIPPOLYTUS: I sought her not: you brought her to these shores,
And when you left entrusted to the banks
Of Troezen, Aricia and the Queen,
I was instructed to look after them.
But what can now delay me? In my youth
I showed enough my prowess in the forests
Against unworthy foes; and could I not,
Escaping an ignoble idleness,
In blood more glorious stain my spears? Before
You reached my present age, already
More than one tyrant, more than one grim monster
Had felt your mighty strength; already you,
Chastiser of insolence, had secured the shores
Of the two seas; the private traveler feared
Outrage no more; and Hercules could rest
From his long labors, hearing of your deeds.
But I, an unknown son of famous sire,
Am even further from my mother's deeds!
Suffer my courage to be used at last;
And if some monster has escaped your arm,
Let me then lay the honorable skin

Before your feet; or by the lasting memory
Of a fine death perpetuate the days
So nobly ended, and prove to all the world
I was your son.

THESEUS: What do I now behold?
What horror makes my frightened family
Flee from my sight? If I return so feared,
So little wanted, why, heaven, from my prison
Did you release me? I had one friend alone;
Imprudently he wished to steal the wife
Of the King of Epirus. I aided, with regret,
His amorous designs; but angry fate
Blinded us both. The King surprised me there,
Defenseless, weaponless. I saw Peirithous,
Sad object of my tears, by this barbarian
Given to cruel monsters whom he fed
With blood of luckless mortals. He shut me up
In dismal caverns underground that neighbored
The empire of the shades. After six months
The gods again looked on me. I deceived
The eyes of those who guarded me. I cleansed
The world of a perfidious enemy;
To his own monsters he became a prey.
And when with joy I approach the dearest things
Now left me by the gods—what do I say?—
When to itself my soul returns and takes its fill
Of that dear sight, for welcome I receive
A shuddering fear and horror. All flee; all shrink
From my embraces. And I feel the terror
That I inspire. I'd like to be again
In the prisons of Epirus. Speak. Phaedra complains
That I am wronged. Who has betrayed me? Why
Have I not been avenged? Has Greece, to whom
So many times my arms proved useful, now
Granted asylum to a criminal?
You do not answer! Is my son, my own son,
Leagued with my enemies? Let us go in.

I cannot stay in doubt that overwhelms me.
Let me know both the offense and the offender.
Let Phaedra tell the cause of her distress. [*Exit* THESEUS.]
(III.6)

HIPPOLYTUS: Where did that speech, which petrified me, tend?
Does Phaedra, still a prey to her mad passion,
Wish to accuse, and so destroy, herself?
What will the King say? What destructive poison
Is scattered over all his house by love.
And I, full of a love he will detest,
How different from the man that he remembers!
What black presentiments affright me now!
But innocence has nought to fear. Let's go:
Seek by what happy art I can awaken
My father's tenderness—speak of a love
That he may wish to crush, though all his power
Will not be able to drive it from my heart.

Act IV

THESEUS *and* ŒNONE.

THESEUS: What do I hear? A traitor, a rash traitor,
To plot this outrage to his father's honor?
How harshly, Destiny, dost thou pursue me!
I know not where I'm going, nor what I am!
O tenderness and bounty ill repaid!
Audacious projects! evil thought! To reach
The goal of his black passion he sought the aid
Of violence. I recognize the sword—
The instrument of his rage—with which I armed him
For nobler purposes. All the ties of blood
Could not restrain him! And Phaedra hesitated
To punish him! Her silence spared the villain!

ŒNONE: She rather spared a pitiable father.

Being ashamed of a violent lover's scheme
And of the wicked fire caught from her eyes,
Phaedra desired to die; her murderous hand
Would have put out the pure light of her eyes.
I saw her raise her arm. I ran to stop her.
Alone I tried to save her for your love,
And, mourning for her troubles and your fears,
I have unwillingly interpreted
The tears you saw.

THESEUS: The villain! He was not able
To stop himself from turning pale. I saw him
Tremble with fear when he encountered me.
I was astonished at his lack of joy;
His cold embraces froze my tenderness.
But was this guilty passion which devours him
Already manifest in Athens?

ŒNONE: My lord,
Recall the Queen's complaints. A criminal love
Was cause of all her hatred.

THESEUS: And did this passion
Kindle again at Troezen?

ŒNONE: O my lord,
I have told you all that passed. Too long the Queen
Has in her mortal grief been left alone;
So let me leave, and hasten to her side. [*Exit* ŒNONE.]

(*Enter* HIPPOLYTUS.) (IV.2)

THESEUS: Ah! here he is. Great Gods! What eye, as mine,
Would not have been deceived? Why should the brow
Of a profane adulterer shine with virtue?
And should one not by certain signs perceive
The heart of villainous men?

HIPPOLYTUS: May I inquire,
My lord, what dismal cloud is on your face?
Dare you confide in me?

THESEUS: Villain! Do you then dare
To show yourself before me? Monster, whom

Too long the thunder's spared, vile brigand,
Of whom I purged the earth, as I believed,
After the transport of a horrible love
Has brought your lust even to your father's bed,
You show your hostile head! You would appear
In places full of your own infamy,
And do not seek, under an unknown sky
A country which my name has not yet reached.
Flee, traitor! Do not come to brave my hatred,
Or try a rage that I can scarcely hold.
I have enough opprobrium that I caused
The birth of such a criminal, without
Your shameful death should come to soil the glory
Of all my noble deeds. Flee! If you do not wish
A sudden death to add you to the villains
This hand has punished, take good care that never
The star that lights us see you in this place
Set a rash foot. Fly, I say; and hasten
To purge my territories forever from
Your horrible aspect. And thou, O Neptune!
If formerly my courage cleansed your shores
Of infamous assassins, remember now,
That for reward of all my happy efforts,
Thou promisedst to grant one prayer of mine.
In the long rigors of a cruel prison
I did not once implore thy immortal power;
Niggardly of the help that I expected,
I saved my prayers for greater needs. Today
I do implore thee. Avenge a wretched father!
This traitor I abandon to thy wrath.
In his own blood stifle his shameless lusts.
And by thy furies I shall recognize
Thy favors.

HIPPOLYTUS: Does Phaedra charge Hippolytus
With love incestuous? Such an excess of horror
Renders me speechless. So many sudden blows
Crush me at once, they take away my words

And choke my utterance.

THESEUS: Traitor, you thought
Phaedra would bury in a cowardly silence
Your brutal conduct. You should not have left
The sword which in her hands has helped to damn you.
Or rather, piling up your perfidy,
You should have bought her silence with her life.

HIPPOLYTUS: With this black falsehood righteously incensed,
I would now speak the truth; but I suppress
A secret that would touch you too. Approve
The respect which seals my lips; and, without wishing
To augment your griefs, I urge you to examine
My life. Remember who I am. Small crimes
Always precede the great. Whoever crosses
The bounds of law may violate at last
The holiest rights. There are degrees of crime
Just as of virtue—never innocence
Changes to utter license at one stroke.
One day alone is not enough to turn
A good man to a treacherous murderer,
Still less to incest. Suckled at the breast
Of a chaste heroine, I have not belied
The fountain of her blood. Pitheus, thought
To be the wisest of all men, did deign
To instruct me. I do not wish to give
Too favorable a picture of myself;
But if some virtue's fallen to my share,
My lord, I think that I have clearly shown
My hatred of the crimes imputed to me.
By this Hippolytus is known in Greece.
I've pushed my virtue to the edge of harshness.
My moral inflexibility is known.
The day's not purer than my inmost heart,
And people wish Hippolytus could be smitten
By some profane love. . . .

THESEUS: Yes, it is that same pride
Which now condemns you. I see the hateful cause

Of your frigidity. Phaedra alone
Charmed your lascivious eyes; your soul, indifferent
To every other object, disdained to burn
With innocent flames.

HIPPOLYTUS: No, father, this my heart—
I cannot hide it longer—has not disdained
To burn with virtuous love. I do confess
My veritable offense. I love. I love
('Tis true) despite your prohibition, sir.
Aricia to her laws holds me enslaved.
The daughter of Pallas has overcome your son.
I worship her; rebellious to your orders
I can neither sigh nor burn, except for her.

THESEUS: You love her? Heavens! But no, the artifice
Is gross. You feign yourself a criminal
To justify yourself.

HIPPOLYTUS: For six months now,
My lord, I shunned her, but I loved. I came
Trembling to tell you. Can nothing disabuse you?
Or by what terrible oath can I convince you?
By earth, and heaven, and by the whole of nature . . .

THESEUS: Rogues always have recourse to perjury.
Cease, cease, and spare me further useless speech,
If your feigned virtue has no other aid.

HIPPOLYTUS: Although to you it may seem false and cunning,
Phaedra, within her heart, will be more just.

THESEUS: Ah! how your impudence excites my wrath!

HIPPOLYTUS: How long my exile? What the place prescribed?

THESEUS: Even if you should go beyond the pillars
Of Hercules, I still would be too near you.

HIPPOLYTUS: Charged with this hideous crime, I should not have
One friend to plead for me when you desert me.

THESEUS: Go seek for friends who morbidly applaud
Adultery and incest, ungrateful traitors,
Dishonorable and lawless, fit protectors
Of such a villain.

HIPPOLYTUS: You speak to me once more
Of incest and adultery. I hold
My peace. Yet Phaedra's mother . . . Phaedra springs
From a race, as you well know, my lord, more filled
With horrors than mine is.

THESEUS: What! will your rage
Lose all restraint before me? For the last time,
Out of my sight! Go, traitor. Do not wait
For a wrathful father to have you driven out
With infamy. [*Exit* HIPPOLYTUS.]

(IV.3)

THESEUS: O wretched man, you run
To inevitable destruction. Neptune, feared
Even by the gods themselves, has given his word,
And he'll perform it. An avenging god
Pursues you, and you'll not escape. I loved you,
And feel that notwithstanding your offense
My heart is yearning for you in advance.
But it was you who forced me to condemn you.
Was ever father more outraged than I?
Just gods, you see the grief that overwhelms me.
How could I father such a guilty child?

(*Enter* PHAEDRA.) (IV.4)

PHAEDRA: My lord, I come to you with fearful heart.
I overheard your wrathful voice, and tremble
Lest your dire threats should have a prompt result.
If there is still time, spare your child, your blood.
I dare to implore you. Save me from the horror
Of hearing his blood cry. O do not cause me
The everlasting grief of spilling it
By a father's hand.

THESEUS: No, madam, in my own blood
My hand has not been steeped. But none the less
He's not escaped me. An immortal hand
Is charged with his destruction. Neptune himself
Owes it to me, and you will be avenged.

PHAEDRA: Neptune owes it to you! Your wrathful prayers . . .

THESEUS: What! do you fear now lest they should be answered?
Rather join yours unto my lawful prayers.
Recount to me his crimes in all their vileness;
Heat up my anger which is too restrained,
Too slow. For you are not acquainted yet
With all his crimes. His mad attempt against you
Has led to further wrongs. Your mouth, he says,
Is full of lies; and he maintains, his heart
And faith are given to Aricia—that he loves her.

PHAEDRA: What, my lord?

THESEUS: That's what he said, but I
Knew how to take this frivolous pretense.
Let's hope from Neptune a swift stroke of justice.
I'm going myself to pray before his altar,
To accomplish his immortal vows with speed.

[*Exit* THESEUS.]

(IV.5)

PHAEDRA: He's gone. What news has beaten on my ears!
What half-extinguished fire within my breast
Revives! What thunderbolt! What dreadful news!
I flew, with all my heart, to save his son,
Breaking away from the restraining arms
Of terrified Œnone; to my remorse
I yielded. And who knows how far it would
Have carried me? Perhaps to accuse myself;
Perhaps, if my voice had failed not, the dread truth
Might have escaped me. . . . Hippolytus feels love,
But not for me. Aricia has his heart!
Aricia has his faith! Gods! When the ingrate,
Pitiless to my pleading, armed himself
With eye so proud and brow so stern, I thought
His heart to love would be forever closed,
Invulnerable to all my sex; and yet
Another has bent his will; and in his eyes
Another has found favor. Perhaps he has

A heart that's easily touched. I am alone
The object of his scorn. And I undertook
The task of his defense!

(*Enter* ŒNONE.) (IV.6)

PHAEDRA: Do you know
Œnone, what I have just learnt?
ŒNONE: No, madam.
But trembling I have come to you, and pale,
Aware of your intentions; and I feared
A madness which might well be fatal to you.
PHAEDRA: Would you believe it, Œnone? I have a rival.
ŒNONE: What?
PHAEDRA: Hippolytus is in love. I cannot doubt it.
That savage enemy no one could conquer
Whom pleading and respect would both annoy,
The tiger I encountered but with fear,
Has recognized a conqueror at least.
Aricia has found the way to his heart.
ŒNONE: Aricia?
PHAEDRA: O pain I never knew before!
To what new torment am I now reserved!
All I have suffered, all my frenzied fears,
My passion's fury and its fierce remorse,
The unbearable insult of his cruel repulse,
Shadowed but feebly what I now endure.
They love each other. By what potent spell
Have I been hoodwinked? How have they met? Since when?
And where? You must have known: why did you hide it?
Could you not tell me of their furtive love?
Were they not often seen to speak together,
To seek each other? Did they go to hide
Deep in the woods? But they, alas, could meet
With perfect freedom. Heaven itself approved
Their innocent desires. They could pursue
Their amorous purposes without remorse,

And every day, for them, broke clear and calm!
While I, sad castaway of Nature, hid
From day and light. Death is the only god
I dared invoke; and I waited him,
Feeding on gall and steeped in tears, but yet
I did not dare (so closely I was watched)
To weep my fill. I tasted that sour pleasure
In fear and trembling; and with brow serene
Disguising my distress, I was deprived
Too often of my tears.

ŒNONE: But their vain loves
Will bear no fruit, for they will meet no more.

PHAEDRA: Forever and forever they will love.
At the moment when I speak—ah! deadly thought!—
They brave the fury of a maddened lover.
Despite the exile which will sunder them,
They vow eternal faith. I cannot bear
A joy which is an outrage to me. Œnone,
Take pity on my jealous rage. That girl
Must be destroyed; the anger of my husband
Against her hateful blood must be aroused
To no light penalty. The sister's crime
Exceeds the brothers'. In my jealous fury
I wish to urge him . . . But what am I doing?
Where has my reason fled? I jealous? I
To beg of Theseus? My husband is not dead,
And I am still aflame. For whom? Each word
Makes my hair stand on end. My crimes already
Have overflowed the measure. Both at once
I breathe the stench of incest and deceit.
My murderous hands, all apt for vengeance, burn
To plunge in innocent blood! Wretch! And I live!
And I endure the sight of sacred Phoebus
From whom I am derived. My ancestor
Is sire and master of the gods; and heaven,
Nay all the universe, is teeming now
With my forbears. Where then can I hide?

Flee to eternal night. What do I say?
For there my father holds the fatal urn,
Put by the Fates in his stern hands, 'tis said.
Minos in Hades judges the pale ghosts.
Ah, how his shade will tremble when his eyes
Behold his daughter there, confessing sins—
Crimes yet unknown in hell! What wilt thou say,
Father, to see this hideous spectacle?
Methinks I now behold the dreadful urn
Fall from thy hand! Methinks I see thee search
For some new punishment, thyself become
The torturer of thine own blood. Forgive:
A cruel god has doomed thy family.
Behold his vengeance in thy daughter's lust.
But yet, alas, never has my sad heart
Once plucked the fruit of the atrocious crime
Whose shame pursues me. Dogged by miseries
To the last gasp, in torture, I render up
A life I long to lose.

ŒNONE: Repel, madam,
An unreal terror! Behold with other eyes
A venial fault. You love. One's destiny
Cannot be overcome, and you were drawn
By a fatal spell. Is it a prodigy
Unknown before amongst us? And has love
Conquered no other hearts than yours alone?
Frailty is but too natural to us all.
You are a mortal—bow to mortals' lot.
The yoke that you bewail is nothing new:
The gods themselves—the dwellers on Olympus—
Who scare us from such crimes, have before now
Been scorched with lawless fires.

PHAEDRA: What do I hear?
What counsels do you dare to give me now?
Would you thus poison me until the end?
Wretch! Thus you ruined me; and when I fled
You brought me back. It was your pleading

Made me forget my duty. When I avoided
Hippolytus, it was you who made me see him.
What have you done? Why has your wicked mouth
Blackened his honor? Perhaps he will be slain,
The father's impious prayer to Neptune answered.
No longer will I hearken to you. Go,
Thou execrable monster, go and leave me
To my unhappy fate. May the just gods
Reward thee with a punishment to fright
Those who by servile arts feed princes' vices,
Urging them down the path they wish to take,
And smoothing it before them—base flatterers,
The most pernicious gift the angry heavens
Can give to kings. [*Exit* PHAEDRA.]

ŒNONE: Ah! Gods! to do her service
I have done all, left all. And I receive
This for reward. I get but my deserts.

Act V

HIPPOLYTUS *and* ARICIA.

ARICIA: How in this mortal danger can you still
Keep silence, and thus leave a loving father
In error? If you scorn my pleading tears,
And easily consent no more to see me,
Go, separate yourself from sad Aricia:
But yet, before you leave, preserve your life;
Defend your honor from a vile reproach,
And force your father to revoke his prayers.
There is still time. Why, by what caprice,
Do you leave the field thus free to your accuser?
Enlighten Theseus.

HIPPOLYTUS: What have I not said?
Should I reveal the soiling of his bed?
Should I, by telling a too truthful tale,

Make flush my father's brow? For you alone
Have pierced the hateful mystery. My heart
Can be unbosomed only to the gods
And you. I could not hide from you—by this
Judge if I love you—all I would conceal
Even from myself. But yet remember, madam,
Under what seal I have revealed it to you.
Forget, if you are able, what I've said,
And may you never open your chaste lips
To tell of this affair. Let us rely
Upon the justice of the gods, for they
Are much concerned to justify me; and Phaedra
Sooner or later punished for her crime
Cannot avoid deserved ignominy.
That's all I ask of you. I permit all else
To my unbounded anger. Leave the serfdom
To which you are reduced, and follow me.
Dare to accompany my flight, Aricia.
Dare to come with me; snatch yourself away
From this unholy place, where virtue breathes
A poisoned air. To hide your disappearance,
Profit from the confusion that is caused
By my disgrace. I can assure the means
For your departure. All your guards are mine,
Powerful upholders of our cause. Argos
Holds out its arms to us, and Sparta calls us.
Let's bear our righteous cries to mutual friends;
And suffer not that Phaedra by our ruin
Should drive us from the throne, and to her son
Promise your spoil and mine. The chance is good;
We must embrace it. . . . What fear now restrains you?
You seem uncertain. Your interest alone
Inspires me to this boldness. When I am
Ablaze, what freezes you? Are you afraid
To tread with me the paths of exile?

ARICIA: Alas!
How dear, my lord, would such an exile be!

Tied to your fate, with what delight would I
Live, by the rest of mortals quite forgotten!
But since I'm not united by such ties,
Can I, with honor, flee with you? I know
That without blemish I can free myself
From Theseus' hands—it would not be to leave
The bosom of my family—and flight
Is lawful if we flee from tyrants. But,
My lord, you love me, and my startled honor . . .

HIPPOLYTUS: No, no, I've too much care of your renown.
A nobler plan has brought me in your presence:
Flee from your enemies, and follow me,
Your husband. Free in our misfortunes, since
Heaven has ordained it so, our troth depends
Upon ourselves alone. Hymen need not
Be ringed with torches. At the gates of Troezen,
Among the tombs, the ancient sepulchers
Of the princes of my line, is a holy temple
Dreadful to perjurers. 'Tis there that mortals
Dare not make empty vows, lest they receive
Swift punishment; and, fearing there to meet
Inevitable death, the lie has not
A sterner bridle. There, if you will trust me,
We will confirm the solemn oath, and take
To witness it the god who's worshipped there,
Praying that he will act as father to us.
I'll call to witness the most sacred gods,
The chaste Diana, Juno the august,
And all the gods who, witnessing my love,
Will guarantee my holy promises.

ARICIA: The King is coming. Fly, Prince; leave at once.
I will remain a moment, to conceal
My own departure. Go, but leave with me
Some faithful guide to lead my timid steps
To where you wait for me. [*Exit* HIPPOLYTUS.]

(*Enter* THESEUS *and* ISMENE.) (V.2)

THESEUS (*aside*): O Gods! enlighten
My troubled heart, and deign to show the truth
That I am seeking here.
ARICIA (*to* ISMENE): Remember all,
My dear Ismene, and prepare for flight. [*Exit* ISMENE.]

(V.3)

THESEUS: You change your color, and seem speechless, madam.
What was Hippolytus doing here?
ARICIA: My lord,
To bid me an eternal farewell.
THESEUS: Your eyes
Have learnt to conquer that rebellious spirit,
And his first sighs were your accomplishment.
ARICIA: My lord, I cannot hide the truth from you.
He's not inherited your unjust hate;
He does not treat me as a criminal.
THESEUS: I see. He vows you an eternal love.
Do not rely on his inconstant heart,
For he would swear as much to others.
ARICIA: He,
My lord?
THESEUS: You ought to have made him less inconstant.
How can you bear this horrible division
Of his affections?
ARICIA: And how do you endure
That a horrible tale should smirch a blameless life?
Have you so little knowledge of his heart?
Do you discriminate so ill, my lord,
'Twixt crime and innocence? Must a hateful cloud
Conceal his virtue from your eyes alone,
Which brightly shines for others? It is wrong
To give him up to lying tongues. Cease now:
Repent your murderous prayers. Fear lest the heavens
Should bear you so much hatred as to grant
What you implored. For often in their wrath
They take our proffered victims; and their gifts
Are but the punishments of our own crimes.

THESEUS: No. You wish in vain to hide his outrage.
You're blinded by your love. I put my trust
In sure and irreproachable witnesses:
I've seen, I've seen a stream of genuine tears.

ARICIA: Take care, my lord. Your hands invincible
Have freed mankind of monsters without number,
But all are not destroyed, and you have left
One still alive. . . . Your son, my lord, forbids me
To tell you more. And knowing the respect
He wishes to retain for you, I would
Afflict him sorely if I dared to speak.
I imitate his modesty, and flee
Out of your presence, lest I should be forced
To break my silence. [*Exit* ARICIA.]

(V.4)

THESEUS: What is in her mind?
What does it hide, this speech of hers, begun
So many times, and always interrupted?
Would they distract me with an empty feint?
Have they agreed together to torture me?
But I myself, in spite of my stern rigor,
What plaintive voice within my heart cried out?
I am afflicted by a secret pity,
And stand amazed. Let me a second time
Interrogate Œnone. I want to have
A clearer picture of the crime. Guards,
Send for Œnone. Let her come alone.

(*Enter* PANOPE.) (V.5)

PANOPE: My lord, I know not what the Queen is planning,
But yet I fear her violent distress.
Mortal despair is painted on her face,
Marked with Death's pallor. Œnone, from her presence
Driven away with shame, has thrown herself
Into the deep sea: it is not known why
She took her desperate action; and the waves
Have hidden her forever.

THESEUS: What do I hear?

PANOPE: The Queen has not been calmed by this dread deed.
Distress still grows within her doubtful soul.
Sometimes, to ease her secret griefs, she takes
Her children, bathing them with tears,
And then, renouncing her maternal love,
She suddenly repels them with her hand.
Then here and there she walks irresolute,
Her wandering eyes no longer knowing us.
Thrice she has written; then, with change of mind,
Thrice she has torn the letter she began.
Deign to see her, my lord, and try to help her.

THESEUS: O heavens! Œnone dead! and Phaedra now
Desires to die. Recall my son. Let him
Defend himself. Let him come and speak with me.
I'm ready to hear him. O Neptune, do not hasten
Thy deadly blessings. I would now prefer
That they should never be fulfilled. Perhaps
I have believed unfaithful witnesses
And raised too soon towards thee my cruel hands.
By what despair now will my prayers be followed!

[*Exit* PANOPE.]

(*Enter* THERAMENES.) (v.6)

THESEUS: Theramenes, is it you? What have you done
With Hippolytus? I entrusted him to you
From a tender age. But what has caused these tears
I see you shedding? What is my son doing?

THERAMENES: O tardy and superfluous cares, vain love!
Hippolytus is no more.

THESEUS: O Gods!

THERAMENES: I have seen
The most lovable of mortals die, and I must add,
My lord, the least guilty.

THESEUS: My son is dead?
When I hold out my arms to him, the gods
Have hastened his destruction. What dread blow

Has snatched him from me? What sudden thunderclap?
THERAMENES: Scarce had we passed the gates of Troezen,
He rode upon his chariot; his sad guards,
Around him ranged, were silent as their lord.
Brooding, he followed the Mycenæ road,
And loosely held the reins. His splendid steeds,
Which once with noble zeal obeyed his voice,
Now with dejected eye and lowered head
Seemed to adapt themselves to his sad thoughts.
Then suddenly from out the waves there came
A dreadful cry which broke the silent air
And from the bosom of the earth a voice
With dreadful groans replied. Our blood was frozen,
Even to our hearts. The manes of the listening steeds
Stood up. Then on the liquid plain arose
A watery mountain which appeared to boil.
The wave approached, then broke, and vomited
Among the foamy seas a raging monster:
His huge head armed with menacing horns, his body
Covered with yellow scales, half-bull, half-dragon,
With his croup curved in involuted folds.
The seashore trembled with his bellowing;
The sky with horror saw that savage monster;
The earth was moved, the air infected with it;
The sea which brought it started back amazed.
Everyone fled; seeing all courage vain,
They sought asylum in a neighboring temple.
Hippolytus alone, a worthy son
Of a heroic father, stopped his horses,
Seized his javelins, approached the monster,
And, with a dart, thrown with unerring aim,
Wounded it in the flank. With rage and pain,
The monster leapt, and at the horses' feet
Fell roaring, rolled itself, and offered them
Its flaming mouth, which covered them with fire,
And blood and smoke. Then terror seized them; deaf,
This time, nor voice nor bridle did they know.

Their master spent himself in useless efforts;
Their bits were reddened with a bloody foam.
'Tis said, that in this terrible confusion
A god was seen who spurred their dusty flanks.
Fear hurtled them across the rocks. The axle
Screeched and snapped. The bold Hippolytus
Saw all his chariot shiver into splinters;
And tangled in the reins, he fell. Excuse
My grief. That cruel sight will be for me
An everlasting source of tears. I've seen,
My lord, I've seen your most unlucky son
Dragged by the horses which his hands had fed.
He tried to check them; but, frightened by his voice,
They ran; and soon his body was a single wound.
The plain resounded with our grievous cries.
At last they slackened speed; they stopped not far
From those old tombs where his royal ancestors
Are the cold relics. There I ran, in tears,
And his guard followed me. A trail of blood
Showed us the way. The rocks were stained with it.
The loathsome brambles carried bloodstained scraps
Of hair torn from his head. I reached him, called
To him; he stretched his hand to me, and opened
His dying eyes, then closed them suddenly.
"The heavens," said he, "now snatch my guiltless life.
Look after Aricia when I am dead.
Dear friend, if my father one day learns the truth,
And weeps the tragic ending of a son
Falsely accused, in order to appease
My blood and plaintive ghost, tell him to treat
His captive kindly, to give her . . ." At this word
The hero died and left within my arms
Only a corpse, disfigured, where the wrath
Of the gods had triumphed, one which his father's eyes
Would fail to recognize.

THESEUS: My son! dear hope
Now taken from me! Inexorable gods,

Too well indeed you have fulfilled your word!
To what remorse my life is now reserved!
THERAMENES: Then gentle Aricia arrived; she came,
My lord, escaping from your wrath, to take him
Before the gods as husband. She approached.
She saw the red and reeking grass; she saw
(What an object for a lover's eyes!)
Hippolytus lying there a shapeless mass.
A while she wished to doubt of her disaster
And failed to recognize the man she loved.
She saw Hippolytus—and asked for him still.
At last too sure that he was lying there,
She with a mournful look reproached the gods;
Cold, moaning, almost lifeless, she fell down
At her lover's feet. Ismene was beside her;
Ismene, weeping, brought her back to life,
Or rather, back to grief. And I have come,
Hating the light, to tell you the last wish
Of a dead hero; and discharge, my lord,
The unhappy task his dying heart reposed
Upon me. But I see his mortal foe
Approaching.

(*Enter* PHAEDRA, PANOPE, *and* GUARDS.) (v.7)

THESEUS: Well, you triumph, and my son
Is lifeless. Ah! how I have cause to fear!
A cruel suspicion, excusing him, alarms me.
But, madam, he is dead. Receive your victim,
Joy in his death, whether unjust or lawful.
I'll let my eyes forever be abused,
Believe him criminal, since you accuse him.
His death alone gives matter for my tears
Without my seeking harsh enlightenment,
Which could not bring him back, and might increase
The sum of my misfortunes. Let me, far from you,
Far from this coast flee from the bloody image
Of my rent son. Perplexed and persecuted

By deadly memories, I would banish me
From the whole world. Everything seems to rise
Against my injustice. Even my very fame
Augments my punishment. Less known of men,
I could the better hide. I hate the honors
The gods bestow upon me; and I'm going
To mourn their murderous favors, and no more
Tire them with useless prayers. Whate'er they granted,
Would never compensate me for the loss
Of what they've taken away.

PHAEDRA: No, Theseus.
I must break an unjust silence; to your son
Restore his innocence. He was not guilty.

THESEUS: Unhappy father! It was by your word
That I condemned him. Cruel! do you think
That you can be excused . . . ?

PHAEDRA: My time is precious.
Hear me, Theseus. It was I myself
Who cast upon your chaste and modest son
Unholy and incestuous eyes. The heavens
Put in my breast that fatal spark—the rest
Was undertaken by the vile Œnone.
She trembled lest Hippolytus should disclose
A passion he abhorred. The traitress then,
Relying on my utter weakness, hastened
To accuse him to your face. She's punished for it.
Fleeing my wrath she sought amidst the waves
Too soft a punishment. The sword by now
Would have cut short my life, had I not left
Virtue suspected. Baring my remorse
Before you, I wished to take a slower road
To the house of Death. I have taken—I have made
Course through my burning veins a deadly poison
Medea brought to Athens. Already the venom
Has reached my dying heart, and thrown upon it
An unimagined cold. Already I see,
As through a mist, the sky above, the husband

My presence outrages; and Death, that robs
My eyes of clearness, to the tarnished day
Restores its purity.

PANOPE: She is dying, my lord.

THESEUS: Oh! that the memory of her black deed
Could perish with her! Of my error now
Only too well enlightened, let us go
To mix the blood of my unhappy son
With tears; to embrace the little that remains
Of that dear son, and expiate the madness
Of my detested prayer; to render him
The honors that he has too much deserved;
And, the better to appease his angry spirit,
Despite her family's plotting, from today
I'll hold Aricia as my own true child.

Athaliah

by RACINE

TRANSLATED BY *Kenneth Muir*

PREFACE

Everyone knows that the kingdom of Judah was composed of the two tribes of Judah and Benjamin, and that the other ten tribes who rebelled against Rehoboam composed the kingdom of Israel. As the kings of Judah were of the house of David, and as they had in their territory the town and Temple of Jerusalem, all the priests and Levites settled near them and remained attached to them: for, since the building of Solomon's Temple, it was not permitted to sacrifice elsewhere; and all those other altars which were erected to God on the mountains, called in the Scriptures for that reason the high places, were not agreeable to Him. So the legitimate cult existed no longer except in Judah. The ten tribes, except for a very few people, were either idolaters or schismatics.

Yet these priests and Levites were themselves a very numerous tribe. They were divided into different classes to serve in turn in the Temple, from one sabbath to another. The priests were of the family of Aaron; and only those of this family could perform the office of sacrificer. The Levites were subordinate to them, and had the task, among other things, of singing, of the preparation of the victims, and of guarding the Temple. This name of Levite is sometimes given indifferently to all those of the tribe. Those who were on their weekly turn of duty had, together with the High Priest, their lodging in the porches or galleries with which the Temple was surrounded, and which were a part of the Temple itself. All the building was called in general the holy place; but that part of the inner temple where the golden candlestick, the altar of the incense, and the tables of the shewbread were, was called more particularly by that name; and that part was again distinguished from the Holy of Holies, where the Ark was, and where the High Priest alone had the right to enter once a year. There was a tradition, almost without a break, that the mountain on which the Temple was built was the same mountain where Abraham had once offered his son Isaac in sacrifice.

I thought I should explain these details, so that those to whom the story of the Old Testament is not familiar will not be held up in reading this tragedy. Its subject is Joas recognized and placed on the throne; and according to the rules I should have entitled it *Joas*; but most people having heard of it only under the name of *Athaliah*, I have not thought it proper to offer it to them under another title, since in addition Athaliah plays so considerable a part in it, and since it is her death which concludes the play. She is a party to the principal events which precede this great action.

Joram,[1] King of Judah, son of Jehoshaphat, and the seventh king of the race of David, married Athaliah, daughter of Ahab and Jezebel, who reigned in Israel, both famous, but especially Jezebel, for their bloody persecutions of the prophets. Athaliah, not less impious than her mother, soon drew the King, her husband, into idolatry, and even had a temple built in Jerusalem to Baal, who was the god of the country of Tyre and Sidon, where Jezebel was born. Joram, after having seen perish by the hands of Arabs and Philistines all the princes, his children, except Ahaziah, died himself of a long malady which burnt up his entrails. His dreadful death did not prevent Ahaziah from imitating his impiety and that of Athaliah, his mother. But this prince, after reigning for only a year, while on a visit to the King of Israel, brother of Athaliah, was enveloped in the ruin of the house of Ahab, and killed by the orders of Jehu, whom God had anointed to reign over Israel and to be the minister of his vengeance. Jehu exterminated all the posterity of Ahab and caused

[1] [Jehoram in the King James Bible.—Trans.]

Jezebel to be thrown from the window, who, according to the prophecy of Elijah, was eaten by the dogs in the vineyard of the same Naboth who had been slain formerly so as to deprive him of his inheritance. Athaliah, having learned of all these massacres at Jerusalem, undertook on her part to extinguish completely the royal race of David, by causing to be slain all the children of Ahaziah, her own grandsons. But luckily Josabeth, sister of Ahaziah and daughter of Joram, but a different sort of mother from Athaliah, arriving during the massacres of the princes, her nephews, found means to snatch from the midst of the dead the infant Joas, still at the breast, and entrusted him with his nurse to the care of the High Priest, her husband, who hid them both in the Temple, where the child was brought up secretly till the day he was proclaimed King of Judah. The *Book of Kings* says that this was seven years afterwards. But the Greek text of *Chronicles*, which Severus Sulpicius has followed, says it was eight. It is this which authorizes me to make the prince nine or ten, to make him old enough to reply to the questions put to him.

I believe I have made him say nothing beyond the capacity of a child of this age with a good intelligence and memory. But even if I have, it must be considered that this is a quite exceptional child, brought up in the Temple by a High Priest who, looking on him as the unique hope of his nation, has instructed him from an early age in all the duties of religion and royalty. It was not the same with the children of the Jews as with most of ours: they were taught the sacred writings, not merely before they had attained the use of reason, but, to use Saint Paul's expression, from the breast. Every Jew was obliged to write once in his life, with his own hand, the whole book of the Law. The kings were even obliged to write it twice, and enjoined to have it continually before their eyes. I can say here that France sees in the person of a prince of eight and a half years, who delights us even now, an illustrious example of what a child, of natural ability aided by an excellent education, can do; and that if I had given to the child Joas the same vivacity and the same discernment which shines in the repartees of this young prince, I should have been accused with reason of having transgressed the rules of verisimilitude.

The age of Zachariah, son of the High Priest, not having been mentioned, one can suppose him, if one likes, to be two or three years older than Joas.

I have followed the explanation of several skillful commentators, who prove by the actual text of Scripture, that all the soldiers whom Jehoiada (or Joad, as he is called in Josephus) armed with the weapons consecrated to God by David, were as much priests and Levites as the five centurions who commanded them. Indeed, say the interpreters, everyone had to be holy in so holy an action, and no profane person should be employed. What was at stake was not merely keeping the scepter in the house of David, but also keeping for that great king the line of descendants of whom the Messiah should be born. "For this Messiah promised so many times as the son of Abraham, should also be the son of David and of all the kings of Judah." From this it follows that the illustrious and learned prelate from whom I have borrowed these words calls Joas the precious remnant of the house of David. Josephus speaks of him in the same terms; and Scripture states expressly that God did not exterminate all the family of Joram, wishing to conserve for David the lamp which he had promised him. For what else was this lamp but the light which should one day be revealed to the gentiles?

History does not specify at all the day on which Joas was proclaimed. Some interpreters claim that it was a feast day. I have chosen that of Pentecost, which was one of the three great feasts of the Jews. In it was celebrated the memory of the publication of the Law on Mount Sinai, and in it was also offered to God the first loaves of the new harvest: which made it called still the feast of the first fruits. I thought that these circumstances would furnish me with some variety for the songs of the chorus.

This chorus is composed of maidens of the tribe of Levi, and I have put at their head a girl whom I have given as sister to Zachariah. It is she who introduces the chorus into her mother's house. She sings with them, speaks for them, and performs the functions of the person of the ancient choruses who was called the coryphaeus. I have also tried to imitate from the ancients that continuity of action which makes their stage never left empty, the intervals between the acts being marked by the hymns and moralizing of the chorus, who are in touch with all that passes.

I shall perhaps be found a little audacious in having dared to put on the stage a prophet inspired by God, who predicts the future. But I have taken the precaution to put into his mouth only expressions taken from the prophets themselves. Although the Scriptures do not state expressly that Jehoiada had had a spirit of prophecy, as they do of his son, they represent him as a man full of the spirit of God. And besides, would it not appear by the gospel that he would have been able to prophecy in the capacity of sovereign pontiff? I suppose, therefore, that he sees the fatal change of Joas who, after twenty years of a reign of great piety, abandoned himself to the evil counsels of flatterers, and stained himself with the blood of Zachariah, son and successor of the High Priest. This murder, committed in the Temple, was one of the principal causes of the wrath of God against the Jews and of all the misfortunes which happened to them afterwards. It is even maintained that since that day the responses of God ceased entirely in the sanctuary. That has given me the opportunity to make Joad depict the destruction of the Temple and the ruin of Jerusalem. But as the prophets ordinarily joined consolations to their threats, and as also the action was concerned with putting on the throne one of the ancestors of the Messiah, I have taken occasion to give a glimpse of the coming of this comforter, for whom all the righteous men of ancient times sighed. This scene, which is a kind of episode, brings in music very naturally, by the custom which several prophets had of entering into their holy trances to the sound of instruments: witness that troop of prophets who came before Saul with the harps and lyres which were borne before them; and witness Elisha himself, who being consulted on the future by the King of Judah and the King of Israel, said, as Joad does here: *Adducite mihi psaltem*. Add to that, that this prophecy serves greatly to augment the tension of the drama, by the consternation it causes and by the different reactions of the chorus and the principal actors.

Dramatis Personae

ABNER, *one of Athaliah's principal officers*
JOAD, *High Priest*
JOSABETH, *his wife, aunt to Joas*
ZACHARIAH, SALOMITH } *their children*
AGAR, *woman of Athaliah's suite*
MATHAN, *priest of Baal*
ATHALIAH, *widow of Joram*
JOAS, *her grandson, the rightful King, called Eliacin*
NABAL, *confidant of Mathan*
AZARIAS, ISMAEL, *and other* LEVITES
NURSE *of Joas*
ATHALIAH'S GUARDS
CHORUS *of girls of the Tribe of Levi*

Scene—The Temple of Jerusalem, in a vestibule of the apartment of the High Priest.

Act I

ABNER *and* JOAD *discovered.*

ABNER: Yes, I have come into this Temple now
To adore the Everlasting; I have come,
According to our old and solemn custom,
To celebrate with you the famous day
When on Mount Sinai the Law was given us.
How times have changed! As soon as the trumpet blast
Proclaimed the day's return, the chosen people
Poured into the sacred porticos in crowds,
And in the Temple, garlanded with flowers,
They stood before the altar rank by rank,
And to the God of the universe they offered
The first fruits of their fields. The sacrifices
By priests alone were not sufficient then.
A woman's presumption now has put a stop
To that great concourse; and to days of darkness
Has changed those happy days. Only a handful
Of zealous worshippers enable us
To trace a shadow of those former times;
While for their God the rest of them display
Fatal forgetfulness. They even flock
To Baal's altars, there to be initiated
Into his shameful mysteries, and blaspheme
The name their sires invoked. I tremble now
That Athaliah—I will hide nothing from you—
Has not yet perfected her dire revenge.
She plans to snatch you from the altar, and . . .
JOAD: Whence comes this black presentiment of yours?
ABNER: Do you imagine that you can be just
And holy with impunity? For long
She has detested that rare constancy
Which gives a double glory to your crown;
For long she's looked on your religious zeal
As rank sedition; and this jealous queen
Hates above all the faithful Josabeth,

Your wife, even for her virtues. If you are
Aaron's successor, Josabeth's the sister
Of our last king. Mathan, moreover, Mathan,
That sacrilegious priest, who is more vile
Than Athaliah herself, at every hour
Besieges her—Mathan, the foul deserter
From the Lord's altars, ever the zealous foe
Of every virtue. 'Tis little that this Levite,
His brows encircled with an alien miter,
Now ministers to Baal: to him this Temple
Is a reproach, and his impiety
Would bring to nought the God that he has left.
There are no means to which he'll not resort
To ruin you; at times he'll pity you
And often he will even sing your praises;
Affecting for you a false tenderness,
And screening so the blackness of his rancor,
He paints you to the Queen as terrible;
Or else, insatiable for gold, he feigns
That in some place that's known to you alone
You hide King David's treasure. But Athaliah
Has seemed for two days to be plunged in gloom.
I watched her yesterday, and saw her eyes
Dart furious glances on the holy place,
As if within this mighty edifice
God hid an avenger, armed for her destruction.
Believe me, Joad, the more I think of it,
The more I am convinced her wrath is ready
To burst upon you, that the bloody daughter
Of Jezebel will soon attack our God,
Even in His sanctuary.

JOAD: He who can bridle
The fury of the waves knows how to foil
The plots of the wicked. Submissive to His will,
I fear the Lord, and have no other fear.
Yet, Abner, I am grateful for the zeal
Which has awakened you to all my perils.

I see injustice vexes you in secret;
That you are still an Israelite at heart.
Heaven be praised! But can you be content
With secret wrath and with an idle virtue?
And can the faith that acts not be sincere?
Eight years ago an impious foreigner
Usurped all the rights of David's scepter,
And with impunity imbrued herself
In the blood of our true kings—foul murderess
Of the children of her son, and even against God
Her treacherous arm is raised:
While you a pillar of this tottering State,
Brought up within the camps of Jehoshaphat,
That holy king, and under his son, Joram,
Commander of his hosts, who reassured
Our fearful towns when Ahaziah was slain,
And all his army at the sight of Jehu
Scattered in panic—"I fear the Lord," you say;
"His truth concerns me." By me that God replies:
"For what use is the zeal that you profess?
Think'st thou to honor me with barren vows?
What do I get from all your sacrifices?
Do I require the blood of goats and heifers?
The blood of your kings cries out and is not heard.
Break off all compact with impiety!
Root out the evil from among my people
And then approach me with your burnt offerings."
ABNER: What can I do among this beaten people?
Judah and Benjamin are powerless now:
The day that saw their race of kings extinguished
Extinguished too their ancient bravery.
God, they say, has withdrawn Himself from us:
He, who was jealous of the Hebrews' honor,
Now, careless, sees their greatness overthrown,
And in the end His mercy is exhausted.
The countless miracles He worked for us
To terrify mankind are seen no more.

The holy Ark is dumb, and renders now
Its oracles no longer.

JOAD: And what time
Was e'er so fertile in its miracles?
When has God shown His power to such effect?
Will you forever, O ungrateful people,
Have eyes which see not? Will great miracles
Forever strike your ears, but leave your heart
Untouched? Abner, must I recall the course
Of prodigies accomplished in our days?
The woes that fell on Israel's tyrants—God
Found faithful in his threats! The impious Ahab
Destroyed, and that field sprinkled with his blood,
Which he usurped by murder; and nearby
Jezebel slain and trampled by the horses,
So that the dogs lapped up her savage blood
And tore her frightful body limb from limb;
The troop of lying prophets all confounded,
And fire from heaven descended on the altar;
Elijah speaking to the elements
As sovereign master; the skies by him locked up
And turned to brass, so that the earth three years
Had neither rain nor dew; at Elisha's voice
The dead reanimated? Recognize,
Abner, in these deeds that still resound,
A God who is indeed the same today
As in the days of old. He manifests
His glory when He wills; His chosen people
Is always present to His memory.

ABNER: But where are those honors oft to David promised,
And prophesied for Solomon, his son?
Alas! we hoped that of their happy race
There would descend a line of kings, of whom
One would at last establish his dominion
Over all tribes and nations, who would make
Discord and war to cease, and at his feet
Behold all kings of the earth.

JOAD: Wherefore renounce
The promises of heaven?
ABNER: Where shall we find
The royal son of David? Can heaven itself
Repair the ruins of this tree that's withered
Even to the very roots? For Athaliah
Stifled the child in his cradle. Can the dead,
Now eight years have gone by, come from the grave?
If in her rage she had mistook her aim,
If of our royal blood there has escaped
One drop to . . .
JOAD: Well, what would you do?
ABNER: O joyous day for me! How ardently
I'd recognize my king. You need not doubt
The tribes would hasten at his feet to lay
Their tribute. But why delude myself
With such vain thoughts? The lamentable heir
Of those triumphant monarchs, Ahaziah
Alone remained—he and his children only.
I saw the father stabbed by Jehu; you
Beheld the sons all butchered by the mother.
JOAD: I'll not explain; but when the star of day
Has traced a third of its course across the sky,
And when the third hour summons us to prayer,
Return to the Temple with the selfsame zeal,
And God may show, by signal benefits,
His word is firm, and never can deceive.
Go now, I must prepare for this great day,
And even now the pinnacle of the Temple
Is whitened by the dawn.
ABNER: What will this be—
This blessing that I cannot comprehend?
The noble Josabeth is coming towards you.
I'll join the faithful flock the solemn rite
Of this day has attracted. [*Exit* ABNER.]

Enter JOSABETH. (I.2)

JOAD: The time is ripe,
Princess, and we must speak. Your happy theft
No longer can be hidden. The insolence
Of the Lord's foes who take His name in vain
From this deep silence has accused too long
His promises of error. What do I say?
Success has fanned their fury; and on our altar
Your evil stepmother would offer Baal
Idolatrous incense. Let us show this king—
The boy your hands have saved, to be brought up
Beneath the Lord's protecting wing. He'll have
Our Hebrew princes' courage, and already
His mind's outstripped his age. Before I speak
Of his high destiny, I'll offer him
To the God by whom kings reign, and soon before
The assembled priests and Levites, I'll declare
Their master's heir.

JOSABETH: Has he himself been told
Of his real name and noble destiny?

JOAD: Not yet. He answers only to the name
Of Eliacin, and thinks he is a child
Abandoned by his mother, to whom I deigned
To act as father.

JOSABETH: Alas! from what dire peril
I rescued him, and into what more peril
Is he about to enter!

JOAD: Is your faith
Already wavering?

JOSABETH: To your wise advice,
My lord, I do submit. For from the day
I snatched this child from death, into your hands
His life and fate were placed. I even feared
The violence of my love; and therefore tried
To shun his presence, lest in seeing him,
My tears for some grief not to be suppressed
Would let my secret out. To tears and prayers
I've consecrated three whole days and nights,

As duty bid; but may I ask today
What friends you have prepared to give you aid?
Will Abner, the brave Abner, fight for us?
And has he sworn that he'll be near his king?

JOAD: Although his faith is sure, he does not yet
Know that we have a king.

JOSABETH: To whom will you
Entrust the guard of Joas? Obed or Amnon?
My father showered his benefits upon them. . . .

JOAD: They're sold to Athaliah.

JOSABETH: Whom have you then
To oppose her satellites?

JOAD: Have I not told you?
Our priests, our Levites.

JOSABETH: I know indeed
That by your foresight secretly assembled
Their number is redoubled; that, full of love
For you, and full of hate for Athaliah,
A solemn oath has bound them in advance
To this son of David who will be revealed.
But though a noble ardor burns in them,
Can they alone their king's cause vindicate?
Can zeal alone for such a work suffice?
Do you doubt that Athaliah—when first 'tis bruited
That Ahaziah's son is cloistered here—
Will mass her foreign cohorts, to surround
The Temple and break in the doors. 'Gainst them
Will these your holy ministers suffice,
Who lifting innocent hands unto the Lord
Can only weep and pray for all our sins,
And ne'er shed blood, save of the sacrifice?
Joas, perhaps, pierced through with hostile spears,
Will in their arms . . .

JOAD: Is God who fights for us
By you accounted nothing? God who protects
The orphan's innocence, and makes his power
Displayed in weakness; God who hates the tyrant;

Who in Jezreel did vow to extirpate
Ahab and Jezebel; God, who striking Joram,
Their son-in-law, pursued the family,
Even to his son; God, whose avenging arm,
Suspended for a time, is still outstretched
Over this impious race?

JOSABETH: And His stern justice
Meted to all these kings is cause for me
To fear for my unlucky brother's son,
For who can tell, if by their crime enmeshed,
This child from birth was not condemned with them?
If God, for David's sake, dividing him
From all that odious race would grant him favor?
Alas! the horrible scene when heaven offered
The child to me again and again returns
To terrify my soul. The room was filled
With murdered princes. Relentless Athaliah,
A dagger in her hand, urged to the kill
Her barbarous soldiers, and pursued the course
Of all her murders. Joas, left for dead,
Suddenly struck my eyes; and even now
I see his frightened nurse throwing herself
In vain before his butchers, holding him
Head downwards on her breast. I took him, steeped
In blood. I bathed his face in tears. And then
I felt his innocent arms go round my neck,
In fear, or to caress me. O great God!
Let not my love be fatal to him now—
This precious relic of the faithful David
Here in thy house nourished upon the love
Of thy great Law. He knows as yet no father
Save Thee alone. Though in the face of peril,
When we're about to attack a murderous queen,
My faith begins to waver, though flesh and blood,
Faltering today, have some part in the tears
I shed for him, preserve the heritage
Of Thy sacred promises, and do not punish

Any save me for all my weaknesses.
JOAD: Your tears are guiltless, Josabeth; but God
Wills us to hope in his paternal care.
He is not wont to visit in his rage
The impiety of the father on the son
Who fears him. The faithful remnant of the Jews
Come to renew their vows to him today.
Even as David's race is still respected,
So is the daughter of Jezebel detested.
Joas will touch them with his innocence
In which the splendor of his blood reshines;
And God by His voice upholding our example
Will speak unto their hearts. Two faithless kings
Successively have braved Him. To the throne
A king must now be raised who'll not forget
God, by his priests, has placed him in the rank
Of his great ancestors, by their hand snatched him
From the tomb's oblivion, and lit again
The torch of David. Great God, if Thou foreseest
He'll be unworthy of his race, and leave
The ways of David, let him be as the fruit
Torn from the branch, or withered in its flower
By a hostile wind! But if this child should prove
Docile to Thy commands, an instrument
Useful to Thy designs, then hand the scepter
To the rightful heir; deliver into my hands
His powerful enemies; frustrate the counsels
Of this cruel queen; and grant, O grant, my God,
That upon her and Mathan shall be poured
Error and rashness, of the fall of kings
Fatal vaunt-courier! The time is short.
Farewell! Your son and daughter bring you now
The damsels of the holiest families. [*Exit* JOAD.]

(*Enter* ZACHARIAH, SALOMITH, *and* CHORUS.) (I.3)

JOSABETH: Dear Zachariah, go now. Do not stop.
Accompany your noble father's steps. [*Exit* ZACHARIAH.]

Daughters of Levi, young and faithful flock,
Kindled already by the zeal of the Lord,
Who come so often all my sighs to share,
Children, my only joy in my long sorrows,
These garlands and these flowers upon your heads
Once suited with our solemn festivals;
But now, alas, in times of shame and sorrow,
What offering suits better than our tears?
I hear already, I hear the sacred trumpet;
The Temple soon will open. While I prepare,
Sing, praise the Lord whom you have come to seek.

[*Exeunt* JOSABETH *and* SALOMITH.]

(I.4)

ALL THE CHORUS: All the universe is full of His glory!
Let us adore this God, and call upon Him!
His Empire was before the birth of Time!
O let us sing, his benefits to praise!
A VOICE: In vain unrighteous violence
Upon his worshippers imposeth silence:
His name will live always.
Day telleth day of His magnificence.
All the universe is full of His glory:
O let us sing, His benefits to praise.
ALL: All the universe is full of His glory:
O let us sing, His benefits to praise.
A VOICE: He gives unto the flowers their lovely hues,
He slowly ripens fruits upon the tree,
And gives them warmth by day and nightly dews;
The field repays his gifts with usury.
ANOTHER: The sun all nature doth reanimate
At His command; He gives the blessed light;
But His best gift to those He did create
Is still His holy Law, our pure delight.
ANOTHER: O Sinai, preserve the memory
Renowned forevermore of that great day
When from a thick cloud on thy flaming peak
The Lord made shine to mortal eyes a ray

Of His eternal glory! Why those flames,
The lightning flash, the eddying clouds of smoke,
Trumpets and thunder in the resounding air?
Came He to overturn the elemental order,
And shake the earth upon its ancient base?

ANOTHER: No, no, He came to reveal the eternal light
Of His holy laws to the children of the Jews;
He came to that happy people, to command them
To love Him with an everlasting love.

ALL: Divine and lovely Law,
O bounteous and just!
How right, how sweet to pledge
To God our love and trust!

A VOICE: He freed our fathers from the tyrant's yoke;
Fed them on manna in the wilderness;
He gives His laws, He gives Himself to us:
And for these blessings asks for love alone.

ALL: O bounteous and just!

A VOICE: For them He cleft the waters of the sea;
He made streams gush out from the arid rock.
He gives His laws, He gives Himself to us,
And for these blessings asks for love alone.

CHORUS: Divine and lovely Law!
How right, how sweet to pledge
To God our love and trust!

A VOICE: Ingrates, who only know a servile fear,
Cannot a God so gracious touch your heart?
Is love so stony and so hard a path?
It is the slave who fears the tyrant's wrath,
But filial love remains the children's part.
You wish this God to shower His gifts on you,
And never give the love that is His due.

CHORUS: Divine and lovely Law!
O bounteous and just!
How right, how sweet to pledge
To God our love and trust.

Act II

JOSABETH, SALOMITH, *and* CHORUS.

JOSABETH: Enough, my daughters. Cease your canticles.
'Tis time to join us now in public prayers.
The hour is come. Let's celebrate this day
And appear before the Lord. But what do I see?

(*Enter* ZACHARIAH.) (II.2)

JOSABETH: My son, what brings you here? Where do you run,
All pale and out of breath?
ZACHARIAH: O Mother . . .
JOSABETH: Well?
What is it?
ZACHARIAH: The Temple is profaned. . . .
JOSABETH: How?
ZACHARIAH: The altar of the Lord abandoned!
JOSABETH: I tremble.
Hasten to tell me all.
ZACHARIAH: Even now my father,
The High Priest, had offered, according to the Law,
The first loaves of the harvest to our God
Who feeds us all. And then he held aloft
The smoking entrails of the sacrifice
In bloodstained hands, while young Eliacin,
Like me, stood by his side and ministered,
Clad in a linen robe, and while the priests
Sprinkled the altar and the congregation
With blood of the offerings—suddenly there was
A noise which made the people turn their eyes.
A woman . . . Can I name her without blasphemy? . . .
A woman . . . It was Athaliah herself.
JOSABETH: Great heaven!
ZACHARIAH: Into a sanctuary reserved for men
Entered that haughty woman, head held high,
And made to pass into the holy precincts

Open to Levites only. Struck with terror
The people fled away. My father— Ah! what wrath
Shone in his countenance, more terrible
Than Moses before Pharaoh. "Queen," he said,
"Go from this holy place, from whence thy sex
And thy impiety alike are banished.
Com'st thou indeed to brave the majesty
Of the living God?" Forthwith the Queen, upon him
Turning a fierce glance, opened her mouth to speak,
And doubtless to blaspheme. I know not whether
The Angel of the Lord appeared to her
Bearing a flaming sword; but this I know—
Her tongue was frozen in her mouth, and all
Her boldness seemed to crumble; while her eyes,
Affrighted, dared not turn away. She seemed
Amazed by Eliacin.

JOSABETH: How so? Did he
Appear before her?

ZACHARIAH: Both of us beheld
This cruel queen, and with an equal dread
Our hearts were struck. But soon the priests stood round us,
And led us forth. And that is all I know
Of this ominous disorder.

JOSABETH: Ah! from our arms
She comes to snatch him; and 'tis he her fury
Seeks even at the altar. Perhaps even now
The object of so many tears . . . O! God,
Who seest my fears, remember David now.

SALOMITH: For whom do you weep?

ZACHARIAH: Is Eliacin's life
In danger now?

SALOMITH: Could he have attracted
The anger of the Queen?

ZACHARIAH: How could they fear
A child without defense, and fatherless?

JOSABETH: She's here. Come, let us go. We must avoid her.

[*Exeunt.*]

(*Enter* ATHALIAH, ABNER, AGAR, *and* GUARDS.) (II.3)

AGAR: Your Majesty, why do you stay within
These precincts, where all objects vex and wound you?
O leave this Temple to the priests who dwell
Within its walls. Flee all this tumult now,
And in your palace strive to give back peace
To your o'ertroubled senses.

ATHALIAH: No. I cannot.
You see my weakness and disquiet. Go,
Send Mathan hither: let him come with speed. . . .
Happy if I by his aid can obtain
The peace I seek, which still eludes my grasp.

[*Exit* AGAR. ATHALIAH *sits.*]

(II.4)

ABNER: Forgive me, madam, if I dare defend
The zeal of Joad, which should not surprise you.
Such is the eternal order of our God,
For He himself marked out for us His Temple,
To Aaron's children only did entrust
His sacrifices; both their place and functions
Appointed to the Levites; and forbad
To their posterity all intercourse
With any other God. Are you, O Queen,
The daughter and the mother of our kings,
So alien to us? Know you not our laws?
And is it necessary that today . . . ?
But here is Mathan. I will leave you with him.

ATHALIAH: I need your presence, Abner. Leave at that
The reckless insolence of Joad, and all
That empty heap of superstitions
Which bars your Temple to all other peoples.
Something more urgent has aroused my fears.
I know that Abner, raised from infancy
To be a soldier, has a noble heart;
And that he renders what he owes to God,
And renders what he owes unto his kings.
Remain with us.

(*Enter* MATHAN.) (II.5)

MATHAN: Great Queen, is here your place?
What has disquieted you? What terror now
Turned you to ice? What have you come to seek
Among your enemies? Do you dare approach
This impious Temple? Have you shed your hatred?
ATHALIAH: Both of you lend me an attentive ear.
I do not wish here to recall the past,
Nor give you reasons for the blood I've shed.
What I have done I thought was necessary.
Abner, I'll not accept a headstrong people
To be my judge. Whatever their insolence
Has dared to claim, I have been justified
By heaven itself. My power that is established
On my successful deeds has made the name
Of Athaliah held in great respect
From sea to sea. By me Jerusalem
Enjoys an absolute peace. The Jordan sees
No more the wandering Arab, and no more
The haughty Philistine with endless raids
(As in your kings' days) desolate her banks.
The Syrian treats me as a queen and sister:
At last the vile oppressor of my house,
Whose savagery I myself have felt,
Jehu, proud Jehu, trembles in Samaria,
On every side hemmed in by neighboring powers
Which I have raised against that murderer.
In these domains he leaves me sovereign mistress.
I now enjoy in peace my wisdom's fruits.
But yet, for some days past, a nagging fear
Has stopped the course of my prosperity.
A dream (why should a dream disturb me so?)
Brought to my heart a gnawing pain. I tried
To escape, but everywhere it followed me:
Methought that in the dreadful deep of night
My mother Jezebel rose up before me,
All gorgeously arrayed as when she died.

Her sorrows had not quenched her pride, but still
Her face was decked and painted to repair
The irreparable ravages of time.
"Tremble, my daughter, worthy of me," she said;
"The cruel God of the Jews will soon prevail
Over you also, and I mourn that you
Are falling into His relentless hands,
My child." In uttering these frightful words,
Her ghost, it seemed, bent down towards my bed;
But when I stretched my hands out to embrace her,
I found instead a horrible heap of bones,
And mangled flesh, and tatters soaked in blood
Dragged through the mire, and limbs unspeakable
For which voracious dogs were wrangling there.

ABNER: Great God!

ATHALIAH: In this confusion there appeared
Before my eyes a child with shining robes,
Like those of the Hebrew priests. On seeing him
My spirits revived, my deadly fear subsided.
But while I wondered at his noble bearing,
His charm and modesty, then all at once
I felt a murderous dagger which the traitor
Plunged deep into my heart. Perhaps you think
This mingling of such diverse images
In my strange dream was but the work of chance.
And I myself, ashamed of my own fear,
Have thought at times they must be the effect
Of some dark vapor. But my soul, possessed
With this remembrance, saw the selfsame sights
Twice visit me in sleep. Twice did my eyes
Behold this child prepare again to stab me,
Until worn down by these pursuing terrors
I went to pray to Baal for his protection,
And seek for peace of mind before his altars.
What cannot panic do to mortal minds?
Urged by a sudden impulse to this Temple
I came instead, thus hoping to appease

The Jewish God, and calm His wrath with gifts.
I thought that God, whoever He may be,
Might become merciful. Pontiff of Baal,
Forgive this strange infirmity of purpose.
I entered; the people fled; the sacrifice ceased.
The High Priest came towards me white with fury.
While he was speaking to me, I beheld—
With terror and astonishment beheld—
The very child of whom I had been warned
By such a fearful dream. I saw him there—
His air, his linen garments, his gait, his eyes,
And all his traits the same. 'Twas he. He walked
Beside the High Priest: but, on seeing me,
They made him disappear; and it is this
That troubles me and brings me to a stop.
It was on this I wished to consult you both.
What, Mathan,
Does this incredible prodigy presage?

MATHAN: Your dream and story fill me with amazement.

ATHALIAH: But, Abner, have you seen this fatal child?
What is he? Of what blood? And of what tribe?

ABNER: Two children at the altar ministered:
One is the son of Joad and Josabeth,
The other I know not.

MATHAN: Why hesitate?
Of both, madam, you need to be assured.
You know the moderation and respect
I have for Joad, that I do not seek
To avenge my wrongs, that equity alone
Reigns ever in my counsels. But, after all,
Would he himself permit a criminal
To live a moment, were it his own child?

ABNER: Of what crime can a child be capable?

MATHAN: Heaven made us see him brandishing a dagger;
Heaven is wise, and nothing does in vain.
What more do you seek?

ABNER: But on the evidence

Of a mere dream, will you imbrue your hands
In a child's blood? You do not even know
His parentage, or what he is.

MATHAN: We fear him.
That's all we need to know. For if he stems
From famous stock, the splendor of his lot
Should hasten now his ruin; and if fate
Has given him humble birth, what does it matter
If a vile blood at random should be spilt?
Should kings be slow in justice, when their safety
Often depends on speedy punishment?
Let us not hamper them with awkward caution;
For from the moment one is suspect to them,
He's innocent no longer.

ABNER: What! Mathan!
Is this the language of a priest? 'Tis I,
Inured to slaughter in my trade of war,
Stern minister of royal vengeances,
Who lend a voice for the unfortunate child;
While you who owe him a paternal kindness,
You, minister of peace in times of wrath,
Covering resentment with a specious zeal—
Blood flows not fast enough in your opinion.
You have commanded me, O Queen, to speak
Without reserve. What then is the great cause
Of all your fear? A dream, a harmless child
Your eye, forewarned, believed to recognize,
Perhaps mistakenly.

ATHALIAH: I wish to think so.
I well may be mistaken. An empty dream
May too much have obsessed me. Ah, well! I must
See once again this child at closer view,
And at my leisure scrutinize his traits.
Let both appear before me.

ABNER: I am afraid . . .

ATHALIAH: That they will not comply? But what could be
Their reasons for refusal? That would cast me

Into some strange suspicions. Let Josabeth
Or Joad bring them. I can, when I wish,
Speak as a queen. Abner, I must avow
Your priests have every reason to extol
Athaliah's favors. I know that in their preaching
They abuse my power and conduct. Yet they live,
And still their Temple stands. But now I feel
My kindness nears its end. Let Joad bridle
His savage zeal, and not provoke my heart
By a second outrage. Go. [*Exit* ABNER.]

(II.6)

MATHAN: Now I can speak
Freely, and put the truth as clear as day.
Some newborn monster, Queen, is being raised
Within this Temple. Wait not for the cloud
To burst. I know that Abner before daybreak
Came to the High Priest's house. You know his love
For the blood of his kings; and who knows if Joad
Has not some plan to place upon the throne
This child with whom the heavens have menaced you,
His own son, or some other?

ATHALIAH: Yes, you open
My eyes, and clearly I begin to see
The meaning of this portent. But I wish
To clear my mind of doubt. A child's unable
To hide his thoughts, and oft a single word
Will let us guess at mighty purposes.
Let me, dear Mathan, see and question him.
And you meanwhile, without causing alarm,
Order my Tyrians to take up arms. [*Exit* MATHAN.]

(*Enter* JOAS, JOSABETH, ABNER, CHORUS, *etc.*) (II.7)

JOSABETH: O servants of the Lord, upon these children,
So dear, so precious, keep your eyes.

ABNER: Princess,
Assure yourself, I will protect them.

ATHALIAH: O Gods!

The more I scrutinize him . . . It is he!
And all my senses now are seized with horror.
Wife of Joad, is this boy your son?
JOSABETH: Who? He, madam?
ATHALIAH: He.
JOSABETH: I am not his mother.
There is my son.
ATHALIAH: And you, who is your father?
Answer me, child.
JOSABETH: Heaven, until this day . . .
ATHALIAH: Why do you hasten to reply for him?
I speak to him.
JOSABETH: From such a tender age
What information can you hope to get?
ATHALIAH: This age is innocent; his artlessness
Will not pervert the simple truth. Leave him
To answer freely everything I ask.
JOSABETH (*aside*): O put Thy wisdom in his mouth, O Lord!
ATHALIAH: What is your name?
JOAS: Eliacin.
ATHALIAH: Your father?
JOAS: They tell me I'm an orphan, thrown since birth
Upon the arms of God. I never knew
My parents.
ATHALIAH: You have no parents?
JOAS: No:
They abandoned me.
ATHALIAH: Since when?
JOAS: Since I was born.
ATHALIAH: Do you not know, at least, which is your country?
JOAS: This Temple is my country. I know no other.
ATHALIAH: Where did they find you?
JOAS: Among the cruel wolves
Ready to eat me up.
ATHALIAH: Who brought you here?
JOAS: An unknown woman, who did not tell her name
And was not seen again.

ATHALIAH: In your earliest years
Who looked after you?
JOAS: Has God ever left
His children in want? He feeds the tiniest birds;
His bounty stretches to the whole of nature.
I pray to him daily, and with a father's care
He feeds me with the gifts placed on his altar.
ATHALIAH: What new prodigy disturbs me now?
The sweetness of his voice, his childlike ways,
His grace, make to my enmity succeed . . .
Could I be moved by pity?
ABNER: Is this, madam,
Your terrible foe? Your dreams are plainly liars,
Unless your pity is the deadly stroke
Which made you tremble.
ATHALIAH: You're going?
JOSABETH: You've heard his fortunes.
He need intrude no longer on your presence.
ATHALIAH: No. Come back. What do you do each day?
JOAS: I worship the Lord and listen to His Law.
I have been taught to read His holy book,
And I am learning now to copy it.
ATHALIAH: What says this Law?
JOAS: That God demands our love;
That He takes vengeance, soon or late, on those
Who take His name in vain; that He defends
The timid orphan; that He resists the proud
And punishes the murderer.
ATHALIAH: I see.
But all the people shut up in this place,
How do they spend their time?
JOAS: They praise and bless
The Lord.
ATHALIAH: Does God exact continual prayer
And worship?
JOAS: Everything profane is banished
Out of His Temple.

ATHALIAH: What are your pleasures then?
JOAS: Sometimes to the High Priest at the altar
I offer salt or incense. I hear songs
Of the infinite greatness of Almighty God;
I see the stately order of His rites.
ATHALIAH: Have you no sweeter pastime? I am sorry
That such a child should lead so sad a life.
Come to my palace! See my glory there!
JOAS: And lose the memory of God's benefits?
ATHALIAH: Why, no. I would not force you to forget them.
JOAS: You do not pray to Him.
ATHALIAH: But you could pray.
JOAS: I should see people pray to other gods.
ATHALIAH: I have my god, and serve him. You would serve yours.
There are two powerful gods.
JOAS: Mine must be feared:
He is God alone, madam, and yours is none.
ATHALIAH: Near me you'd find a host of pleasures, boy.
JOAS: The happiness of the wicked passeth away
Even as a torrent.
ATHALIAH: Who are these wicked?
JOSABETH: Oh, madam,
Excuse a child . . .
ATHALIAH: I like to see your teaching.
So, Eliacin, you please me. You are not
An ordinary child. I am the Queen,
And have no heir. Take off this robe, and leave
This mean employment. I would have you share
In all my riches. From this very day
Make trial of my promises. At my table,
Everywhere, seated at my side, I mean
To treat you as my son.
JOAS: As your son?
ATHALIAH: Yes?
You're silent?
JOAS: What a father I should leave!

And for . . .
ATHALIAH: Well?
JOAS: For what a mother!
ATHALIAH: His memory is faithful; and in all
That he has said I recognize the spirit
Of you and Joad. This is how you use
(Infecting his simple youth) the peace wherein
I leave you; and you cultivate so young
Their hate and fury. You pronounce my name
Only with horror to them.
JOSABETH: Can we conceal
From them the story of our woes? The world
Knows them; and you yourself take glory in them.
ATHALIAH: Yes, my just fury—and I boast of it—
Avenged my parents' deaths upon my sons.
I saw my father and my brother butchered,
My mother cast down from her palace window,
And in one day (what a spectacle of horror!)
Saw eighty princes murdered! For what reason?
To avenge some prophets whose immoderate frenzies
My mother justly punished; and I, a queen
Without a heart, a girl without a friend,
Slave to a cowardly and futile pity,
Would not, transported by blind rage, commit
Murder for murder, outrage for outrage,
And treat all the posterity of David
As they have treated Ahab's luckless sons?
Where would I be today had I not conquered
My weakness, stifled a mother's tenderness,
Had I not shed a stream of my own blood
With my own hand, and by this dauntless stroke
Have quelled your plots? And now the vengeance
Of your implacable God has snapped forever
All bonds between our houses. David I hold
Abhorred, and that king's sons, yea even those
Born of my blood, are strangers to me.
JOSABETH: All

Has prospered for you. May God see and judge us!
ATHALIAH: This God, who has been long your only refuge,
What will become of his predictions?
Let Him give you this king, this child of David,
Your hope and expectation, who is promised
To all the nations. . . . But we shall see. Farewell.
I leave you, satisfied. I wished to see.
I have seen.
ABNER: As I have promised you
I give you back what you entrusted me.
[*Exeunt* ATHALIAH *with her* GUARDS.]

(*Enter* JOAD.) (II.8)

JOSABETH: Did you o'erhear this haughty queen, my lord?
JOAD: Yes, I heard all, and shared your grief and fears.
These Levites and myself, prepared to help you,
Resolved to perish with you. (*To* JOAS) May the Lord
Watch over you, my child, whose courage gives
A noble witness to your name. I'm grateful,
Abner, for what you've done. Do not forget
The hour when Joad expects you. As for us,
Whose looks are sullied and whose prayer's disturbed
By this impious murderess, let us go in,
And with a pure blood that my hands will shed
Cleanse even the marble where her feet have touched.
[*Exeunt* ALL, *except* CHORUS.]
(II.9)
ONE OF THE CHORUS: What star is shining on us now?
What will this wondrous child become one day?
He braved the splendor of the proud,
And not allowed
Its perilous lures to lead his feet astray.
ANOTHER: While others are to alien altars hasting
To offer incense, this child, indomitable,
Proclaims that God alone is everlasting,
A new Elias before a Jezebel.

ANOTHER: Who will reveal to us your secret birth,
Dear child? Are you some holy prophet's son?
ANOTHER: So in the shadow of the tabernacle
Beloved Samuel grew,
Till he became our hope and oracle;
O may thou too
Console the children of Israel!
ANOTHER (*singing*): O bless'd a thousand times
The child whom the Lord loveth,
Who hears his voice betimes,
And whom that God instructeth.
Secluded from the world, from infancy,
With all the gifts of heaven graced,
The contagion of wickedness has not defaced
His spotless innocency.
ALL: Happy, O happy, is the infancy
The Lord doth teach and takes beneath his wing!
THE SAME VOICE (*alone*): Thus in a sheltered valley
A crystal stream beside,
There grows a tender lily,
Kind Nature's love and pride.
Secluded from the world from infancy,
With all the gifts of heaven graced,
The contagion of wickedness has not defaced
His spotless innocency.
ALL: O bless'd a thousand times the child
Whom the Lord makes obedient to his laws!
A VOICE (*alone*): O God! that virtue humble
Down perilous paths must stumble;
That he who seeks Thee, longing to preserve
His innocence of mind,
Such obstacles should find,
Pitfalls and perils that may make him swerve.
How manifold are Thy foes!
Where can Thy saints repose?
The wicked cover all the face of the earth.
ANOTHER: Palace of David, and his city dear!

O famous mount where God so long has dwelt,
Why hast thou felt
The wrath of heaven? Zion, what dost thou say
When thou beholdst an impious foreigner
Seated upon thy true kings' throne today?

ALL: Zion, dear Zion, what dost thou say,
When thou beholdst an impious foreigner
Seated upon thy true kings' throne today?

THE SAME VOICE (*continuing*): Instead of beauteous songs, expressing
The holy joys of David, blessing
His God, his father, and his Lord,
Dear Zion, thou beholdst men hymning
The impious stranger's god, blaspheming
The holy name thy kings adored.

A VOICE (*alone*): How long, O Lord, how long shall we behold
The wicked rise up against Thee?
For in Thy Temple, impiously bold,
They dare to come before Thee,
Treating as mad the people who adore Thee.
How long, O Lord, how long shall we behold
The wicked rise up against Thee?

ANOTHER: What is the use (they say)
Of your harsh virtue? And why should you shun
Countless sweet pleasures? Since your God has done
Nothing for you, 'tis foolish to obey.

ANOTHER: Come, let us sing (they say)
And take the flowery way,
From pleasure unto pleasure, as they fly;
Mad is it on the future to rely,
For the uncertain-numbered years slip by,
Bringing their inevitable sorrow:
Then let us hasten while we may
To enjoy this life today:
Who knows if we shall live tomorrow?

ALL: They shall weep, O God, and they shall tremble,

Those wretches who will never once behold
Thy holy city's splendor long foretold.
It is for us to sing, here in Thy Temple,
To whom Thou hast shown Thy everlasting light,
To sing of all Thy gifts, and praise Thy might.

A VOICE (*alone*): Of all these vain delights in which they swim
What will remain? The memory of a dream
Whose fond deceit is known.
When they awake—awakening full of horror!—
While the poor at Thy throne
Shall taste the ineffable sweetness of Thy peace,
They'll drink in the day of Thy wrath the cup of terror
Thou shalt present to all that guilty race.

ALL: Awakening full of horror!
O dream that quickly fades!
O blind and dangerous error!

Act III

Enter MATHAN *and* NABAL *to* CHORUS.

MATHAN: Go, children. One of you tell Josabeth
Mathan would speak with her, in secret, here.

ONE OF THE CHORUS: Mathan! O God of heaven, may'st thou confound him!

NABAL: What! fled without response?

MATHAN: Let us approach. [*Exit* CHORUS.]

(*Enter* ZACHARIAH.) (III.2)

ZACHARIAH: Presumptuous man, where would you pass? Approach
No further. This is the sacred dwelling place
Of holy ministers. The laws forbid

Any profane to enter. Whom do you seek?
Upon this solemn day my father shuns
The criminal sight of curst idolaters;
And prostrate now before the Lord, my mother
Fears to be interrupted.

MATHAN: We will wait.
Cease to perturb yourself, my son. I wish
To speak with your noble mother. I have come here
Bearing the Queen's command. [*Exit* ZACHARIAH.]

(III.3)

NABAL: Even their children
Display their haughty boldness. But tell me now:
What does the Queen desire on this occasion?
And whence has sprung confusion in her counsels?
Insulted by the insolent Joad today,
And in a nightmare threatened by a child,
She would have slaughtered Joad in her wrath,
And in this Temple set both Baal and you.
You told me of your joy, and I had hoped
To have my share of the spoils. What then has changed
Her wavering will?

MATHAN: My friend, these last two days
I have not known her. She is now no more
That bold, clear-sighted Queen, uplifted high
Above her timid sex, who crushed her foes
At once and unawares, and knew the price
Of a lost instant. Now fear of vain remorse
Troubles that lofty soul. She hesitates;
She drifts, and (in a word) she is a woman.
With bitterness and rancor I had filled
Her heart, already struck by heaven's threats;
Entrusting her revenge to me, she bade me
Muster the guard. But whether that same child—
A luckless waif, they say—when brought before her,
Appeased the terror of her dream, or whether
She found some charm in him, I've seen her wrath
Turn hesitant; and she postpones revenge

Until tomorrow. All her plans, it seems,
Destroy each other. "I have made inquiries,"
I told her, "of this child. They have begun
To boast his ancestry. From time to time,
Joad displays him to the factious mob,
Almost as though he were a second Moses,
And with false oracles supports his claims."
The blood at these words mounted to her face,
And never did a happy lie produce
Such prompt effect. "Is it for me to languish
In this uncertainty?" she said at once.
"Away with this disquietude! Go now:
Pronounce this sentence unto Josabeth:
The fires are kindled, and the sword prepared.
Nought can prevent the ravage of their Temple
Unless I have that child as hostage."

NABAL: Well,
For a child they do not know, whom chance perhaps
Has flung into their arms, would they permit
Their Temple to be razed? . . .

MATHAN: But Joad is
Proudest of mortals. Rather than deliver
Into my hands a child he has dedicated
Unto his God, you will see him undergo
The worst of deaths. Besides, it is apparent
They love this child; and if I've understood
The Queen's account, Joad knows something more
About the child's birth than he's yet revealed.
Whoever he is, he will be fatal to them—
That I can well foresee. They will deny him.
The rest is mine. And now I hope at last
That sword and fire will take away the sight
Of this obnoxious Temple.

NABAL: What can inspire
So strong a hatred in you? Does the zeal
Of Baal transport you? As for me, you know,
I am an Ishmaelite, and do not serve

Either Baal or the God of Israel.
MATHAN: Do you suppose, my friend, that with vain zeal
I let myself be blinded for an idol,
A fragile wooden idol which the worms
Upon his altar—in spite of all my care—
Consume each day? I was born a minister
Of the God they worship here, and I perhaps
Would serve Him still, could but the love of greatness,
The thirst for power, be accommodated
Within His narrow yoke. There is no need
For me to remind you of the famous quarrel
Between myself and Joad, when I strove
To supersede him—my intrigues, my struggles,
My tears, and my despair. Vanquished by him,
I entered then a new career: my soul
Attached itself entirely to the court,
Till, by degrees, I gained the ear of kings,
And soon became an oracle. I studied
Their hearts and flattered their caprice. For them
I sowed the precipice's edge with flowers;
Nothing, except their passions, was sacred to me:
I changed both weight and measure at their whim:
When Joad's harsh inflexibility
Wounded their proud and delicate ear, I charmed them
With my dexterity, veiling from their eyes
The dismal truth, depicting all their passions
In favorable colors, and, above all,
Prodigal with the blood of the poor. At last
To the new god the Queen had introduced
A temple was built by her. Jerusalem wept
To see herself profaned. The children of Levi
In consternation howled towards the heavens.
Myself alone, setting a good example
To the timid Jews, deserter from their Law,
Approved the enterprise—and thereby earned
The primacy of Baal. I became
Terrible to my rival: I too wore

The tiara on my brows, and went his equal.
Yet sometimes, I confess, in all my glory,
The memory of the God whom I have left
Importunes me with terror: this it is
Feeds and augments my fury. I shall be happy
If I achieve my vengeance on His Temple,
And thus convict His hate of impotence;
And amidst ruin, ravage, and the dead,
By deeds of horror lose all my remorse.
But here is Josabeth.

(*Enter* JOSABETH.) (III.4)

MATHAN: Sent by the Queen,
To re-establish peace and banish hatred,
Princess, whom heaven has given a gentle spirit,
Marvel not if I address you now.
A rumor I myself believe is false
Supports the warning she received in dreams,
And it has turned on Joad (who's accused
Of dangerous plots) the current of her wrath.
I will not brag here of my services.
Joad, I know, has treated me unjustly,
But one should always render good for evil.
So charged with words of peace I come to you.
Live, solemnize your feasts without reproof.
She only asks a pledge of your obedience.
It is—although I've done my best to dissuade her—
That orphan child she saw here.

JOSABETH: Eliacin?

MAHAN: I'm somewhat ashamed for her. Of an empty dream
She takes too much account, but nonetheless
You would declare yourselves her mortal foes
If in the hour this child is not delivered
Into my hands. The Queen, impatiently,
Awaits your answer.

JOSABETH: And that then is the peace
Which you announce?

MATHAN: How can you hesitate
To accept? And is the small compliance asked
Too much to pay?

JOSABETH: I would have been surprised
If Mathan, putting off deception, could
Have overcome the injustice of his heart,
And if the inventor of so many evils
Could now at last come forward as the author
Of even the shadow of good.

MATHAN: Of what do you complain?
Is someone coming in rage to tear your son
Out of your arms? What is this other child
Who seems so dear to you? This great attachment
Surprises me in turn. Is he a treasure
So precious and so rare? A liberator
That heaven prepares for you? Well, think of it.
Should you refuse, it would confirm for me
A rumor that begins to circulate.

JOSABETH: What rumor?

MATHAN: That this child is nobly born,
Destined for some great project by your husband.

JOSABETH: And by this rumor which must fan her fury
Mathan . . .

MATHAN: Princess, it is for you to draw me
Out of my error. I know that Josabeth,
The implacable foe of falsehood, would resign
Even her life, if saving it would cost
One word against the truth. Have you no trace
Of this child's origin? Does a dark night
Conceal his race? And are you ignorant
Both of his parents and from whose hands Joad
Received him to his arms? Speak. I am listening
And apt to give you credence. To the God
You serve, Princess, give glory!

JOSABETH: Wicked man,
'Tis fitting you should name in such a way
A God your mouth instructs men to blaspheme.

Is it possible His truth can be attested
By you who sit on the plague-ridden throne
Where falsehood reigns, disseminating poison;
You, villain, fed on perfidy and treason?

(*Enter* JOAD.) (III.5)

JOAD: Where am I? See I not the priest of Baal?
Daughter of David, speak you to this traitor?
Allow him speak with you? Do you not fear
That from the abyss which opens at his feet
Flames will rush out to set you in a blaze?
Or that the walls, in falling, crush you too?
What does he want? How dares the foe of God
Come to infect the air we breathe?

MATHAN: This rage
Is like you, Joad. Yet you ought to show
More prudence; and you should respect a queen,
And not insult the man she deigns to use
To bear her high commands.

JOAD: What evil tidings
Come from her now? What terrible command
That such an envoy brings?

MATHAN: I have conveyed
To Josabeth Queen Athaliah's will.

JOAD: Go from my presence then, thou impious monster:
Heap up the measure of thy monstrous crimes.
Go, pile up all thy horrors. God prepares
To join thee with the perjured race—with Doeg,
Abiron, Dathan, and Achitophel.
The dogs to whom He handed Jezebel,
Awaiting but His rage to be unleashed,
Are at the door and howling for their prey.

MATHAN: Before nightfall . . . it will be seen which one of us
Will . . . But let us go, Nabal.

NABAL: Where are you going?
What has bewildered and amazed your senses?

There lies your way. [*Exeunt* NABAL *and* MATHAN.]

(III. 6)

JOSABETH: The storm has broken.
Now Athaliah in her fury asks
For Eliacin. Already they have started
To pierce the mystery of his birth, my lord,
And of your plan—for Mathan nearly named
His father.

JOAD: Who could have revealed his birth
To the perfidious Mathan? Could he guess
Too much from your confusion?

JOSABETH: I did my best
To master it. But yet, my lord, believe me,
The danger presses. Let us keep the child
For a happier time: while the wicked confer,
Before he is surrounded and they seize him,
Let me hide him for a second time.
The gates, the roads, are open still. If he
Must be transported to most fearful deserts,
I am prepared. I know a secret path
By which with him unseeing and unseen
I'll cross the falls of Kedron; I will go
Into the desert where weeping once, and seeking
Safety in flight, as we do now, King David
Escaped pursuit by his rebellious son.
I shall, because of him, fear less the bears
And lions. But why refuse King Jehu's help?
I'll offer now some salutary advice:
Let Jehu now be the depositary
Of this our treasure. We could leave today.
The journey is but short. The heart of Jehu
Is neither savage nor inexorable
And he is well disposed to David's name.
Alas! is there a king so harsh and cruel—
Or one at least without a Jezebel
For mother—who'll not pity the misfortune
Of such a suppliant? Is not his cause

Common to every king?

JOAD: What timid counsels
Do you dare offer me? How could you hope
For Jehu's succor?

JOSABETH: Does the Lord forbid
All care and forethought? Does one not offend Him
By too much confidence? In His sacred plans
Employing human means, has He not armed
The hands of Jehu?

JOAD: Jehu, whom He chose
In His deep wisdom, Jehu, on whom I see
Your hope is founded, has repaid His blessings
With an ingrate forgetfulness. He leaves
Ahab's vile daughter in peace. He follows now
The ungodly example of the kings of Israel,
Preserves the temples of the god of Egypt;
And now at last in the high places dares
To offer an incense God cannot endure.
He has not served His cause, avenged His wrongs;
His heart's not upright, and his hands not pure.
No, no, in God alone must be our trust.
Let us show Eliacin openly—the royal
Circlet upon his head. I even wish
To advance the hour we had determined on,
Ere Mathan's plot is hatched.

(*Enter* AZARIAS, CHORUS, *and* LEVITES.) (III.7)

JOAD: Well, Azarias,
Is the Temple closed?

AZARIAS: Yes, all the doors are shut.

JOAD: Only your sacred cohorts now remain?

AZARIAS: Twice have I gone through all the sacred courts.
All, all have fled, and they will not return—
A miserable troop dispersed with fear.
The holy tribe alone remain to serve
The Lord of Hosts. I think that since this people
Escaped from Pharaoh, they have not been struck

By such a terror.

JOAD: A coward race indeed,
And born for slavery—brave against God alone.
Let us pursue our task. But who has kept
These children still among us?

A GIRL: Could we, my lord,
Divide us from you? Are we strangers here
In the Temple of God? You have beside you now
Our fathers and our brothers.

ANOTHER: Alas, for us!
If to avenge the shame of Israel
Our hands cannot, as Jael's in former days,
Pierce through the impious head of God's own foes,
At least for Him we could give up our lives.
When you, with arms, fight for His threatened Temple,
We can at least invoke Him with our tears.

JOAD: See what avengers arm them for Thy quarrel,
O everlasting Wisdom—priests and children!
But if Thou dost uphold them, who can shake them?
Thou canst, at pleasure, call us from the tomb;
Strike us, and heal; destroy and resurrect.
They do not trust now in their own deserts,
But in Thy name, invoked so many times.
And in Thine oaths, sworn to their holiest kings,
And in this Temple, Thy holy dwelling place,
Which shall endure as long as doth the sun.
Whence comes it that my heart with holy dread
Begins to tremble? Is it the Holy Spirit
Who takes possession of me? It is He.
He kindles me, and speaks. My eyes are opened,
And the dark centuries unroll before me.
You Levites, with the concord of your sounds,
Accompany the raptures He inspires.

CHORUS: May the voice of the Lord be heard, His will revealed,
And as in springtime the sweet morning dew
Refreshes the grass of the field,

May His oracle divine our hearts renew.
JOAD: O heavens, hear my voice; O earth, give ear!
O Jacob, say no more the Lord doth sleep.
Sinners, begone. The Lord awakens now!
[*Music.* JOAD *soon continues.*]
How is the pure gold turned to vilest lead?
Who is this High Priest slaughtered without pity
In the holy place? Weep, Jerusalem, weep!
Slayer of holy prophets, perfidious city!
Now God has turned away His love from thee:
Thy incense in His eyes is now polluted.
Where are these women and children led?
God has destroyed the queen of cities:
Her priests are captives, and her kings are fled.
Men come no more to her solemnities.
The Temple overturns;
The sacred cedar burns!
O Zion, that in vain my sorrow pities,
What hand has ravished all your loveliness?
My eyes have changed now into water-springs
To weep for thy distress.
AZARIAS: O holy Temple!
JOSABETH: O David!
CHORUS: O God of Zion,
Remember now Thy ancient promises.
[*Music again; after a moment* JOAD *interrupts.*]
JOAD: What new Jerusalem rises now
From out the desert shining bright,
Eternity upon her brow,
Triumphing over death and night?
Sing, peoples, Zion now is more
Lovely and glorious than before.

Whence come these children manifold
She did not carry at her breast?
Lift up thy head, O Zion, behold
These princes with thy fame possesesd;

The earthly kings all prostrate bow
And kiss the dust before thee now.

Peoples to walk within thy light
Shall strive; and happy those who feel
Their souls for Zion burning bright
With fervent and with holy zeal;
Rain down, O heavens, thy sacred dew!
Earth, may a savior spring from you!

JOSABETH: How may this signal favor be vouchsafed
If David's line, from which this savior springs
Shall be . . .

JOAD: Prepare the gorgeous diadem
Which David wore upon his sacred brow.
And you, to arm yourselves, now follow me
To the secret chambers, far from eyes profane,
Where a great store is hid of swords and spears,
Once steeped in Philistinian blood, and then
By conquering David, laden with years and fame,
All consecrate to God. Could we employ them
In a nobler cause? Come, I myself desire
To share them now amongst you.

[*Exeunt* ALL, *except* SALOMITH *and* CHORUS.]

(III.8)

SALOMITH: Sisters, how many fears and mortal troubles!
Are these the first fruits, O omnipotent God,
Perfumes and sacrifices which should be
Offered upon Thy altar?

A VOICE: What a sight
For timorous eyes! For who would have believed
That we should ever see the murderous swords
And lances gleaming in the house of peace?

ANOTHER: Why does Jerusalem, to God indifferent,
Now hold her peace while pressing danger threatens?
Whence comes it, sisters, that to protect us all
Even brave Abner does not break his silence?

SALOMITH: But in a court where justice is unknown

And all the laws are force and violence,
Where honor's bought with base obedience,
Who will speak up for luckless innocence?
ANOTHER: In this peril and extreme confusion
For whom is the sacred diadem prepared?
SALOMITH: The Lord has deigned to speak unto His prophet:
But who can understand what is revealed?
Are they arming now in our defense?
Or will they bring destruction on us all?
ALL: O promise! O menace! O dark mystery!
According to the prophecy,
How many ills and blessings will there be?
How may the future for us prove
So much of anger with so much of love?
FIRST VOICE: Zion will be no more—a cruel flame
Will leave of all her glory but a name.
SECOND VOICE: Founded upon His everlasting word,
Zion will be protected by the Lord.
FIRST VOICE: My eyes behold her glory disappear.
SECOND VOICE: I see her brightness spreading everywhere.
FIRST VOICE: Zion has fallen into the abyss.
SECOND VOICE: Aspiring Zion and the heavens kiss.
FIRST VOICE: What sad abasement!
SECOND VOICE: What immortal glory!
FIRST VOICE: How many cries of sorrow!
SECOND VOICE: What songs of triumph!
THIRD VOICE: Peace, sisters, trouble not yourselves:
Some day the mystery will be revealed.
ALL THREE: Let us revere His wrath, hope in His love.
FOURTH VOICE: Who can disturb the peace,
Of a heart that loves Thee, Lord?
In Thy will is its peace,
Its trust is in Thy word.
Can there be happiness
In earth or heaven
Except the tranquil peace
That Thou hast given?

Act IV

JOAS, JOSABETH, ZACHARIAH, SALOMITH, *a* LEVITE, *and* CHORUS.

SALOMITH: Beside his mother with majestic pace
Young Eliacin advances with my brother.
What do they bear between them in those cloths?
What is that sword that's borne before them?
JOSABETH: My son,
Upon that table reverently place
The dread book of our Law. Dear Eliacin,
Put the royal fillet near the holy book.
Levite, the sword of David must be placed
Beside his crown. So Joad has ordained.
JOAS: What is the meaning, Princess, of this sight?
Wherefore the sword, the crown, the holy book?
For since the Lord received me in His Temple,
I have not seen a ceremony like it.
JOSABETH: All your doubts, my son, will soon be cleared.
JOAS: You wish to try this crown upon my brows?
Princess, take care that you do not profane
Its glory and respect the memory
Of the King who wore it. I, a luckless child,
Abandoned to the bears . . .
JOSABETH: Let be, my son.
I know what is ordained.
JOAS: But yet I hear
A sob escape you. You are weeping, Princess.
What pity moves you? Must I, as Jephthah's daughter,
Be sacrificed to appease the wrath of God?
Alas! a son has nothing not his father's.
JOSABETH: Here comes the one who will expound heaven's will.
Fear nothing. Now let all the rest depart.

[*Exeunt* ALL, *except* JOAS.]

(*Enter* JOAD.) (IV.2)

JOAS: Father!
JOAD: My son?
JOAS: What means this preparation?
JOAD: 'Tis right, my son, that I should tell you all;
You must be first to hear God's great designs
For you and for His chosen. Arm yourself
With courage and new faith. 'Tis time to show
The ardor and the zeal which in your heart
I have implanted, and to pay to God
That which you owe him. Do you feel, my son,
That generous desire?
JOAS: I am prepared,
If he should wish, to give my life to Him.
JOAD: You've often heard the story of our kings.
Do you recall, my son, what narrow laws
A king who is worthy of the diadem
Should self-impose?
JOAS: God himself has pronounced
That a wise king does not rely on wealth.
He fears the Lord his God, and walks before Him,
Keeping His precepts, laws, and His strict judgments;
And with excessive burdens does not load
His brethren.
JOAD: But if you had to take as model
One of our kings, my son, which would you choose
To resemble?
JOAS: David, full of faithful love
Of the Lord, appears to me the perfect model
Of a great king.
JOAD: And so, in their excess,
You would not imitate the faithless Joram,
The impious Ahaziah?
JOAS: Oh, father!
JOAD: Go on:
How does it seem to you?
JOAS: May all like them
Perish as them! Why do you kneel before me?

JOAD: I render you the reverence that I owe
  Unto my king. Make yourself worthy, Joas,
  Of David, your great ancestor.
JOAS: Joas?
  I?
JOAD: You shall know now by what signal grace
  God overthrew the murderous design
  Of a mad mother. Her knife was in your breast
  When, choosing you, God saved you from the slaughter.
  You have not yet escaped from her fierce rage:
  Just as in former days she wished to kill
  In you the last of her son's children, now
  Her cruelty is bent to make you perish,
  Pursuing you still under the name which hides you.
  But now beneath your standards I have mustered
  A loyal people, ready to avenge you.
  Enter, you noble chiefs of sacred tribes,
  Who have the honor to perform in turn
  The holy ministry.

(*Enter* AZARIAS, ISMAEL, *and three* LEVITES.) (IV.3)

JOAD: King, these are
  Thy champions against thy enemies.
  Priests, here is the King that I have promised.
AZARIAS: What? Eliacin?
ISMAEL: This beloved child?
JOAD: Is of the kings of Judah the true heir,
  Last born of the unhappy Ahaziah,
  Named Joas, as you know. This tender flower,
  Cut down so soon, all Judah mourned as you,
  Believing that he shared his brothers' fate.
  He was indeed struck with the treacherous knife,
  But God preserved him from a fatal blow
  And kept some warmth within his beating heart,
  Let Josabeth deceive the vigilant eye
  Of the assassins, bear him at her breast,

All bleeding, with myself the sole accomplice,
And in the Temple hide both child and nurse.
JOAS: Father, alas! How can I ever pay
So much of love and such great benefits?
JOAD: For other times reserve your thanks. Behold
Therefore, you ministers of God, your king,
Your cherished hope. For you I have preserved him,
Until this hour, and here begins your part.
As soon as the murderous daughter of Jezebel
Learns that our Joas sees the light of day,
She will return, to plunge him once again
Into the horror of the tomb. Already,
Before she knows him, she would murder him.
Now, holy priests, it is for you today
Her fury to forestall, and end at last
The shameful slavery of the Jews; avenge
Your murdered princes, raise again your Law,
And make the two tribes recognize their king.
The enterprise is great and perilous,
For I attack a proud queen on her throne.
Under her flag there is a numerous host
Of doughty foreigners and renegades:
But yet my strength is in the living God
Whose interest is my guide. Think, in this child
All Israel resides. The God of wrath
Already vexes her. Despite her spies,
Already I have gathered you together.
She thinks we have no arms, and no defense.
Let us crown Joas, and proclaim him King;
And then, intrepid warriors of your prince,
Let us invoke the arbiter of battles,
And, waking in our hearts our dormant faith,
Even in her palace let us seek our foe.
And then what hearts though sunk in cowardly slumber
On seeing us advance in this array
But will not haste to follow our example?
A king whom God has brought up in His Temple,

Aaron's successor followed by his priests,
Leading the sons of Levi to the combat,
And in these same hands, reverenced by the people,
The arms of the Lord by David consecrated!
God will spread terror in his enemies.
Now without horror in the infidel blood
Imbrue yourselves. Strike down the Tyrians,
And even Israelites: for are you not
Descended from those Levites, famed in story,
Who when the fickle Israelites in the desert
To the god of the Nile gave unlawful worship,
Their hands they sanctified in traitors' blood—
Holy murderers of their dearest kin—
And by this noble deed acquired for you
The signal honor to be alone employed
At the Lord's altars? But I see that you
Already burn to follow me. Swear then, first,
Upon this solemn book, to live, to fight,
And perish for this king whom heaven today
Has given back to you.

AZARIAS: Yes, here we swear
For us and for our brethren to restore
King Joas to his fathers' throne. We swear
Never to sheathe the sword till we've avenged him
On all his enemies. If one of us
Should break this vow, let him, great God, be struck
With Thy avenging wrath, that he and his children,
Excluded from Thy heritage, may be
Among the dead Thou dost not know!

JOAD: O King!
Wilt thou not swear to be forever faithful
Unto this Law, thy everlasting rule?

JOAS: Why should I not conform me to this Law?

JOAD: My son—I still dare call you by that name—
Suffer this tenderness; forgive the tears
That flow from me in thinking of your peril.
Nurtured far from the throne, you do not know

The poisonous enchantment of that honor.
You do not know yet the intoxication
Of absolute power, the bewitching voice
Of vilest flattery. Too soon they'll tell you
That sacred laws, though rulers of the rabble,
Must bow to kings; that a king's only bridle
Is his own will; that he should sacrifice
All to his greatness; that to tears and toil
The people are condemned, and must be ruled
With an iron scepter; that if they're not oppressed,
Sooner or later they oppress—and thus,
From snare to snare and from abyss to abyss,
Soiling the lovely purity of your heart,
They'll make you hate the truth, paint virtue for you
Under a hideous image. Alas! the wisest
Of all our kings was led astray by them.
Swear then upon this book, and before these
As witnesses, that God will always be
Your first of cares; that stern towards the wicked,
The refuge of the good, you'll always take
Between you and the poor the Lord for judge,
Remembering, my son, that in these garments
You once were poor and orphaned, even as they.

JOAS: I swear to keep that which the Law ordains.
Punish me, Lord, if I depart from You.

JOAD: Come:
We must anoint you with the holy oil.
Here, Josabeth: you now can show yourself. . . .

(*Enter* JOSABETH, ZACHARIAH, *and* CHORUS.) (IV.4)

JOSABETH: O King! O son of David!

JOAS: My only mother!
Dear Zachariah, kiss your brother, come.

JOSABETH: Kneel down, my son, before your king.
[ZACHARIAH *kneels*.]

JOAD: My children,
May you be always thus united.

JOSABETH: You know
What blood has given you life?
JOAS: I know as well
What hand, except for you, had snatched it from me.
JOSABETH: I now can call you by your name—Joas.
JOAS: Joas will never cease to love you.
CHORUS: What!
Is he . . . ?
JOSABETH: 'Tis Joas.
JOAD: Let us hear this Levite.

(*Enter* LEVITE.) (IV.5)

LEVITE: I do not know what project against God
Is meditated; but the warning bronze
Clangs everywhere; among the standards now
They kindle fires; and doubtless Athaliah
Musters her army. We are even now
Cut off from succor; and the sacred mount
On which the Temple stands is everywhere
Hemmed in by insolent Tyrians. One of them,
Blaspheming, has informed us even now
That Abner is in irons and cannot shield us.
JOSABETH: Dear child, whom heaven in vain has given me,
Alas! to save you I have done my best.
God has forgotten now your father, David.
JOAD: Do you not fear to draw His wrath upon you
And on the King you love? And should God tear him
Forever from your arms, and seem to will
That David's house should be extinguished quite,
Are we not here upon the holy mount
Where Abraham above his innocent son
Lifted obedient arm without complaint,
And placed upon a pyre the precious fruit
Of his old age, leaving to God the task
Of carrying out his promise, sacrificing
All hope of issue with this son and heir
In whom it was bound up? Friends, let us share

The various posts between us. Let Ismael
Guard all the side that faces east. And you,
Take the north side; you the west; and you
The south. Let no one, whether priest or Levite,
Through hasty zeal discover my designs
Or leave before 'tis time. Let each one then,
Urged by a common ardor, guard the post
Where I have placed him, even to the death.
The foe in his blind rage regards us all
As flocks reserved for slaughter; and believes
He will meet nought but chaos and dismay.
Let Azarias accompany the King.
Come now, dear scion of a valiant race,
And fill your warriors with new bravery.
Put on the diadem before their eyes,
And die, if die you must, at least as King.
Follow him, Josabeth. Give me those arms.
Children, now offer God your innocent tears.

[*Exeunt* ALL, *except* SALOMITH *and* CHORUS.]

(IV.6)

CHORUS: Children of Aaron, go!
Never did nobler cause
Your fathers' zeal incite.
Children of Aaron, go!
'Tis for your rightful king
And for your God you fight.

A VOICE: Where are the darts you throw,
Great God, in Thy righteous anger?
Wilt Thou not take vengeance on Thy foe?
Art Thou a jealous God no longer?

ANOTHER: Where, God of Jacob, are Thy ancient blessings?
In the horror which surrounds our lives
Hear'st Thou but the voice of our transgressions?
Art Thou no more the Lord God who forgives?

ALL: Where, God of Jacob, are Thy ancient blessings?

A VOICE: Against Thee, Lord, O even against Thee
The wicked bends his bow.

The feasts of God (they say) shall cease to be
Upon the earth; men from His yoke we'll free;
His altars overthrow;
His saints we'll slay; so that there will remain
Of His name and of His glory
Only a fading story,
And neither God nor His Anointed reign.

ALL: Where are the darts You throw,
Great God, in Thy righteous anger?
Wilt Thou not take vengeance on Thy foe?
Art Thou a jealous God no longer?

A VOICE: Sad remnant of our kings, the dear last bloom
Of a lovely stem, shall we behold you fall
Once more beneath a cruel mother's knife?
Did some bright angel then avert thy doom,
Or did the voice of the living God recall,
From the night of the tomb thy spirit back to life?

ANOTHER: O God, dost Thou impute to him the sins
Of father and of grandfather? Has Thy pity
Abandoned him, and will it not return?

ALL: Where, God of Jacob, are Thy ancient blessings?
Art Thou no more the Lord God who forgives?

VOICE: Dear sisters, hear you not the trumpet sound
Of the cruel Tyrians?

SALOMITH: Yes, I also hear
The shouts of barbarous soldiers, and I shudder.
Quick, let us flee to the protecting shade
Of the strong sanctuary.

Act V

ZACHARIAH, SALOMITH, *and* CHORUS.

SALOMITH: Dear Zachariah, what can you tell us now?

ZACHARIAH: Redouble your ardent prayers to the Lord.

Perhaps our last hour's come. The order's given
For the dreadful battle.
SALOMITH: What is Joas doing?
ZACHARIAH: Joas has just been crowned, and the High Priest
Has poured the consecrated oil upon him.
O heavens! What joy in every eye was painted
To see this king who from the tomb was snatched.
Sister, the scar from the knife can still be seen.
The faithful nurse is there, who had been hidden
In this vast edifice, and kept her charge,
And had no other witness of her cares
Than Mother and our God. Our Levites wept
With joy and tenderness, and mingled sobs
With cries of joyfulness. Among it all,
Friendly and without pride, he stretched a hand
To one, and blessed another with his glance;
He swore he would be ruled by their advice,
And called them all his fathers and his brethren.
SALOMITH: But has the secret yet been spread abroad?
ZACHARIAH: No, it is kept within the Temple still.
The Levites in deep silence guard the doors,
Waiting to act together, and cry as signal
"Long live King Joas." Our father forbids
The King to risk his life, makes Azarias
Remain with him as guard. Yet Athaliah,
A dagger in her hand, now laughs to scorn
The feeble ramparts of our brazen doors;
To break them she awaits the fatal engines,
And breathes forth blood and ruin. Some of the priests
At first proposed that in a secret place,
A subterranean cell our fathers hollowed,
We should at least conceal our precious Ark.
"O fear," my father cried, "unworthy of you,
Insulting to our cause. The Ark which made
So many lofty towers to fall, and forced
Jordan to stay her course, so many times
Triumphant over alien gods, to flee

The aspect of an insolent woman!" Mother,
Beside the King in terrible distress,
Sometimes on him and sometimes on the altar
Fastened her eyes, sinking beneath the weight
Of her dumb fears. She would have made the eyes
Of even the cruelest to weep. The King at whiles
Embraced her, soothed her. Follow me, dear sisters,
And if today the King must perish, come,
Let us share his fate.

SALOMITH: What insolent hand is this
Redoubling knocks, which makes these Levites run
In apprehension? What precaution makes them
To hide their arms? O is the Temple forced?

ZACHARIAH: Banish your needless fears. God sends us Abner.

(*Enter* ABNER, JOAD, JOSABETH, ISMAEL, *and* LEVITES.) (V.2)

JOAD: Can I believe my eyes, dear Abner? By what path
Have you, despite the host that hems us in,
Gained access to this place? For it was said
That Ahab's sacrilegious daughter had,
To make assurance of her cruel purpose,
Laden with shameful irons your generous hands.

ABNER: Yes, my lord. She feared my zeal and courage;
This was the least reward she kept for me;
Shut in a horrid dungeon by her order,
I waited—when the Temple had been burnt
And streams of blood poured forth—for her to come
And free me from a weary life, to cut short
My days, and thus to end the pain I suffered,
That I'd outlived my kings.

JOAD: What miracle
Obtained for you your pardon?

ABNER: God only knows
What passes in that heart. She sent for me
And said distractedly: "You see this Temple
Encompassed by my host; the avenging sword

Stands poised above it, and your God's unable
Against me to defend it. But His priests
Can still—but time is short—redeem themselves.
On two conditions: that with Eliacin
Is put into my power the royal treasure—
I'm sure they know its hiding place—that treasure
Which David heaped together, and under pledge
Of secrecy, bequeathed to the High Priest:
Tell them that for this price I'll spare their lives.

JOAD: What counsel, Abner, should we follow now?

ABNER: If it is true you guard some secret hoard
Of David, give her all this gold, and all
You have been able from her greedy hands
To save of rich and rare, give it her now.
Would you that unclean murderers should break
The altar, burn the Cherubim, lay their hands
Upon the Ark, and with our proper blood
Pollute the sanctuary?

JOAD: But does it suit
Abner, with generous hearts, thus to deliver
A luckless child to death, a child which God
Confided to my care, redeem our lives
At the expense of his?

ABNER: God sees my heart:
And would that Athaliah, by His power,
Forgot this child, and that her cruelty,
Contented with my blood, thought thus to appease
Heaven which torments her. But what avails
Your useless care for him? When all will perish,
Will this boy perish less? Does God ordain
You should attempt the impossible? You know
That Moses, to obey a tyrant's law,
Was by his mother left beside the Nile,
Seeing himself from birth condemned to peril;
But God preserving him against all hope
Brought it to pass that he from infancy
Was nurtured by the tyrant. And who knows

What life he has reserved for Eliacin?
And if preparing for him a like fate,
He has made the implacable murderess of our kings
Already capable of pity? At least—
And Josabeth, perhaps, beheld it too—
I saw her so much moved at sight of him,
Her anger's violence declined. Princess,
You're silent in this peril. What! for a child
Who is a stranger to you, would you suffer
That Joad should allow you to be slain,
You, and your son, and all this people too,
And that the one place on the earth where God
Desires to be adored should be consumed
With fire? Were this young child a precious relic
Of the kings, your fathers, what would you do more?

JOSABETH (*aside*): For his king's blood you see his tenderness.
Why don't you speak to him?

JOAD: 'Tis not yet time,
Princess.

ABNER: Time is more precious than you think,
My lord. While you debate what to reply,
Mathan, near Athaliah, with flashing rage
Demands the signal, urges on the slaughter.
O must I kneel now at your sacred knees?
In the name of the holy place which you alone
May enter, where God's majesty resides,
However hard the law imposed on you
Let us consider how we may ward off
This unexpected blow. O give me but
The time to breathe! Tomorrow, even tonight,
I will take measures to assure the Temple
And to avenge its injuries. But I see
My tears and my vain words are means too weak
Your virtue to persuade. Well, find me then
Some sword, some weapon; at the Temple gates
Where the foe waits me, Abner can at least
Die fighting.

JOAD: I surrender. You have given
Advice that I embrace. Let us avert
The threat of all these ills. 'Tis true indeed
Committed to my trust—the final hope
Of the sad Jews, and I with vigilant care
Concealed it from the light. But since it must
To your queen be disclosed, I will content her.
Our doors will open to admit the Queen,
Her bravest captains too; but let her keep
Our holy altars from the open fury
Of a gang of foreigners. Spare me the horror
Of the pillage of the Temple. Would they fear
Children and priests? Let her arrange with you
The number of her suite. As for this child,
So feared, so dreadful, Abner, I know well
The justice of your heart; I will explain
About his birth before her, and to you.
You will see if we must put him in her power,
And you shall judge between the Queen and him.
ABNER: My lord, I take him under my protection.
Fear nothing. I return to her who sent me. [*Exit* ABNER.]
(V.3)
JOAD: O God! This is Thy hour. They bring to Thee
Thy prey. Listen Ismael.
JOSABETH: Blindfold her eyes
Once more, O master of the heavens, as when
Thou rob'st her of the profit of her crime
And hid that tender victim in my breast.
JOAD: Go, Ismael, lose no time, and carry out
These orders to the letter; above all
At her entry, and when she passes through,
Show her the image of an absolute calm.
You, children, make you ready now a throne
For Joas. Accompanied by our sacred soldiers,
Let him come forth. And tell his faithful nurse
To come here also. Princess, may the source
Of these your tears, dry up. (*To a* LEVITE) You, when the Queen,

Drunk with mad pride, has crossed the Temple threshold,
That she may not retreat the way she came
See that the warlike trumpet at that instant
Startles the hostile camp with sudden fear.
Call everyone to aid their king; and make
Even to his ear the miracle resound,
That Joas is preserved. Behold he comes.

(*Enter* JOAS.) (V.4)

JOAD: Ye holy Levites, priests of the living God,
Surround this place on every side. Keep hidden;
And leaving me to regulate your zeal,
Show not yourselves until you hear my voice.
King, I believe this hope may be allowed
In answer to your vows: that at your feet
Your enemies will fall. She who pursued
Your infancy with fury to this place
Now strives to kill you. But be not afraid:
Think that around you, and on our side, stands
The Angel of Death. Ascend your throne and wait. . . .
The door is opening. Allow this veil
To cover you a moment. You change color,
Princess.

JOSABETH: How can I see the Temple filled
With murderers, and not turn pale? Look now,
Do you not see with what a numerous escort . . . ?

JOAD: I see the Temple doors are closed again,
All is well.

(*Enter* ATHALIAH *and* SOLDIERS.) (V.5)

ATHALIAH: There thou art, seducer,
Vile author of conspiracies and plots,
Who only in sedition set'st thy hopes,
Eternal enemy of absolute power;
Thou hast reposed upon thy God's support;
Art thou yet disabused of that vain hope?
He has put thy Temple and thy life itself
Into my power. On the altar where thy hand

Is wont to sacrifice, I should . . . But I must be
Contented with the price that's offered me.
What you have promised, see you execute.
This child, this treasure, you must now deliver
Into my hands—where are they?

JOAD: Immediately
Thou shalt be satisfied. I am going to show them
Both at one time.

[*The curtain is drawn.* JOAS *is seen on his throne. His nurse on her knees,* R. AZARIAS, *sword in hand, stands* L. *Near him,* ZACHARIAH *and* SALOMITH *are kneeling on the steps of the throne. Several* LEVITES, *sword in hand, are ranged on both sides.*]

JOAD: Appear, dear child,
Blood royal of our kings. Dost know, O Queen,
Our holiest monarch's heir? Dost know at least
These marks thy dagger made? There is thy king,
Thy grandson and the son of Ahaziah.
All people, and thou, Abner, recognize
King Joas!

ABNER: Heavens!

ATHALIAH: Traitor!

JOAD: Dost thou see
This faithful Jewess, at whose breast he fed,
As well thou knowest? He was by Josabeth
Delivered from thy rage; and in this Temple
God has preserved him. This is what remains
To me of David's treasure.

ATHALIAH: Thy knavery,
Thou traitor, will be fatal to the child.
Deliver me, soldiers, from an odious phantom!

JOAD: Soldiers of the living God, defend your king.

[*The back of the stage opens. The inside of the Temple is seen; and the armed* LEVITES *enter from all sides.*]

ATHALIAH: Where am I? Treason! O unlucky Queen!
With arms and enemies I am beset.

JOAD: Thine eyes will seek in vain. There's no escape,

And God has hemmed thee in on every side.
That God thou bravedst has now delivered thee
Into our hands. Now render an account
To Him of the blood with which thou has been drunk.
ATHALIAH: What! fear has frozen my unworthy soldiers!
Into what snare, base Abner, hast thou led me?
ABNER: God is my witness, Queen . . .
ATHALIAH: Swear not by thy God,
Traitor! Avenge me.
ABNER: On whom? On Joas?
On my master?
ATHALIAH: He, Joas? He, thy king?
Know, wicked men, my arms besiege you still,
And all my camp is shouting for me now.
They are coming to my rescue. Tremble now,
You troop of rebels.

(*Enter* ISMAEL.) (v.6)

ISMAEL: My lord, the Temple's freed
Of all its enemies. The stranger's fled;
The Jew submits. And even as the wind
Scatters the smoke, the voice of the Almighty
That army has dispersed. From the Temple gates
Our Levites have proclaimed the rightful King,
Have told how he was snatched in infancy
From the fatal sword, and how the daughter of Ahab
Is fallen in the snare. On every side
The trumpet sounded; mingled with its noise
The cries of the astounded host have spread
The sudden terror with which Gideon struck
The haughty Midian. The Tyrians,
Throwing away their swords and bucklers, fled
By diverse routes. They disappeared the first.
Some Jews, dumbfounded, also took to flight.
Wondering at God's mercy showered on Joas,
The rest, with acclamation, hailed him King.
Till all the people with the selfsame spirit

Inspired, women, old men, and children,
Embraced with joy, and blessed the Lord their God
For what He gave. All sing of David's son
Brought back to life; while in the holy city
Baal is struck with horror; and the doors
Of his sacrilegious temple are broke in.
Mathan is slain.

ATHALIAH: Thou hast conquered, O God of the Jews!
Yes, it is Joas, and I seek in vain
To deceive myself. I recognize the place
Where he was pierced. I see the mien and gesture
Of Ahaziah. Everything recalls
The blood which I detest. David has triumphed,
Ahab's alone destroyed. Remorseless God,
Thou hast brought everything to pass. 'Tis Thou,
Who flattering me with easy vengeance, made me
A score of times in a day oppose myself,
Sometimes arousing pity for a child,
And sometimes dazzling me with Thy rich treasures,
So that I've feared to give to flame and pillage
This Temple; so that this son reigns, Thy care
And the work of Thy hands; so that to signalize
His new gained empire, he will now be made
To plunge the dagger in my breast. This is
My dying wish for him. What said I? Wish?
Nay, I am confident that he will be
Repugnant to Thy yoke, tired with Thy Law,
Faithful to Ahab's blood he took from me;
That he will do what his grandfather did,
Be like his father. It shall come to pass
That this hated heir of David will abolish
Thy honors and profane Thy altar—to avenge
Ahab and Jezebel and Athaliah. [*Exit* ATHALIAH, *guarded.*]
(V.7)

JOAD: Let her at once be taken from the Temple,
So that its sanctity is not profaned.
Go, you avengers of your murdered princes,

And stop their blood's cries even with her death.
If any rash men should embrace her quarrel,
Deliver him, too, to the fury of the sword.

JOAS (*descending*): O God, who seest my trouble and affliction,
Turn far from me her curse. Suffer it not
To be accomplished, and let Joas die
Ere he forget You.

JOAD: Assemble all the people;
Show them their king, who comes to renew his oath.
King, priests, and people, filled with thankfulness,
Let us confirm the covenant of Jacob
With God, and penitent for our misdeeds,
Let us now re-engage ourselves to Him
With a new oath. Abner, beside the King
Take up your place again.

(*Enter a* LEVITE.) (v.8)

JOAD: Well? Have they punished
This rash and impious woman?

LEVITE: The sword has expiated
The horrors of her life. Jerusalem,
For long a prey to her unbridled rage,
Freed from her odious yoke at last with joy
Beheld her weltering in her blood.

JOAD: Her end
Was terrible, but well deserved. Learn from it,
King of the Jews, and ne'er forget that kings
Have a stern judge in heaven, that innocence
Has an avenger, the fatherless a father.

MODERN LIBRARY COLLEGE EDITIONS

T 74 AQUINAS, ST. THOMAS: *Introduction*
T 73 ARISTOTLE: *Introduction*
T 72 AUGUSTINE, SAINT: *The Confessions*
T 87 AUSTEN, JANE: *Pride and Prejudice*
T 1 AUSTEN, JANE: *Pride and Prejudice* and *Sense and Sensibility*

T 2 BALZAC, HONORÉ DE: *Père Goriot* and *Eugénie Grandet*
T 42 BELLAMY, EDWARD: *Looking Backward*
T 86 BLAKE, WILLIAM: *Selected Poetry and Prose*
T 62 BOSWELL, JAMES: *The Life of Samuel Johnson*
T 3 BRONTË, CHARLOTTE: *Jane Eyre*
T 4 BRONTË, EMILY: *Wuthering Heights*
T 43 BROWNING, ROBERT: *Selected Poetry*
T 5 BUTLER, SAMUEL: *The Way of All Flesh*
T 44 BYRON, GEORGE GORDON, LORD: *Selected Poetry*

T 57 CAESAR, JULIUS: *The Gallic War and Other Writings*
T 69 CAMUS, ALBERT: *The Plague*
T 6 CERVANTES, MIGUEL DE: *Don Quixote*
T 84 CHEKHOV, ANTON: *Best Plays*
T 55 CICERO, MARCUS TULLIUS: *Basic Works*
T 52 COLERIDGE, SAMUEL TAYLOR: *Selected Poetry and Prose*
T 63 CONRAD, JOSEPH: *Nostromo*
T 45 CRANE, STEPHEN: *The Red Badge of Courage*

T 7 DANTE ALIGHIERI: *The Divine Comedy*
T 8 DEFOE, DANIEL: *Moll Flanders*
T 9 DICKENS, CHARLES: *A Tale of Two Cities*
T 10 DICKENS, CHARLES: *David Copperfield*
T 89 DONNE, JOHN: *Poetry and Prose*
T 11 DOSTOYEVSKY, FYODOR: *Crime and Punishment*
T 12 DOSTOYEVSKY, FYODOR: *The Brothers Karamazov*

T 66 Dostoyevsky, Fyodor: *Best Short Stories*

T 13 Eight Famous Elizabethan Plays
T 80 Eighteenth-Century Plays
T 14 Emerson, Ralph Waldo: *Selected Writings*

T 68 Faulkner, William: *Light in August*
T 78 Faulkner, William: *Absalom, Absalom!*
T 88 Faulkner, William: *Intruder in the Dust*
T 94 Faulkner, William: *The Sound and the Fury*
T 61 The Federalist
T 15 Fielding, Henry: *Tom Jones*
T 16 Fielding, Henry: *Joseph Andrews*
T 17 Flaubert, Gustave: *Madame Bovary*
T 18 Franklin, Benjamin: *Autobiography and Selected Writings*

T 19 Goethe, Johann Wolfgang von: *Faust*
T 82 Gogol, Nicholai: *Dead Souls*

T 20 Hardy, Thomas: *The Mayor of Casterbridge*
T 46 Hardy, Thomas: *Tess of the d'Urbervilles*
T 90 Hardy, Thomas: *Jude the Obscure*
T 21 Hawthorne, Nathaniel: *The Scarlet Letter*
T 76 Hegel, Georg Wilhelm Friedrich: *Philosophy*
T 54 Herodotus: *The Persian Wars*
T 22 Homer: *The Iliad*
T 23 Homer: *The Odyssey*
T 56 Howells, William Dean: *The Rise of Silas Lapham*

T 24 Ibsen, Henrik: *Six Plays*
T 83 Ibsen, Henrik: *The Wild Duck and Other Plays*

T 47 James, Henry: *The Portrait of a Lady*
T 59 James, Henry: *The Bostonians*

T 48 Keats, John: *Complete Poetry and Selected Prose*

T 25 Machiavelli, Niccolo: *The Prince* and *The Discourses*
T 75 Malraux, André: *Man's Fate*
T 93 Mann, Thomas: *The Magic Mountain*
T 70 Medieval Romances
T 26 Melville, Herman: *Moby Dick*

T 27 Meredith, George: *The Ordeal of Richard Feverel*
T 28 Milton, John: *Complete Poetry and Selected Prose*
T 29 Molière: *Eight Plays*
T 65 Montaigne: *Selected Essays*

T 91 O'Neill, Eugene: *Later Plays*

T 81 Pascal's Pensées
T 71 Plato: *Works*
T 58 Poe, Edgar Allan: *Selected Poetry and Prose*
T 49 Pope, Alexander: *Selected Works*
T 67 Proust, Marcel: *Swann's Way*

T 79 Restoration Plays

T 30 Seven Famous Greek Plays
T 77 Seventeenth-Century French Drama
T 50 Shelley, Percy Bysshe: *Selected Poetry and Prose*
T 85 Six Modern American Plays
T 31 Sterne, Laurence: *Tristram Shandy*
T 92 Swift, Jonathan: *Gulliver's Travels*
T 32 Swift, Jonathan: *Gulliver's Travels and Other Writings*

T 53 Tacitus: *Complete Works*
T 60 Tennyson, Alfred Lord: *Selected Poetry*
T 33 Thackeray, William Makepeace: *Vanity Fair*
T 34 Thackeray, William Makepeace: *Henry Esmond*
T 35 Thoreau, Henry David: *Walden and Other Writings*
T 51 Thucydides: *Complete Writings*
T 36 Tolstoy, Leo: *Anna Karenina*
T 37 Trollope, Anthony: *Barchester Towers* and *The Warden*
T 38 Turgenev, Ivan S.: *Fathers and Sons*

T 39 Virgil: *The Aeneid, Eclogues and Georgics*
T 64 Voltaire: *Candide and Other Writings*

T 40 Whitman, Walt: *Leaves of Grass and Selected Prose*
T 41 Wordsworth, William: *Selected Poetry*

The Best of the World's Best Books

COMPLETE LIST OF TITLES IN
THE MODERN LIBRARY

A series of handsome, cloth-bound books, formerly available only in expensive editions.

76 ADAMS, HENRY: *The Education of Henry Adams*
310 AESCHYLUS: *The Complete Greek Tragedies,* Vol. I
311 AESCHYLUS: *The Complete Greek Tragedies,* Vol. II
101 AIKEN, CONRAD (Editor): *A Comprehensive Anthology of American Poetry*
127 AIKEN, CONRAD (Editor): *20th-Century American Poetry*
145 ALEICHEM, SHOLOM: *Selected Stories*
104 ANDERSON, SHERWOOD: *Winesburg, Ohio*
259 AQUINAS, ST. THOMAS: *Introduction to St. Thomas Aquinas*
248 ARISTOTLE: *Introduction to Aristotle*
228 ARISTOTLE: *Politics*
246 ARISTOTLE: *Rhetoric and Poetics*
160 AUDEN, W. H.: *Selected Poetry*
263 AUGUSTINE, ST.: *Confessions*
264 AUSTEN, JANE: *Pride and Prejudice* and *Sense and Sensibility*

256 BACON, FRANCIS: *Selected Writings*
299 BALZAC: *Cousin Bette*
193 BALZAC: *Droll Stories*
245 BALZAC: *Père Goriot* and *Eugénie Grandet*
116 BEERBOHM, MAX: *Zuleika Dobson*
22 BELLAMY, EDWARD: *Looking Backward*
184 BENNETT, ARNOLD: *The Old Wives' Tale*
231 BERGSON, HENRI: *Creative Evolution*
285 BLAKE, WILLIAM: *Selected Poetry and Prose*
71 BOCCACCIO: *The Decameron*
282 BOSWELL, JAMES: *The Life of Samuel Johnson*
64 BRONTË, CHARLOTTE: *Jane Eyre*
106 BRONTË, EMILY: *Wuthering Heights*
198 BROWNING, ROBERT: *Selected Poetry*
15 BUCK, PEARL: *The Good Earth* *[Italy*
32 BURCKHARDT, JACOB: *The Civilization of the Renaissance in*
241 BURK, JOHN N.: *The Life and Works of Beethoven*
289 BURKE, EDMUND: *Selected Writings*
136 BUTLER, SAMUEL: *Erewhon* and *Erewhon Revisited*
13 BUTLER, SAMUEL: *The Way of All Flesh*
195 BYRON, LORD: *Selected Poetry*
24 BYRON, LORD: *Don Juan*

295 CAESAR, JULIUS: *The Gallic War and Other Writings*
51 CALDWELL, ERSKINE· *God's Little Acre*

249 CALDWELL, ERSKINE: *Tobacco Road*
352 CAMUS, ALBERT: *The Fall & Exile and the Kingdom*
109 CAMUS, ALBERT: *The Plague*
349 CAMUS, ALBERT: *Notebooks 1935–1942*
339 CAMUS, ALBERT: *Resistance, Rebellion and Death*
353 CAPOTE, TRUMAN: *Selected Writings*
79 CARROLL, LEWIS: *Alice in Wonderland,* etc.
165 CASANOVA, JACQUES: *Memoirs of Casanova*
150 CELLINI, BENVENUTO: *Autobiography of Cellini*
174 CERVANTES: *Don Quixote*
161 CHAUCER: *The Canterbury Tales*
171 CHEKHOV, ANTON: *Best Plays*
50 CHEKHOV, ANTON: *Short Stories*
272 CICERO: *Basic Works*
279 COLERIDGE: *Selected Poetry and Prose*
251 COLETTE: *Six Novels*
235 COMMAGER, HENRY STEELE & NEVINS, ALLAN: *A Short History of the United States*
306 CONFUCIUS: *The Wisdom of Confucius*
186 CONRAD, JOSEPH: *Lord Jim*
275 CONRAD, JOSEPH: *Nostromo*
34 CONRAD, JOSEPH: *Victory*
105 COOPER, JAMES FENIMORE: *The Pathfinder*
194 CORNEILLE & RACINE: *Six Plays by Corneille and Racine*
130 CRANE, STEPHEN: *The Red Badge of Courage*
214 CUMMINGS, E. E.: *The Enormous Room*

236 DANA, RICHARD HENRY: *Two Years Before the Mast*
208 DANTE: *The Divine Comedy*
122 DEFOE, DANIEL: *Moll Flanders*
92 DEFOE, DANIEL: *Robinson Crusoe* and *A Journal of the Plague Year*
43 DESCARTES, RENÉ: *Philosophical Writings*
173 DEWEY, JOHN: *Human Nature and Conduct*
348 DEWEY, JOHN: *John Dewey on Education*
110 DICKENS, CHARLES: *David Copperfield*
204 DICKENS, CHARLES: *Pickwick Papers*
308 DICKENS, CHARLES: *Our Mutual Friend*
189 DICKENS, CHARLES: *A Tale of Two Cities*
25 DICKINSON, EMILY: *Selected Poems*
23 DINESEN, ISAK: *Out of Africa*
54 DINESEN, ISAK: *Seven Gothic Tales*
12 DONNE, JOHN: *Complete Poetry and Selected Prose*
205 DOS PASSOS, JOHN: *Three Soldiers*
293 DOSTOYEVSKY, FYODOR: *Best Short Stories*
151 DOSTOYEVSKY, FYODOR: *The Brothers Karamazov*
199 DOSTOYEVSKY, FYODOR: *Crime and Punishment*
55 DOSTOYEVSKY, FYODOR: *The Possessed*
5 DOUGLAS, NORMAN: *South Wind*
206 DOYLE, SIR ARTHUR CONAN: *The Adventure and Memoirs of Sherlock Holmes*
8 DREISER, THEODORE: *Sister Carrie*
69 DUMAS, ALEXANDRE: *Camille*
143 DUMAS, ALEXANDRE: *The Three Musketeers*
227 DU MAURIER, DAPHNE: *Rebecca*

338 Ellison, Ralph: *Invisible Man*
192 Emerson, Ralph Waldo: *The Journals*
91 Emerson, Ralph Waldo: *Essays and Other Writings*
331 Erasmus, Desiderius: *The Praise of Folly*
314 Euripides: *The Complete Greek Tragedies*, Vol. V
315 Euripides: *The Complete Greek Tragedies*, Vol. VI
316 Euripides: *The Complete Greek Tragedies*, Vol. VII

271 Faulkner, William: *Absalom, Absalom!*
175 Faulkner, William: *Go Down, Moses*
351 Faulkner, William: *Intruder in the Dust*
88 Faulkner, William: *Light in August*
61 Faulkner, William: *Sanctuary* [*Dying*
187 Faulkner, William: *The Sound and the Fury* and *As I Lay*
324 Faulkner, William: *Selected Short Stories*
117 Fielding, Henry: *Joseph Andrews*
185 Fielding, Henry: *Tom Jones*
28 Flaubert, Gustave: *Madame Bovary*
102 Forester, C. S.: *The African Queen*
210 France, Anatole: *Penguin Island*
298 Frank, Anne: *Diary of a Young Girl*
39 Franklin, Benjamin: *Autobiography*, etc.
96 Freud, Sigmund: *The Interpretation of Dreams*

36 George, Henry: *Progress and Poverty*
327 Gide, André: *The Counterfeiters*
177 Goethe: *Faust*
40 Gogol, Nicholai: *Dead Souls* [*Writings*
291 Goldsmith, Oliver: *The Vicar of Wakefield and Other*
20 Graves, Robert: *I, Claudius*
286 Gunther, John: *Death Be Not Proud*

265 Hackett, Francis: *The Personal History of Henry the Eighth*
163 Haggard. H. Rider: *She* and *King Solomon's Mines*
320 Hamilton, Edith: *The Greek Way*
135 Hardy, Thomas: *Jude the Obscure*
17 Hardy, Thomas: *The Mayor of Casterbridge*
121 Hardy, Thomas: *The Return of the Native*
72 Hardy, Thomas: *Tess of the D'Urbervilles*
233 Hart & Kaufman: *Six Plays*
329 Hart, Moss: *Act One*
250 Harte, Bret: *Best Stories*
93 Hawthorne, Nathaniel: *The Scarlet Letter*
239 Hegel: *The Philosophy of Hegel*
223 Hellman, Lillian: *Six Plays*
26 Henry, O.: *Best Short Stories*
255 Herodotus: *The Persian Wars*
328 Hersey, John: *Hiroshima*
334 Hesse, Herman: *Steppenwolf*
166 Homer: *The Iliad*
167 Homer: *The Odyssey*
141 Horace: *Complete Works*
302 Howard, John Tasker: *World's Great Operas*
277 Howells, William Dean: *The Rise of Silas Lapham*
89 Hudson, W. H.: *Green Mansions*
35 Hugo, Victor: *The Hunchback of Notre Dame*

340 Hume, David: *Philosophy*
209 Huxley, Aldous: *Antic Hay*
48 Huxley, Aldous: *Brave New World*
180 Huxley, Aldous: *Point Counter Point*

305 Ibsen, Henrik: *Six Plays*
307 Ibsen, Henrik: *The Wild Duck and Other Plays*
240 Irving, Washington: *Selected Writings*

16 James, Henry: *The Bostonians*
107 James, Henry: *The Portrait of a Lady*
169 James, Henry: *The Turn of the Screw*
269 James, Henry: *Washington Square*
244 James, Henry: *The Wings of the Dove*
114 James, William: *The Philosophy of William James*
70 James, William: *The Varieties of Religious Experience*
234 Jefferson, Thomas: *The Life* and *Selected Writings*
355 Johnson, Samuel: *Johnson's Dictionary: A Modern Selection*
124 Joyce, James: *Dubliners*
300 Jung, C. G.: *Basic Writings*

318 Kafka, Franz: *The Trial*
283 Kafka, Franz: *Selected Stories*
297 Kant: *Critique of Pure Reason*
266 Kant: *The Philosophy of Kant*
233 Kaufman & Hart: *Six Plays*
273 Keats: *Complete Poetry and Selected Prose*
303 Kierkegaard, Søren: *A Kierkegaard Anthology*
99 Kipling, Rudyard: *Kim*
74 Koestler, Arthur: *Darkness at Noon*

262 Laotse: *The Wisdom of Laotse*
148 Lawrence, D. H.: *Lady Chatterley's Lover*
128 Lawrence, D. H.: *The Rainbow*
333 Lawrence, D. H.: *Sons and Lovers*
68 Lawrence, D. H.: *Women in Love*
252 Lewis, Sinclair: *Dodsworth*
221 Lewis, Sinclair: *Cass Timberlane*
325 Livy: *A History of Rome*
56 Longfellow, Henry W.: *Poems*
77 Louys, Pierre: *Aphrodite*
95 Ludwig, Emil: *Napoleon*

65 Machiavelli: *The Prince* and *The Discourses*
321 Mailer, Norman: *The Naked and the Dead*
317 Malamud, Bernard: *Two Novels*
33 Malraux, André: *Man's Fate*
309 Malthus, Thomas Robert: *On Population*
182 Marquand, John P.: *The Late George Apley*
202 Marx, Karl: *Capital and Other Writings*
14 Maugham, W. Somerset: *Best Short Stories*
270 Maugham, W. Somerset: *Cakes and Ale*
27 Maugham, W. Somerset: *The Moon and Sixpence*
176 Maugham, W. Somerset: *Of Human Bondage*
98 Maupassant, Guy de: *Best Short Stories*
46 Maurois, André: *Disraeli*
119 Melville, Herman: *Moby Dick*
253 Meredith, George: *The Egoist*